W9-AQX-158

Praise for
CRISIS AHEAD

"With real-time social media available to billions of people, a crisis is just one tweet or YouTube video away. However, when something does occur that has potential to affect your reputation, 'no comment' is not a savvy response. *Crisis Ahead* prepares you for effectively managing threats to your business. It's your guide to the strategies and tactics of effective real-time communications. Read it so you will be ready when (not if) a crisis hits your organization."

David Meerman Scott, marketing strategist, entrepreneur, and
bestselling author of 11 books including
The New Rules of Marketing and PR

"Having dealt with a crisis or two and maybe causing a few on my own, I appreciate Edward Segal's primer on how to prepare for and respond to a crisis. Every organization, business,, or political candidate will face some sort of crisis. It is inevitable and probably unavoidable. But there are successful strategies, tactics, and techniques for dealing with crisis situations, and Segal presents them here clearly and succinctly with his memorable '10 Rs of crisis management' and useful guidance on how communicators can rise to the challenges they will face."

Mike McCurry, former State Department and
White House Spokesman (1993–1998), Professor/Director,
Wesley Theological Seminary

"*Crisis Ahead* is the ultimate and invaluable survival guide for business executives who are knee-deep in a crisis and a handy reference book for company officials who want to prepare for the inevitable. Edward Segal helps you assess your readiness to handle a crisis and provides a practical handbook—packed with exciting real-world examples that required real-world solutions—for crisis communication planning everyone can benefit from. Edward's conversational writing style makes *Crisis Ahead* a quick and easy read and its innovative design ensures you can immediately find the advice and information you need before, during, or after a crisis."

Mitchell E. Marovitz, Ph.D., APR, Fellow PRSA, Chair,
Public Relations Program, Business and Management Department,
The Graduate School, University of Maryland Global Campus

"Edward Segal has drawn from his experience as a CEO and an experienced crisis-communication counselor to produce an insightful and practical book that will be useful to leaders and managers in companies and nonprofit organizations alike. The book considers myriad scenarios that could lead to a crisis situation, and the checklists and exercises he has included well-support application of the thought processes and practices he suggests. As Edward notes, crises ignore no organization, and the key to responding well is preparing well. His new guide is designed to support just that."

John H. Graham IV, former FASAE, CAE, President and CEO, American Society of Association Executives: The Center for Association Leadership

"*Crisis Ahead* is the one book every CEO and other company officials should have in easy reach on their desks before, during, and after a disaster, scandal, or other emergency strikes. This is a quick and easy read with important advice and insights for anyone who helps lead or manage a business or organization. Don't wait until there is a crisis to figure out how to respond and recover from it. Do yourself and your organization a big favor and start reading *Crisis Ahead* today."

Arnold Sanow, author, *Get Along with Anyone, Anytime, Anywhere*

"In *Crisis Ahead*, Edward Segal puts his wealth of experience and knowledge about crisis management and communication at your fingertips. He has written a lively, engaging, and practical handbook that provides invaluable insights and advice for preventing, managing, and recovering from dozens of crisis situations. *Crisis Ahead* is like having your own personal crisis management expert available and on call 24/7."

Karen Friedman, Karen Friedman Enterprises, author, *Shut Up And Say Something* and *Ordinary People: Extraordinary Lessons*

"Great CEOs know the importance of contingency planning. They are ready for the crisis before it strikes. Edward Segal's *Crisis Ahead* provides a practical and realistic guide that reflects his diverse background as a PR consultant, CEO, corporate spokesperson, journalist, and astute observer of how others have responded to a variety of crisis situations. Edward is an authority on crisis management whose deep knowledge and extensive expertise is on full display in *Crisis Ahead*. All CEOs, managers, and boards of directors should read it as soon as possible."

Jerry Matthews, author, *Reach Zenith: The 10 Intangible Skills of Great CEOs*

"Associations and nonprofit organizations sometime wrongly believe they are immune from a crisis, or that its impact will be minimal. It is not difficult to find news about organizations that have had to deal with million dollar embezzlements, violations of the law ('We didn't know') or a death at their planned event. Having a crisis response plan and resources is critical for survival for leaders, staff, and boards of directors. *Crisis Ahead*, and the expertise and examples provided by author Edward Segal, are valuable tools."

Bob Harris, CAE, The Nonprofit Center, www.nonprofitcenter.com

"I know from my experience and research that proactive planning is critical in order for companies and organizations to successfully weather a crisis and come out even stronger on the other side. The bad news is that crises are inevitable. The good news is that in *Crisis Ahead* Edward Segal provides the protocols that are necessary to help ensure the survival of a business and the resiliency of its brand."

Sweta Chakraborty, Ph.D., Risk and Behavioral Scientist,
Millennium Leadership Fellow, The Atlantic Council

"Edward Segal's newest book is nothing short of crisis management gold. It is the smart, straight-forward, comprehensive, "how to" guide you need to get ready for and manage the unexpected and the unthinkable. *Crisis Ahead* is the one-stop, go-to reference guide on crisis management for anyone who starts, runs, or helps lead any business or organization. Why put your company or organization at risk by ignoring or denying problems that can impact your reputation, operations, and bottom line? By following Edward's comprehensive and practical advice, you can have the confidence and peace of mind that you are as ready as you can be for any crisis and can bounce back from it as soon as possible."

David Nellis, Principal, Executive Creative Director,
Return on Investment marketing and communication agency

"In my book *A Setback Is A Setup For A Comeback*, I write that 'In every journey to success you will experience setbacks, and those setbacks often come in the form of a crisis! And those who win, are those who are able to turn those crisis moments into spectacular comebacks!' Edward Segal is a battle-tested crisis management expert who had spent years in the trenches dealing with scores of crisis situations and providing advice and counsel to organizations who have found themselves in the fire pit of crisis. In this new book, *Crisis Ahead*, he shares his time tested secrets to help you turn your setbacks (crisis moments) into stellar comebacks and help you WIN!"

Dr. Willie Jolley, Hall of Fame Speaker, bestselling author,
A Setback Is A Setup For A Comeback & An Attitude of Excellence,
Nationally Syndicated Radio & TV Personality

"Is your business confronting a product recall or allegations of sexual misconduct? You'll gain valuable advice on how to respond in Edward Segal's *Crisis Ahead*. Hit by a cyberattack? He walks you through that, too. A wide range of crises from a wayward CEO to a natural disaster to a shooting incident are covered here. Keep this book close. You never know when your crisis will strike."

Ed Barks, President, Barks Communications, author, *A+ Strategies for C-Suite Communications* and *The Truth About Public Speaking*

"In an age of constant crisis, everyone needs to think differently and garner new skills. Think like legendary broadcast journalist Edward R. Murrow, act like a social media guru, lead like General Patton, take risks like Pulitzer Prize-winning reporter Ernie Pyle, and understand human motivations like the Dalai Lama. *Crisis Ahead* adroitly leads you on that path to being a patient teacher and visionary for your company or organization."

Richard Levick, Esq. Chairman & CEO, LEVICK, the global crisis communications agency, author, *The Communicators: Leadership in the Age of Crisis* and other books

"*Crisis Ahead*, Edward Segal's dynamic guide to survival when a disaster strikes your company or organization, is a much-needed wake-up call that can help you avoid or recover from a wide range of unexpected events. It features a 'book within a book' (see Chapter 6) that takes the reader on a fascinating journey via case studies about the crises experienced by some of the biggest corporations (think Boeing and Sears), celebrities, and high-profile individuals (Kevin Spacey, Leslie Moonves, and more). Each case study quickly captures your attention, gets to the heart of the crisis, and summarizes how well or poorly they were managed. *Crisis Ahead* is a practical tool for leaders and managers that takes you on an entertaining and educational journey. It is a timely and welcome reminder about the value of having a plan of action and mapping out appropriate responses for overcoming any crisis that your business could face. I only wish this book had been available in the aftermath of a deadly and destructive earthquake that I went through in California several years ago. Segal's advice and insights would have made my road to recovery from this crisis—a natural disaster—that much easier."

Pat "Ziggy" Zicarelli, GRI, CRS, Past President, California Association of REALTORS®, 2020 National Association of REALTORS® Liaison to the REALTOR® Party Political Action Committee

"If you are a leader of any type of organization, then Edward Segal's *Crisis Ahead* is a must-have. In this book, he lays out potential scenarios, lessons, and best practices for responding to dozens of different crisis scenarios. He begins with a vulnerability questionnaire that forces you to stop and think about all the things that could easily become a crisis in a minute's time, and his crisis scenarios provide a reality check about how prepared you are to deal with them. He then walks you through how to prepare a crisis plan. Segal presents this critical information in an easy to follow format. He shares dozens of in-depth examples of different crises that organizations have endured and provides valuable advice on how to handle similar situations. I will provide copies of *Crisis Ahead* to the companies I work with to help them prepare to deal with natural disasters. Any executive who wants to learn how to avoid, manage and recover from a crisis will find Segal's ideas and suggestions invaluable."

Coni K Meyers, LMC, CBLC, CDC, Kickbutt Leadership Visionary & Mentor, international bestselling author, *Crystalline Moments, Success Chronicles, Resilience in the Storm,* and *Conceived to Lead*

"This book is a must-read for anyone who might deal with a organizational or company crisis at some point in their career. WARNING: a crisis will happen to all of us...we just don't know when. Edward Segal's *Crisis Ahead: 101 Way to Prepare for and Bounce Back from Disasters. Scandals, and Other Emergencies* is not just another book on crisis communications, it's an engaging A-to-Z road map on how to avoid a crisis early on, and when faced with one, it offers thought-provoking and real-life examples of how to engage all stake-holders that can help the organization survive (even thrive after) the crisis. This book will also help prepare a CEO and internal teams to know what to look for and ask when considering outside counsel from a crisis communications firm."

Danny Selnick, Communication Consultant and former executive of two press release news wire services

CRISIS AHEAD

101 WAYS TO PREPARE FOR AND BOUNCE BACK FROM DISASTERS, SCANDALS, AND OTHER EMERGENCIES

EDWARD SEGAL

NICHOLAS BREALEY
PUBLISHING

BOSTON • LONDON

First published in the United States of America in 2020 by Nicholas Brealey Publishing

An Hachette company

24 23 22 21 20 1 2 3 4 5 6 7 8

Copyright © Edward Segal, 2020

The right of Edward Segal to be identified as the Author of the Work has been asserted by him in accordance with the Copyright, Designs and Patents Act 1988.

All rights reserved. No part of this publication may be reproduced, stored in a retrieval system, or transmitted, in any form or by any means without the prior written permission of the publisher, nor be otherwise circulated in any form of binding or cover other than that in which it is published and without a similar condition being imposed on the subsequent purchaser.

Library of Congress Control Number: 2019949164

ISBN 978-1-5293-6142-1
US eBook ISBN 978-1-5293-6196-4
UK eBook ISBN 978-1-5293-6195-7

Printed in the United States of America

Nicholas Brealey Publishing policy is to use papers that are natural, renewable, and recyclable products and made from wood grown in sustainable forests. The logging and manufacturing processes are expected to conform to the environmental regulations of the country of origin.

Nicholas Brealey Publishing
Carmelite House
50 Victoria Embankment
London EC4Y 0DZ
Tel: 020 7122 6000

Nicholas Brealey Publishing
Hachette Book Group
53 State Street
Boston, MA 02109, USA
Tel: (617) 523 3801

www.nbuspublishing.com

To Pamela Kervin Segal:

My best friend and traveling companion—no matter where we go or what we do.

Contents

The Coronavirus Crisis

This is not the introduction I intended when I completed the draft manuscript for *Crisis Ahead*. After COVID-19 grew from a regional outbreak to a full-blown international crisis, I felt a new sense of purpose and urgency in publishing the book. I want to share my thoughts with you about how the coronavirus crisis compares with other crisis situations and what we can learn from it—even as the crisis continues to unfold.

Questions

Currently, there are many unanswered or unanswerable questions about the crisis, including:

- Are we at the beginning of the end or the end of the beginning of this global public health emergency?
- Is this a one-time crisis or will the virus return every year like the flu?
- How will the virus change the ways we live and work?
- Is the effect the crisis is having on the national and global economies going to be temporary?

The coronavirus crisis has several things in common with many of the 100+ crisis situations I discuss in the following pages.

- It was sudden and unexpected.
- No one had prepared or trained for it.
- Even if companies had crisis plans in place, they realized too late they needed. comprehensive contingency plans to deal with this particular crisis.
- People scrambled to respond quickly and in the best ways they could.
- Experts were consulted for guidance on what to do, when to do it, and how to do it.
- It is not clear how we will recover or how long it will take to return to normal.

This Is Not the First Time

We've had to deal with several health crisis situations in our history, such as the 1918 flu pandemic, polio, AIDS, and Ebola. The response by governments to these and other public health emergencies has often followed a similar and disappointing pattern: ignore it, deny it, hope it goes away, finally acknowledge the severity of the crisis, then play catch-up to deal with it. In the private sector, some companies have taken a wait-and-see attitude, preferring to follow the government's lead or monitor the activities of competitors before responding. Other businesses and organizations have been proactive and wasted no time in taking action.

There are early lessons to be learned from this virus crisis. Together with the best practices for managing any crisis that are covered in Chapter 6 of this book, the lessons include:

- The importance of having a plan and testing to ensure it will work
- Heeding early warnings
- Having enough of the right resources
- Responding quickly
- Telling the truth
- Accurately gauging the impact of the crisis
- Learning from the experiences of others
- Adhering to the facts
- Setting realistic deadlines

How to Respond to COVID-19

Most companies have not dealt with a crisis before, and certainly not one like the COVID-19 crisis. As it unfolds, it's clear many businesses and organizations are flying blind. They run the risk of going against the dozens of best practices for managing *any* crisis that you can find in Chapter 6.

Unfortunately, every day the crisis continues means companies may be at risk of making crisis management mistakes they will soon regret. Along with the best practices that are summarized beginning on page 229, here are some recommendations to help you avoid making those mistakes:

- Don't say or do anything that may add to people's anxieties, fears, or concerns about the pandemic. Everything that is said and done should help provide as much confidence and accurate information as possible.

- Express empathy and understanding for what others may be thinking or feeling.
- Obtain the facts about the crisis from credible sources, such as the US Centers for Disease Control and Prevention and the World Health Organization.
- Follow the news and developments about the virus. Keep a close eye on how COVID-19 is affecting any and all aspects of your business, including employees, sales, inventory, and customers.
- Don't repeat rumors, speculation, or questionable social media posts. Cite the source of the information and alerts you share with others.
- Communicate often. Let people know exactly how the crisis is affecting your company or organization and what is being done or will be done about it. You should be the source of reliable information about how the disease is impacting your business.
- Be transparent. Post and distribute updates and key messages about the impact of the virus on your company. If appropriate, establish a 24/7 hotline as another way to help answer questions or concerns from worried customers, investors, or the public.
- Don't minimize or sugarcoat bad news. Remember that people can find information about your business—or inaccurate information—from a variety of sources.
- Always tell the truth—no matter how much it may hurt. Otherwise your credibility and the trust people have placed in your organization will suffer.
- If you have a crisis plan, follow it, then test and update it on a regular basis to address the current situation.
- If you don't have a plan, make one now. Letting people know you have a plan for dealing with this or any other crisis can help provide a level of confidence that you know what you are doing and are doing it in a logical, comprehensive, and coordinated fashion. If you need it, there's a template for a generic crisis management/communication plan on page 34. You can access templates of the plan on my website at PublicRelations.com. Go to the Customized Crisis Plan page and enter this case-sensitive password (don't include the period): CrisisPlan2020. From there, you can copy or download a template, then fill in the blanks and customize, update, and test it periodically.
- Secure the help you need. This is not the time to wing it. If there is any aspect of your crisis management plan for which you need help implementing, don't hesitate to bring in the expertise you need to get the job done, and get it done right.
- Stay ahead of the curve. As the crisis continues, work up your own confidential and worst-case projections about how the virus may impact your company, and plan your next steps accordingly—including how you will bounce back after the crisis is over.
- Don't assume the coronavirus crisis will end soon. You may be in for a long and bumpy ride.

Delivering Bad News

The pandemic quickly changed not only how and where people work, but how and when they are laid off. Thanks to email, Zoom, and other web-based video tools, it's possible to deliver the bad news about the impact of the crisis to employees, consultants, and independent contractors from anywhere and at any time.

But when delivering the virtual version of pink slips, business executives should exercise caution in what they say and how they say it. Keep these crisis management-related tips in mind:

- Remember the big picture. Place your difficult-to-make decisions within the context of the hard and challenging choices companies and organizations around the country and world are making.
- Show empathy and compassion. Put yourself in the shoes of the people who are being laid off. If you were on the receiving end of an email or video conferencing session, what would you want to be told? Before you push "send" or make the call, write down what you want to say, then read it aloud to a trusted colleague, friend, or family member for their feedback and guidance.
- What you say may not be what they hear. While being laid off in this difficult time may not come as a total shock, the bad news may still be hard to absorb. Your message may be misconstrued by people who are having their own crisis—a crisis that could be made much worse because you are laying them off.
- You will be talking to multiple audiences. What you say and how you say it may be shared with friends, family members, colleagues, neighbors, social media, and news organizations.
- Give people hope—if you can. When appropriate and possible, provide some hope that, after the crisis is over, there may be a chance they will be rehired. But don't give them false hope if there is no hope at all—honesty is always the best policy.

A Sure Thing

Even as the world grapples with the COVID-19 crisis, it is not too early for businesses and organizations to start preparing for the *next* crisis. History shows there is *always* a next crisis. And the sooner you are ready for it, the better.

About this Book

Crisis Ahead provides quick, practical advice and expert guidance to help your business or organization prepare for, prevent, manage, and recover from a crisis, scandal, disaster, or other emergency. This book is for CEOs, senior staff, corporate communication professionals, HR and legal teams, boards of directors, and front-line employees who need to know what to do in the moment: what levers to pull and what moves to make in real time when faced with a crisis or situation.

Some situations could result in nothing more than a temporary embarrassment, while others could cause long-term harm or threaten the existence of your organization. No matter what kind of crisis you face or how long it lasts, you must be ready to respond strategically, efficiently, and effectively.

When, why, and how you read this book depends on your need, priority, and situation.

- If you want a reality check and to gauge your readiness for a crisis, start with Chapter 1: How Ready Are You? Find Out Now Before It's Too Late. The quizzes and written exercises in this chapter will help determine the degree to which you are prepared to confront and deal with different situations.
- If you want to take steps now to prepare for a crisis, start with Chapter 2: If You Fail to Plan, You're Planning to Fail. Here you will learn how to develop and implement your crisis management plan, access a free customizable crisis management and communication plan, and receive updates to the examples, anecdotes, lessons, and advice in this book.
- If you have a plan but have not tested it to make sure it works, go to Chapter 3: Put Your Plan to the Test. This chapter includes anecdotes and insights about why and how others practiced their responses to different emergency scenarios and what some of them learned when they put the plans to use in real crisis situations.
- Do you need help dealing with a crisis situation right now? Turn to Chapter 4: When the Sh*t Hits the Fan: Best Practices. This chapter provides guidance for managing and communicating about a variety of crisis situations.
- Has your crisis attracted the attention of news organizations, or do you think that it will? Then check out Chapter 5: How to Work with the Media during a Crisis.
- Would you like to learn from others who have already been through a crisis? Read Chapter 6: Learn from the Successes and Mistakes of Others. If you have crisis management and communication plans in place, the anecdotes and

examples in this chapter will serve as a wake-up call to update those plans, practice responses to different crisis scenarios, and revise your plans and potential responses as needed. Because of the importance of this content, there is a shaded border on either side of the pages in this chapter, making it easier to find if you thumb through the book. Even when the book is closed, the shaded pages will stand out in case you need to refer to them quickly.

- Are you trying to rebound from a crisis? Go to Chapter 7: Bouncing Back: How to Recover from a Crisis. Here you'll find examples of companies, organizations, and high-profile individuals who have recovered from their crisis and the steps you can take to lay the foundation for your own comeback.
- Are you lucky enough not to be under any crisis-related pressures or deadlines and have the luxury of time to prepare for a crisis? Then use the book as an "A-to-Z" reference guide and browse through the topics that most interest you and your colleagues.

The unfortunate truth is that there were thousands of crisis incidents before I wrote this book, and there will be thousands more after it is published. Readers can stay up to date about the lessons learned from crisis incidents after *Crisis Ahead* was published by going to the Crisis Updates page on my website at PublicRelations.com and entering this case sensitive password (do not include the period): CrisisAheadUpdates2020.

Reality Check

This book is based on the following key realities:

- It's easier, faster, and more affordable to learn from the experiences of others than to suffer through a bad situation yourself—only to find out afterward what you *should* have done.
- It's not a matter of *if* companies will face a crisis, but *when* they will, *where* it will happen, *how* bad it will be, and *what* they will do about it.
- Most organizations do not have the knowledge, skills, or resources to face or recover from a crisis. They do not have a crisis plan in place or, even if they do, have not tested it to see how it would hold up in the real world.
- Hope, luck, delay, denial, or stonewalling are not effective strategies for managing a crisis or trying to avoid one. They usually make matters worse.
- A crisis does not respect national boundaries, calendars, clocks, industries, or professions. It can strike any company, organization, or high-profile individual anytime and anywhere.

- You may need specific skills and resources—such as management, public relations, marketing, advertising, legal, HR, and IT—to help get through a crisis. Depending on the situation, you may have to call on assistance from first responders, law enforcement, healthcare providers, financial experts, consultants, or government agencies.
- A lot can be at stake in a crisis, such as:
  o The stock price of publicly traded companies and the value of privately owned ones
  o The image, reputation, stability, and future of the company
  o Revenues, profits, and future earnings
  o Legal liability, lawsuits, and litigation
  o Insurance coverage and premiums
  o Employee morale
  o Retention and recruitment of workers
  o Relations with customers, clients, vendors, and suppliers
  o Participation and membership in nonprofit organizations
  o Your job and career

The recommendations, examples, and anecdotes in this book are based on:

- My 30-plus years of experience as a crisis management expert, public relations consultant, journalist, communications director, and press secretary for members of Congress and political candidates
- Dealing with internal and external crisis situations as the CEO of two trade associations
- Advising and helping others to work through a variety of crisis situations. The issues I worked on included:
  o The arrest and firing of CEOs
  o Allegations of sexual harassment
  o Unethical and unprofessional behavior
  o Hate crimes
  o Forged documents
  o Natural gas leaks and explosions
  o Violation of property rights
  o Seafood safety
  o Skeletons in an individual's past
  o Public backlash to the policies of a trade association
  o Mismanagement of corporate finances

- o The safety of the nation's blood supply
- o Business and personal bankruptcies
- o Defending the image and reputation of an international corporation
- Conducting crisis management and communication training for hundreds of CEOs and other top company officials
- Advice on public relations strategies, tactics, and techniques that was originally published in a different form in my first book, *Getting Your 15 Minutes of Fame and More!* (New York: John Wiley & Sons, 2000). This advice is featured in Chapter 2 (preparing crisis plans) and Chapter 5 (working with the media during a crisis).
- Interviews with those who have prepared for or managed a crisis
- My analysis of thousands of news stories about how corporations, organizations, and individuals in dozens of industries and professions around the world responded to hundreds of different crisis triggers

CHAPTER 1
How Ready Are You?
Find Out Now Before It's Too Late

Three things that never work for avoiding, managing,
or recovering from a crisis are ignorance, denial, and wishful thinking.

You just learned that someone in your IT department has sent an email to all your customers, vendors, and media contacts. The message contains derogatory comments about you and embarrassing photos of you.

What would you do?

Don't wait until you have a crisis to find out whether you are ready for it. You are bound to be disappointed with the answer. It's safe to assume that if you are reading this book, you want to know now what you can or should do when a crisis strikes. The first step is to take a reality check about your vulnerability to a crisis and how prepared you are to deal with one.

The 10 Rs of Crisis Management

There are several major steps you can take to help ensure that you are as ready as you can be for any crisis. I've boiled the steps down to the following 10 rules—"The 10 Rs of Crisis Management."

1. **Risk.** Identify the risk triggers that would cause a crisis for your organization. Some risks may be unique to your company because of the nature of your business. For example, if you're an airline, a risk trigger would be an plane crash. Other triggers could apply no matter what type of business you are in, such as embezzlement or sexual harassment.
2. **Reduce.** Take the steps that are necessary and prudent to lessen known risks. These steps can be as basic as following common-sense accounting procedures in order to help prevent fraud and forgery to more extensive actions such as providing appropriate training or retraining to employees.
3. **Ready.** Have a crisis plan in place and ready to implement when it is needed. Because one size will not fit all companies, the plan should be customized to meet the needs and realities of your organization and industry.

4. **Redundancies.** Have back-up and contingency plans in case they are required. Since it is impossible to plan for every eventuality, a Plan B, Plan C, or Plan D may be needed, just in case.

5. **Research.** Get all the information you can about your crisis, including details about what just happened, is happening now, or you expect to happen. Knowing the who, what, when, where, why, and how of the situation is essential in helping to respond strategically, effectively, and efficiently.

6. **Rehearse.** Practice implementing your plan on a regular basis—at least once a year. Having a plan and not practicing it is not much different than having no plan at all. The more you practice implementing the plan, the more prepared you will be if and when you need to use it.

7. **React.** Activate your plan when necessary. Know what will trigger a crisis and how you would respond to different crisis scenarios. A crisis is no time to try to learn as you go along.

8. **Reach Out.** Immediately communicate with those who are affected by or concerned about the crisis. Your company or organization may have different publics and stakeholders who would be affected by the situation and would be interested in the outcome.

9. **Recover.** Know how you would bounce back from a crisis. Planning your recovery from a disaster, scandal, or other emergency is just as important as planning your response to it. You will need to get back to normal as quickly as possible, and a recovery plan will help you do just that.

10. **Remember.** Keep in mind the experiences of those who have already gone through a crisis. What would you do to repeat their successes and avoid their mistakes? There is no need to reinvent the wheel when it comes to the best ways to respond to, manage, and recover from a crisis. There are plenty of lessons from which you can learn.

How Vulnerable Are You to a Crisis?

Although there is no way to absolutely guarantee you will never have a crisis of any kind, there are ways to determine how vulnerable you are to one. You can get a good idea about your potential exposure by answering the following 26 questions. The answers will help you to address the first of the 10 Rs—Risk: Identify the risk triggers that would cause a crisis for your organization. The threshold for a crisis depends on the risk trigger and how it affects a company or organization. For example, an international conglomerate whose new product underperforms in the market might be able to absorb the failure and move on; a small start-up company might not be as fortunate. But a trigger such as sexual abuse or workplace violence could create a crisis for an organization of any size.

	Yes	No
1. Is your business in an industry or profession where there have been accidents, such as healthcare, chemical processing, transportation, construction, or aviation?	☐	☐

Vulnerability: Because of the nature of your business, it could be more prone to a crisis.

2. Has or will your company introduce a new product or service?	☐	☐

Vulnerability: The product or service may fail, impacting your bottom line, ability to compete, retain employees, etc.

3. Did your company introduce a product or service that did not do well in the marketplace?	☐	☐

Vulnerability: Your bottom line may suffer, as may your image, reputation, credibility, ability to attract and retain employees, etc.

4. Has there been a recent decline in your sales, revenue, or profits?	☐	☐

Vulnerability: Your bottom line may suffer, as may your image, reputation, credibility, ability to attract and retain employees, etc.

5. Are you in a highly competitive industry or profession?	☐	☐

Vulnerability: You may not have the resources you need to compete successfully; you could be the target of an unwanted merger or acquisition by a competitor; or you may lose clients, customers, or employees to your competition.

		Yes	No

6. Is there frequent turnover among your employees or senior managers? ☐ ☐

   Vulnerability: The people who helped make your company successful and competitive may no longer be working for you.

7. Do you hire and fire people on the basis of their age or sex? ☐ ☐

   Vulnerability: You may be sued for gender or age discrimination.

8. Have you been accused of having a hostile work environment? ☐ ☐

   Vulnerability: You may be subject to litigation, key employees may decide to work elsewhere, and it could be harder for you to attract new workers.

9. Do you have a limited portfolio of clients or customers? ☐ ☐

   Vulnerability: The foundation of your business may be too narrow, thereby putting the future of your company at risk.

10. Do the top officials of your organization go on business trips? ☐ ☐

    Vulnerability: They could be injured or die in a travel-related accident. Depending on the country they travel to, robbery or kidnapping may be a possibility. Or they could miss important meetings or appointments because of travel-related delays.

11. Do you require that only one person sign corporate checks? ☐ ☐

    Vulnerability: Without appropriate accounting-related checks and balances, you may be vulnerable to embezzlement or fraud.

	Yes	No

12. Is your company in an industry that is heavily regulated by the government, such as banking, medicine, or petroleum? ☐ ☐

   Vulnerability: The government may propose or implement regulations that are harmful to your company and its ability to compete.

13. Do you make or sell products or services outside of your country? ☐ ☐

   Vulnerability: Your ability to manufacture and market your products or services could be hampered by new rules, laws, regulations, or tariffs in other countries.

14. Do you buy advertising to market your products, services, or expertise? ☐ ☐

   Vulnerability: Advertising-related costs could increase, making it more expensive to market and promote your company.

15. Do you work with consultants, freelancers, vendors, resellers, or franchisees? ☐ ☐

   Vulnerability: They may make mistakes or errors in judgment that can cost you time, money, credibility, and business.

16. Is your organization located in a country where there has been or could be political unrest or violence? ☐ ☐

   Vulnerability: The future of your company may be at risk, and the lives and safety of your employees could be at stake.

17. Are there forests or heavy vegetation nearby? ☐ ☐

   Vulnerability: Your business could be shut down or destroyed because of a forest fire or wildfire.

	Yes	No

18. Do you store your computer files in the cloud?   ☐   ☐

Vulnerability: Your files and documents could be hacked.

19. Are your computers on a network?   ☐   ☐

Vulnerability: The computers could crash or be hacked.

20. Do you allow employees to work from home or on their personal computers?   ☐   ☐

Vulnerability: The computers could crash or be hacked or attacked.

21. Does your organization have a presence on social media?   ☐   ☐

Vulnerability: Your company's social media platforms may not be secure and could be vulnerable to hacking, spyware, and viruses.

22. Is your office or company located near a river or train tracks?   ☐   ☐

Vulnerability: Your company may be impacted by a flood or a train-related accident.

23. Are earthquakes a regular occurrence in your region?   ☐   ☐

Vulnerability: A serious earthquake could cause fatalities, damage or destroy your building, curtail the operations of your business, and make it difficult for employees to get to work.

24. Is your office or building adjacent to natural gas pipelines?   ☐   ☐

Vulnerability: The closer you are to a natural gas pipeline, the more likely it is that your company could be impacted by a gas-related leak, fire, or explosion.

	Yes	No
25. Is your area subject to floods, hurricanes, snowstorms, or other weather-related events?	☐	☐

Vulnerability: Nature-related events could affect the activities and operations of your business.

	Yes	No
26. Is your office or building located near mountains or hills?	☐	☐

Vulnerability: In the aftermath of heavy rains, your building or business could be affected by mudslides or landslides.

How vulnerable are you to the risk of a crisis? Give yourself 4 points for every "yes" response:

Scoring:	80 or higher	Stormy weather ahead
	72–76	I won't be able to sleep at night
	60–68	Don't be surprised when something bad happens
	56 or fewer	Well, it could be a lot worse

Are You Ready for a Crisis?

Now that you know how vulnerable you may be to a crisis, let's see how ready you are to deal with one.

Three things that never work for avoiding, managing, or recovering from a crisis are ignorance, denial, and wishful thinking. The Crisis Hall of Shame is full of people and companies who were convinced they would never face a crisis or were ready for any crisis, disaster, scandal, or emergency—only to find out how wrong they were. Why would you want to join them in this Hall of Shame? It's best that you find out now how prepared—or unprepared—you and your organization are to take on a crisis.

Get a reality check about your crisis readiness by taking this brief quiz:

Are you able to contact the following people within two minutes?

	Yes	No	Don't Know
1. Key staff members	☐	☐	☐
2. Executive committee	☐	☐	☐
3. Board of directors	☐	☐	☐
4. Attorney	☐	☐	☐
5. Webmaster or IT company	☐	☐	☐
6. CPA or financial adviser	☐	☐	☐
7. Insurance agent	☐	☐	☐

Do these people know how to reach you within two minutes?

8. Key staff	☐	☐	☐
9. Executive committee	☐	☐	☐
10. Board of directors	☐	☐	☐
11. Company attorney	☐	☐	☐
12. Webmaster or IT company	☐	☐	☐
13. CPA or financial adviser	☐	☐	☐
14. Insurance agent	☐	☐	☐

Do you have these contacts in your smartphone or other mobile device?

15. Your local first responders	☐	☐	☐
16. Your mayor and other public officials	☐	☐	☐
17. News organizations in your area	☐	☐	☐
18. Your company's healthcare provider	☐	☐	☐

	Yes	No	Don't Know

Do you:

19. Have an updated crisis plan in place? ☐ ☐ ☐

20. Hold annual drills to test your response to a crisis? ☐ ☐ ☐

21. Know what would trigger a crisis for your company? ☐ ☐ ☐

22. Know the key questions to ask in any crisis? ☐ ☐ ☐

23. Have a list of everyone who should be contacted in case of a crisis? ☐ ☐ ☐

24. Have your staff's email addresses and phone numbers? ☐ ☐ ☐

25. Keep back-up and hard copies of key files and documents? ☐ ☐ ☐

26. Know if you have cell phone coverage in your current location? ☐ ☐ ☐

27. Know the location of your laptop, tablet, and smartphone? ☐ ☐ ☐

28. Know where you can access the internet? ☐ ☐ ☐

29. Have a fire alarm in your office or building? ☐ ☐ ☐

30. Have a sprinkler system in your office or building? ☐ ☐ ☐

31. Have a security alarm in your office or building? ☐ ☐ ☐

	Yes	No	Don't Know

Do you have the following policies and procedures in place:

	Yes	No	Don't Know
32. Leadership succession	☐	☐	☐
33. Hiring	☐	☐	☐
34. Terminating employees	☐	☐	☐
35. Background checks for new hires	☐	☐	☐
36. Background checks for corporate officers	☐	☐	☐
37. Code of conduct	☐	☐	☐
38. Employee discipline	☐	☐	☐
39. Sexual harassment	☐	☐	☐
40. Whistle-blower	☐	☐	☐
41. Internet, email, and social media	☐	☐	☐
42. Human resources	☐	☐	☐
43. Equal opportunity	☐	☐	☐
44. Data back up and recovery	☐	☐	☐
45. Office procedures	☐	☐	☐
46. Annual review of investments	☐	☐	☐
47. Anti discrimination	☐	☐	☐
48. Anti fraud	☐	☐	☐
49. Anti embezzlement	☐	☐	☐
50. Annual review of insurance policies	☐	☐	☐

The Bottom Line

How prepared are you? Give yourself 2 points for every "yes" response:

Scoring: 90–100   We are as ready as possible

                    80–88   We are almost ready

                    70–78   We need to do more work

                    60–68   We have a lot of work to do

                    0–58   Let's hope nothing bad happens anytime soon

To improve your score, take steps now to do what's necessary to turn every "no" or "don't know" answer into a "yes." Take this quiz at least once a year to help ensure that you are as prepared as you can be for any crisis.

What Would You Do If...

The bad news is that it is impossible to prevent every conceivable crisis, emergency, or scandal from striking your company or organization.

The good news is that although you can't *prevent* every possible crisis from occurring, at the very least you can be *prepared* to confront all possible crises. One way to prepare is to do some role playing and think through some possible crisis scenarios. The more you are ready today, the more likely it is that you can come through with flying colors if that scenario becomes a reality tomorrow.

Below you'll find dozens of different scenarios based on worst-case situations and actual incidents that have befallen corporations, organizations, and individuals and could create a crisis for your company. Pick any scenario you want—or all of them if you really enjoy a challenge. Answer the following questions of how you would respond to each scenario.

1. What would you do and in what order?
2. What you would say about the crisis to key audiences or stakeholders such as:
    a. Your board of directors
    b. Staff

    c. Customers

    d. Investors/shareholders

    e. Vendors

    f. The public/target audiences

    g. News organizations

3. What actions would you take to help ensure that a similar crisis would not happen to your company?

Go through this exercise anytime you want, and as many times as you want. Complete one or more scenarios now to gauge your "Crisis IQ"—or go through it while reading other parts of the book to put your new knowledge to the test. Or wait until you're done with the entire book and treat the scenarios as if they were your final exam at the end of a course on crisis management and communication.

Scenario: Earthquake

A powerful earthquake strikes your community during the lunch hour, toppling several buildings adjacent to your office. Numerous aftershocks have already occurred, and more are expected. The lights in your office keep flickering, your phone lines are dead, and your computers are not working. Some of your staff members are out of the office having lunch.

Scenario: Product Defect

Government officials today announced that after a series of complaints, investigations, and tests, they have determined one of your products is unsafe and should be recalled immediately. They said that unless you make an immediate announcement to recall the product, they will make their own announcement to the media and impose fines and sanctions on your company for failing to issue a recall.

Scenario: Illness

A thank-you lunch that you hold for employees was a remarkable success. A few hours after the event, you start receiving phone calls and emails that several of them have been taken to the hospital with suspected food poisoning. You realize you are not feeling that well yourself.

Scenario: Fire

According to news reports, demonstrators in a foreign country have set several buildings on fire in the downtown area of the same city where your company's international sales office is located. The office was heavily damaged by the fire, but you are having problems contacting anyone to find out what happened, if your staff is safe, and whether the company's computers are secure.

Scenario: Tornado Warning

Authorities have just issued an alert for tornadoes in the region, and several twisters have already been spotted near your company's headquarters. Your employees have expressed concerns for their personal safety and the safety of their families.

Scenario: Homophobia

A longtime and valued employee announced last month that he is gay. During the past few days some employees and clients have refused to have any interaction with him, saying that they are not comfortable with his sexual orientation. Earlier today an antigay message was found scrawled on a mirror in the restroom.

Scenario: Discrimination

The manager of one of your stores told a transgender customer to leave because "We do not serve people like you." The customer refused to leave, and the manager called the police who, at the manager's insistence, arrested the customer for trespassing. Other customers who were in the store at the time recorded the incident on their cell phones and the video has gone viral.

Scenario: Racial Slurs

Your CEO was secretly recorded at a recent cocktail party using a racial slur to describe the president of your major competitor. The recording was sent to news outlets and excerpts were played on that night's evening news. Civil rights organizations are now demanding that your CEO resign or be fired.

Scenario: Forgery

The vice president of finance of your organization has been accused by one of his assistants of forging your name on checks and other documents. The chairman of your board of directors has learned about the allegation. She demands to know why you have not informed the board about this and what you are doing about the matter.

Scenario: Death

Mary Smith is the wife of Joe Smith, the chief executive officer of your organization. Mary calls in tears to tell you that Joe was killed in an automobile accident on the way to work that morning. Joe had been giving a ride to Fred Jones, who is the president of your company. Mary does not know whether Fred survived. Before you can ask her any questions, she hangs up, crying.

Scenario: Hostage Situation

Your annual appreciation dinner for your most important clients is being held in the ballroom of a major hotel. While the guests are being served dinner, a member of your staff says that there is a big commotion outside in the hallway. You go to investigate and discover there are a lot of police in the lobby and a gunman has taken hostages in another part of the hotel.

Scenario: Floods and Mudslides

Your company's offices are located close to where a recent fire destroyed vegetation and trees that protected the area against mudslides and floods. It has been raining heavily for several days and there are reports that floods and mudslides are a strong possibility.

Scenario: Embezzlement

You are in the middle of an annual audit being conducted by your accounting firm. The CPA calls to alert you to her concerns that someone appears to be embezzling funds from the company. She says she wants to give you a heads-up about the matter before the audit is completed in several weeks.

Scenario: Unethical Behavior

You are a member of a national trade association that requires its members to abide by a stringent set of rules and a code of ethics; all your employees are required to follow the association's laws and regulations. Several members of the public have filed complaints against your company due to allegations of unethical conduct by your sales manager and her staff.

Scenario: Product Tampering

Your company makes a popular brand of snack food. Local hospitals have announced that several people have become extremely ill from eating your product. Government authorities now believe that someone tampered with your product either at the stores where it is sold or at the factory where it is made.

Scenario: Website Post

An employee who was fired last week has posted comments on Glassdoor claiming that she and others lost their jobs because of age discrimination. In support of these claims, the former employee says she has results of her most recent job performance review in which she received high marks and favorable ratings.

Scenario: Criticism

A new product that you launched a few days ago and are heavily promoting is being severely criticized because its design is seen as being racially insensitive. Various groups and organizations are calling for the product to be taken off the market immediately, and negative comments about the product are now trending on Twitter. Online sales of your other products have started to decline because of the controversy.

Scenario: Active Shooter

As you listen to the radio during your drive home after work, there is a news bulletin that a gunman has killed at least nine people near your exhibit booth at a trade show that is being held at a well-known hotel on the other side of the country.

Scenario: Chemical Spill

A police officer on a bullhorn outside your office announces that a tanker truck traveling on a nearby highway has crashed, sending life-threatening chemicals splashing across the road. The officer urges everyone to stay where they are.

Scenario: Power Outage

You are the administrator of a community hospital with more than 500 beds. The lights in the building started to flicker 10 minutes ago, and then all power in the building went out. For some reason the back-up generator has not kicked in yet. Your pager is beeping, and you are receiving several urgent text messages on your smartphone.

Scenario: Hate Speech

After drinking too much at an after-work party last Friday, several of your employees made and posted a video in which they used anti-Semitic and anti-Muslim language to describe colleagues who had refused to join them for drinks. The video was posted on YouTube, where it is now trending; a group of white nationalists has tweeted praise for your company for hiring people who hold opinions that are so like their own.

Scenario: Ransomware

You just received a text message from someone claiming to have taken control of all your computers. They said that unless you arrange to give them 40 bitcoins by 10:00 a.m. tomorrow they will erase all the data on your computers.

Scenario: Deepfake Video

You are a prominent politician running for reelection. Your press secretary just told you that someone posted online an altered video of you in which you "admit" to having an affair with the wife of your opponent in the election.

Scenario: DUI

The celebrity spokesperson who helps promote your company's products was arrested for driving under the influence. He is now in a holding cell at police headquarters downtown. A reporter at a major business publication has learned about the arrest and left a message for you to call her back right away.

Scenario: Child Pornography

Police have just arrested your HR director for having child pornography on his desktop computer at work and laptop computer at home. He claims that he is being framed by someone at the office who is after his job.

Scenario: Protests

An employee you fired last week for poor work performance has organized a group of his friends who are now picketing your building. They claim—falsely—that you discriminate against the LGBTQ community.

Scenario: Bankruptcy

Your company is bleeding money because of a series of failed product launches. Your CPA and banker both say that you should seriously consider declaring bankruptcy as soon as possible.

Scenario: Whistle-blower

A longtime employee in your bookkeeping department claims to have information about fraud and abuse at the company. She told you she is planning to go to law enforcement officials with the evidence.

Scenario: Accident

Your company recently launched a shared e-scooter service in several cities without first obtaining the approval of local governments. You were just told about a news report that a mother and her baby were killed by someone riding one of your electric scooters in one of those cities.

Scenario: Gas Leaks

You are the president of a gas utility company that provides natural gas to several large cities. Your chief safety officer has expressed concerns about the growing number of reported leaks and your reluctance to spend the money necessary to fix and prevent the leaks. He just called a minute ago to report there was a natural gas explosion in one of the communities served by your company.

Scenario: Workplace Safety

The head of the shipping department called to say an employee was injured when a tall stack of heavy boxes toppled over and crushed him. An ambulance has been called and is now on the way.

Scenario: Extortion

A vendor's lawyer, with whom your legal team has been having heated arguments over a multimillion-dollar contract, says he is calling off negotiations. The attorney says that unless you pay him the full amount of the proposed contract within 48 hours, he will go to the press with damaging information he has about you and your board of directors.

Scenario: Backlash

Consumers are not happy that your company increased the price of your best-selling product by 20 percent. They are now expressing their displeasure on Yelp and other social media platforms.

Scenario: Contamination

The US Food and Drug Administration has notified you that their tests have detected some foreign matter in an over-the-counter medicine your company makes. They believe the contamination occurred during the manufacturing process at one of your plants.

Scenario: Plagiarism

You make a popular online game that is played by millions of people around the world. Someone has posted a message claiming that the videos featured in the game are identical to those used in a game that is made by one of your competitors.

Scenario: Advertising

Your advertising department created a social media ad that uses snippets of video from a popular show that is streamed online. You've just received a letter from the streaming service's law firm threatening to sue because you do not have permission to use the video.

Scenario: Romantic Affair

Your company's vice president of finance promised to give one of the women in his department a raise and promotion if she had an affair with him. You have learned about the affair and the fact that she recorded some of those encounters with him, told a colleague about the affair, and now is threatening to inform the board of directors.

Scenario: Attention to Detail

Your company makes maps of the Earth that are only sold online. You just learned that the names of several countries are misspelled in the newest edition of the map.

Scenario: Banning Products

You make the most popular brand of e-cigarettes in the country. The legislature in the state where your company is headquartered just passed legislation that will outlaw all such devices.

Scenario: Industrial Espionage

You just found out that the head of research and development for your organization obtained the plans for a competitor's new product that is rumored to begin production next year.

Scenario: Workplace Violence

One of your employees was angry that he did not receive a satisfactory performance review last week. This morning he brought a gun to work and shot and injured several of his colleagues. He is now threatening to kill others. Someone called the police after the first shots were fired, but they have not yet arrived.

Scenario: Shortages

A company that supplies important parts for one of the products you make has called to say they unexpectedly ran out of the materials they use to make one of those parts.

Scenario: Downsizing

Because of a recent downturn in sales, you've decided that you have no choice but to lay off half of the people on your payroll. It's either that or run the risk of going bankrupt.

Scenario: Transparency

Customers are contacting your call center to complain that the battery in some of the smartphones your company makes will not charge properly. You were aware of the problem when the product was launched last month but hoped no one would notice it.

Scenario: Child Abuse

You are the priest at a small church. A member of the congregation has just told you that a priest at a nearby church is abusing the children of parishioners.

Scenario: Investigation

An investigation revealed that the president of your company abused his expense account by charging family vacations and extravagant meals on a corporate credit card. Some employees have found out about a report that will be made next week to the board of directors concerning the matter, and they are posting comments on Facebook about it.

Scenarios: Equal Pay

Like many organizations, your company pays women a lot less than men for doing the same work. The women, who make up more than half of your workforce, now say they want you to close the pay gap immediately or they will walk off the job.

Scenario: Racial Profiling

A salesman at a new car dealership you own told a Hispanic couple to leave because "people like you can't afford our cars and you don't know how to drive in our country." The couple refused to go, and the general manager called the police to have them arrested for trespassing.

Scenario: Destruction of Documents

The IT department previously assured you that they had digital copies of all the important documents related to the history of your organization. You now learn that only half of the documents were digitized. The rest were destroyed in a warehouse fire last month.

Scenario: Blaming Others

Your company makes one of the most popular passenger planes in the world. One of the planes crashed yesterday, killing all on board. At a news conference this morning the chairman of the company blamed the crash on "idiot pilots who don't know how to fly."

Scenario: Fines

You are president of an oil refinery that has been releasing toxic chemicals into the air for years. Federal officials sued the company for violating antipollution laws and won. This morning a judge imposed a fine of $50 million on the refinery.

Scenario: Lawsuit

Twenty of your current staff members have told news organizations that they are going to sue your company, claiming it discriminates against minority workers.

Scenario: Hoax

Someone calls 911 to report that they heard shots being fired in your office. Police show up with guns drawn and order everyone to put their hands behind their heads and drop to the floor. No shots were fired, everyone is safe, and you think your company is the victim of a malicious hoax.

Scenario: Congressional Testimony

As chairman of a national financial services company, you have been asked to appear before a congressional committee to explain why hackers were able to steal the private and confidential information about and records of millions of customers.

Scenario: Fired

You are the head of a well-known national corporation. The board of directors has just notified you that because of mediocre performance reviews and your failure to generate enough profits for the company, they are going to terminate your contract. The PR department has already prepared a news release about your departure, a copy of which you just received in your email in-box.

Scenario: Price Gouging

Your company makes a one-of-a-kind medication that people take to treat a certain kind of cancer. Because your organization spent so much money to make the drug, you announced today that you will increase the cost of the medicine by 500 percent. There is already a flood of criticism about your decision on all the social media platforms.

Scenario: Taxes

This morning the *Wall Street Journal* published a front-page story about how a dozen corporations—including yours—have avoided paying taxes in each of the past three years. People are complaining on Facebook that your company cheated its way out of paying its fair share of taxes.

Scenario: Financial News

You've just received unwelcomed news from your marketing and sales departments. The latest quarterly sales figures are below projections, and preorders for a new product that will be launched next year are off. You are scheduled to meet with investors next week and will be asking them for more money so you can develop the next generation of the product. The PR department left a message that the *Wall Street Journal* is interested in doing a profile story about your company.

Scenario: Undocumented Immigrants

Your construction company hires undocumented immigrants. The government has just raided all your worksites and arrested dozens of your employees who cannot prove they are in the country legally. Company officials could be fined or imprisoned for hiring undocumented immigrants.

Scenario: Leadership Failure

You are the president of an organization and apparently had too much to drink before you did a live interview with a reporter on a local television station last night. You called the reporter names, tried to hit him, then walked away from the journalist. The company's board of directors had an emergency meeting this morning to discuss the matter and says that, because of your behavior last night, they no longer have confidence that you can lead the company.

Scenario: Reorganization

In a last-ditch effort to prevent your manufacturing company from going out of business, you have decided to restructure. As part of the reorganization, you will have to fire hundreds of employees, close three factories, and consolidate several departments within the corporation.

Scenario: Elections

National elections were just held in one of the countries where your corporation has several factories. To help fulfill his promise to lower the unemployment rate, the newly elected president in that country wants you to hire more people to work in those factories. If you don't, he is threatening to cancel several lucrative contracts his government has with your company.

Scenario: Pranks

You are the marketing director of a consumer products company that makes, among other things, detergent pods for dishwashing machines. A member of your staff just told you that teenagers are posting videos of themselves on YouTube in which they try to swallow as many of the pods as possible.

Scenario: Wildfire

You own a theme park located near a major freeway and not far away from an area of heavy vegetation. Fire crews have been battling an aggressive blaze about a mile away from the park, with no signs that the fire will be controlled anytime soon. The fire department wants you to close the park immediately.

Scenario: Sexual Harassment

Several women on your staff are complaining about the behavior of a supervisor who insists on touching them inappropriately and making sexist jokes and remarks.

Scenario: Funding

Despite your best efforts, your start-up company is not generating enough income to pay for expenses, much less make a profit. The venture capitalists who provided the money you needed to launch the company are threatening to stop investing unless you show a profit in 12 months.

Scenario: Rumors

You own and operate a national chain of fast food restaurants. There are rumors on the internet that you are going to close several of the restaurants because they are not making money. Although there is some truth to the rumors, they are coming at an inconvenient time because you are in the process of building and opening even more restaurants.

Scenario: Leaked Documents

You were asked by a prominent financial publication to provide documents you considered to be confidential for use in a profile story they are working on about your company. You told the reporter that you would not give them the information they wanted, but the journalist found someone else at your company who has leaked the documents.

Scenario: Terrorism

You are the CEO of an international hotel chain. CNN and other news outlets report that terrorists have bombed one of your hotels in a foreign country. Hundreds of your guests are believed to be injured and dozens are likely dead, according to the reports.

Scenario: Publicity Stunt

To help generate news coverage about your chain of regional brick-and-mortar bookstores, you announced you've hidden in the pages of some of the books clues to the location of a treasure chest full of money. Store managers now report that people are ransacking the stores, throwing books off shelves, and creating pandemonium. The police have been called.

Scenario: Lying

You own a national chain of used car dealerships. To help make your cars more marketable, you've told your mechanics to turn back the odometers of high-mileage cars. Some customers, after buying the cars, now suspect that their car has more miles on it than they were led to believe. The customers have started filing complaints with law enforcement agencies.

Scenario: Resignation

You are the chairman of a company whose president was indicted by a grand jury. She has just submitted her resignation to the board of directors, saying she wants to "spend more time with my family." She made no mention of the indictment in her letter.

*   *   *

Any of the scenarios above could put an organization's ability to deal with a crisis to the test. By practicing these potential situations, you'll have a better idea of what you need to do now in order to be prepared for any of them tomorrow.

CHAPTER 2
If You Fail to Plan, You're Planning to Fail

*In preparing for a crisis, it's always best
to assume nothing and prepare for anything.*

10 Reasons Why You Need a Crisis Plan

There are 10 reasons why you need a plan, and why you need it now. Just like an insurance policy, no one hopes that a crisis plan will ever have to be used. But when the need arises, you will be relieved that it is there and available.

You need a plan because when a crisis strikes you need to know:

- What to do
- Who should do it
- When to do it
- Where to do it
- Why you should do it
- How to do it

You also need a plan to:

- Help protect your company's people, assets, credibility, image, and reputation
- Provide confidence to senior staff, employees, and stakeholders
- Lessen the impact of the crisis on your company or organization
- Help put the matter behind you as quickly as possible

Even when you have a plan in place there will be essential information you will need before you can implement it. There are several questions you should ask that can help you to identify and develop that information. Those questions can be found starting on page 55.

Your Early Warning System

It's important to be aware of and sensitive to possible warning signs of a crisis that can come from a variety of sources, such as the internet and social media. Postings by employees, customers, or other members of the public on websites, Twitter, Facebook, and blogs can tip you off to a problem or issue before it's too late and blooms into a full-blown crisis. Or the posts may give you enough time to prepare for and respond to the inevitable. In either case, the sooner you find out about it, the better.

For example, you can track issues and subjects that might lead to a crisis for your company or organization by setting up individual alerts on Google that will automatically send you news and information about key words and topics. And you can find out what people think about your company, products, or services by visiting sites such as Yelp and Glassdoor.

Some companies encourage online conversations with consumers so they can quickly respond to problems, concerns, or criticisms. That kind of dialogue can defuse and prevent bigger problems from cropping up later.

Whatever you do and however you do it, don't be the last one to know what others are saying about your organization.

The Right Approach

There are right ways and wrong ways to plan for and respond to a crisis. The wrong ways include hoping you will get lucky and never have a crisis, ignoring the many risks and realities that can lead to a crisis, denying that a crisis could ever happen to your organization, and winging it when responding to a crisis.

Those ways never work and will make any crisis worse for you, your company, and everyone affected by it. The right way to plan for a crisis is to:

- Be ready to react quickly
- Know all the facts that you can about the crisis
- Decide ahead of time who will do what, when, where, why, and how
- Have back-up and contingency plans
- Know whom to communicate with about a crisis and when, why, and how they will be notified

- Never assume anything
- Expect the unexpected; don't be surprised when things get worse before they get better
- Ensure that the plan will work
- Put the crisis behind you and bounce back as soon as possible

You can use the plan to:

- Prepare for a crisis
- Test your response to different scenarios
- Help get you through a real crisis

Customize Your Crisis Plan

There is a generic crisis plan at the end of this chapter that you can customize to meet the needs and realities of your company or organization. You can also use it to prepare different plan for different crisis situations (see a list of common crisis triggers starting on page 83). The template has various categories of information that can be filled in and customized for your company and crisis.

I've posted a Word version of the template on my website at PublicRelations.com. You can access the plan by going to the Customized Crisis Plan page and entering this case-sensitive password (do not include the period): CrisisPlan2020. From there, you can copy or download the template, then fill in the blanks and customize and update the plan as needed. Be sure to test your plan on a regular basis to help ensure it will work when needed.

Why You Need a Plan B

It is important to prepare for worst-case scenarios—not just for the various types of crises you may face, but also for how you would respond to them. In practical terms, a plan and a team that cannot be accessed or activated is not much different than having no plan or team at all. For example, what would you do if a deadly earthquake hit and:

- The computer network on which your crisis plan is stored crashes?
- Members of the crisis management team are killed or injured in the earthquake or simply have no access to cell phone service?

- The company president, who is responsible for activating the crisis team, is out of the country and cannot be reached?

In preparing for a crisis, it's always best to assume nothing and prepare for anything.

When members of the Apollo 11 crew were the first to land on the moon in 1969, there was no contingency plan if something went wrong when it was time for them to return to Earth. At the very least, you should have a Plan B if something goes wrong. Why? Because you may not be as lucky as the astronauts.

Your Crisis Management Team

You need to act quickly and decisively in a crisis. This means it will be important that there are as few obstacles as possible in making and approving decisions, implementing decisions, and doing what it takes to address and resolve the situation.

It is never too early to start thinking about who would manage a crisis for your organization. It could be you, top officials of your company, a mix of employees and corporate officers, outside experts, or a combination. The point is this: the best crisis plan in the world is useless without anyone to implement it. Waiting until there is a crisis to appoint a response team to manage it means you will lose valuable time that would otherwise be spent on dealing with the situation.

Crisis Management Team. For most crisis situations, you will be best served by having a crisis response team and team leader. Their background, composition, and responsibilities will vary according to the nature of the company and the crisis. Although the team members may change depending on the crisis, likely members include representatives of the IT, HR, legal, marketing, sales, public relations, and other departments or divisions of the organization.

Determine ahead of time where the team will work, have access to communication and staff support, etc. Appoint back-ups for each member of the team in case they are unavailable or cannot be reached in an emergency.

When activated, the team should have access to all relevant available information about the situation, including the who, what, when, where, why, and how of the crisis. Before it is needed for an actual crisis, the team should meet to come up with the worst-case scenarios, and decide what, from a theoretical standpoint, the options or most appropriate response should be.

While actual decisions will be based on real situations, a list of potential alternatives that could be discussed and considered during an emergency will help save valuable time. Refer to the scenarios that start on page 12 and the crisis case studies in Chapter 6 for ideas and inspiration. The practice scenarios and responses should be written down and kept as a ready reference for when the team meets.

Crisis Team Leader. The team leader should be an individual who commands respect and knows how to manage, lead, and communicate clearly and effectively. They should be very familiar with the organization and available 24 hours a day, seven days a week. In case of illness, travel, or vacation, a back-up team leader should be appointed. The team leader should have the authority to deal with the highest-ranking officials in the organization.

Spokesperson. If the crisis becomes known to the media and the public, it makes sense to appoint a spokesperson to interact with the news organizations. In an ideal world, that individual should have prior experience in public relations and working with reporters. At the very least, they should be knowledgeable about the company and the crisis and able to conduct themselves in a calm and professional manner.

Unless your company already has a spokesperson who can interact with reporters and news organizations, or you are too busy or do not want to take on this responsibility, you may find it necessary to appoint someone to serve as the spokesperson during the crisis. The person who represents the company to the media should:

- Have the full trust, faith, and confidence of senior company officials.
- Be "in the loop" to receive the information they need to do their job—they should have an early heads-up of any potential issues or problems that affect the crisis.
- Be a part of the decision-making process for the approval of media materials and statements.
- Have the resources and technology necessary to do the job, from monitoring the news to distributing media materials.
- Have immediate access to the people they need to answer questions from the media.
- Have undergone media relations and spokesperson training.

An organization should speak with only one voice in a crisis. Therefore, it's important that you have policies in place that require employees to refer to the spokesperson any calls or inquiries they receive about the crisis.

Why and How Your Response to a Crisis May Vary

Choose Your Words Carefully

Although communication is important in a crisis, you should exercise caution in what you say, to whom you say it, and why you are saying it. Your words could extend and worsen the crisis or come back to haunt you in the form of investigations and lawsuits. Depending on the nature of your crisis, you may need to defer to others to say or do something about it, such as federal and state officials, the FBI, and local law enforcement agencies.

Location, Location, Location

The culture of the country in which you are located could affect the way you respond to a crisis and how people react to it. An AP story in the *San Francisco Chronicle* discusses the public appearance of Toyota's CEO in the aftermath of a company crisis:

> Japanese protocol for corporate chiefs under fire usually starts with a deep bow, perhaps a resignation to take responsibility...and sometimes sobbing. A show of heartfelt remorse goes a long way in consensus-oriented Japan, where intentions, not just results, carry meaning.
>
> While tears would be a sign of weakness for an American executive, the Japanese public are swayed by emotions because empathy for a weak person is valued as an honorable trait, says Tatsumi Tanaka, president of Risk Hedge, a consultant for major companies.
>
> "It's a special Japanese aesthetic," he said. "It's a virtue to acknowledge one's mistakes and mend one's ways, and crying is seen as a symbol of that."[1]

The Right Way

While you do not have to cry when you do it, saying you're sorry can be an important step in addressing and recovering from a crisis. But be careful about apologizing. Depending on where you're located, there could be legal implications for expressing remorse about or apologizing for your role in a crisis, scandal, or other emergency. In dozens of US states you can say you're sorry without fear of it being used against you in court.[2]

If and when you apologize, do it right. Generally speaking, it's best to apologize as soon as possible, express appropriate levels of remorse and regret, and commit to making things right.[3] Two celebrities knew when and how to apologize after saying or doing things they regretted. Barbra Streisand apologized for her remarks about two individuals who claimed they had been sexually abused by pop star Michael Jackson (read the full story on page 97), and comedian Kathy Griffin expressed remorse for posting a picture that was meant to humorously depict the severed head of President Donald Trump (read the full story on page 162).

Be sure to keep your attorney in the loop about your crisis, and tell them what you want to do about it and what you are going to say about it. You never know how your actions or words might be used against you. As noted elsewhere in this book, you do not want to do anything that makes a crisis worse or prolongs it. An attorney can also advise you whether there are federal or state laws related to your crisis, such as racial, age, and gender discrimination statutes; advance notification of plant closings; and reporting requirements in the case of cyberattacks.

Also, contact your insurance company in case there are any issues related to an apology as it concerns the losses or damages covered by your policy.[4]

While we're talking about insurance, it's wise to talk with your insurer now about your policy to make sure that you have enough insurance to cover you in a crisis. You do not want to be like the Paradise Ridge Winery in California, which suffered major damage from a wildfire, only to discover that it did not have enough insurance to recover (read the full story on page 223).

Document Your Crisis

Although you may have your hands full when dealing with the crisis, try to take notes about the situation and your activities. Prepare a chronology or fact sheet about the crisis. Distribute it as a handout for use by the crisis team and to document the crisis. Keep a log of all calls, text messages, emails, or other communication received during the crisis. It should include the source's name, position, the questions they asked and the answers they were given, etc. Identify all lessons learned from the experience and update your crisis management plan accordingly.

Next Steps

If you have gone through the scenario exercises that start on page 12 and the crisis case studies in Chapter 6, you have a good idea of the dozens of different scenarios—and real crisis situations—that corporations and organizations could and have experienced. But because there are so many events and activities that can lead to a crisis, no single generic plan could work for every organization or in every crisis. Your plan should reflect the realities of your company.

After your crisis plan is in place, do not file it away and forget about it. Conduct a regular series of drills and exercises throughout the year to ensure the plan will work, to find and address any potential issues, and to update the plan as needed to reflect new realities facing your organization, changes in leadership and staff, etc.

See Chapter 3 for examples of how others have tested their crisis plans.

Crisis Management and Communication Plan for [insert name of company] Prepared /Updated on [insert date] by [insert name] This Plan Was Last Tested in a Crisis Exercise on [insert date]

(There is a Word version of this generic plan on my website at PublicRelations.com. You can access the plan by going to the Customized Crisis Plan page and entering this case-sensitive password (do not include the period): CrisisPlan2020. From there, you can copy or download the template, then fill in the blanks and customize and update the plan as needed.)

Crisis Trigger

Insert whether this plan is customized for a particular type of crisis. If not, what events will activate this plan?

Contingency Plan

Insert whether and where there are back-up plans in case this plan does not apply to the crisis.

Crisis Details

Describe what you know about the crisis, and how current the information is.

Who:

What:

When:

Where:

Why:

How:

Impact

What impact will the crisis have on the operations, activities, reputation, market share, or bottom line of your company? What can be done to lessen that impact?

Awareness

Who already knows about the crisis and how they learned about it.

Notifications

Who should know about the crisis and how and when will they be told.

Success

Describe how you will define success in dealing with the crisis.

Priorities

List what must be done and in what order to address and resolve the crisis.

Deadlines

List any deadlines that must be met.

Messaging

List the three or four most important messages that you need to communicate about the crisis.

Describe how you will distribute these messages via your communication tools or channels.

Questions and Answers

List the questions that people will most likely ask about the crisis and how to respond to them. Will the Q&A be posted online or distributed to key audiences? If yes, when?

Hotline

Will a hotline be established to answer questions about the crisis. If yes, when?

Challenges

List the challenges you may face in resolving the crisis.

Opportunities

Describe any unanticipated opportunities created by the crisis and how you will take advantage of them.

Resources

List the internal or external resources that are needed, such as WiFi access points, computers, paper, printers, cell phones, etc.

Important Contact Information

Insert contact information for those who need to be informed about the crisis.

Approvals

Insert the names of those who will need to approve any decisions, actions, or media materials. To help save valuable time, consider preparing preapproved statements and media materials for different crisis scenarios that can be quickly updated or revised for immediate use.

Red Tape

Insert a list of obstacles or resistance that must be dealt with or overcome.

Crisis Team Members

Insert names, contact information, responsibilities, etc.; include back-up team members in case someone is not available.

Crisis Team Leader

Insert name, contact information, responsibilities, etc.; include a back-up person in case the team leader is not available.

Spokesperson

Insert name and contact information of a primary spokesperson; include a back-up spokesperson in case the primary spokesperson is not available.

Location

Insert the address or location from which the crisis will be managed; include a back-up location in case the first location is compromised.

Recovery

What steps must be taken to bounce back from this crisis?

Distribution

Insert a list of those who have a copy of this plan and which version of the plan they have.

Documentation

Insert a chronology of the events and activities associated with the crisis and what was done to address the situation.

* * *

As noted elsewhere in this book, after you've prepared your crisis plan be sure to review, revise, and update it on a regular basis and use it when you conduct your regular series of crisis drills and exercises. And be sure you can access the plan immediately if and when you need it for an actual emergency.

CHAPTER 3
Put Your Plan to the Test

*As others have found out, there are no assurances
when it comes to a crisis.*

Until you practice using your crisis management plan, you will not know for sure if there are areas in which it can be improved or strengthened. Don't wait until a crisis hits to find out if there are any problems with your plan. That's like buying a new car without first making sure that you like how it drives, feels, and looks. Don't sign off on your plan until you have taken it for a test drive and you're confident it will be a good fit for your organization.

Practice Makes Perfect

Those who apparently believed it would be prudent to test their plans included:

- **NASA scientists.** They were concerned about the possibility of an asteroid hitting the Earth in the future. In their crisis simulation, New York City was destroyed by an asteroid and more than one million people were killed.[1]
- **Bank officials from the biggest Western industrial powers.** They thought it was important to test their response to a simulated cyberattack on their financial institutions.[2]
- **Airport agencies and airline officials in India.** They staged an exercise to see how they would respond to the collision of two planes at an international airport in Mumbai.[3]
- **US military leaders.** They wanted to gauge their response to a simulated cyberattack that crippled the operations of a major army base. To make the drill as authentic as possible, almost all of the power at the base was intentionally turned off without any warning for more than 12 hours.[4]
- **New York City.** A cross section of leaders and representatives from the government and private sectors conducted a "digital fire drill" to see how the city's infrastructure would respond to different cyberattack scenarios.[5]

Back to School

I had an opportunity to observe a crisis management training session that was conducted by the Pentagon for all branches of the US armed services. I watched as dozens of officers from the air force, army, coast guard, marines, and navy worked in small groups to respond to an active shooter scenario at a military base.

The goal of the drill was to ensure that the officers understood the importance of having a prepared plan and knew ahead of time what to do and in what order when a crisis strikes. The students were assigned specific roles and responsibilities for managing the crisis. They had to:

- Decide what to do, why, and in what order in response to the unfolding incident
- Track the location of the shooter
- Collect and determine the accuracy of information about the rapidly changing situation
- Notify key audiences, make decisions about responding to social media posts, conduct interviews with reporters, etc.

The one-day crisis management simulation was held at Fort Meade, Maryland, by the Department of Defense's Defense Information School as part of a 45-day curriculum for public affairs officers. The school draws on a variety of real-life situations from the military and private sectors as the basis for their crisis communication exercises and provides similar training for the armed forces of countries around the world.

The instructors have to train before they are allowed to teach at the school. They must attend a one-month course on preparing lesson plans, the classroom environment, and the rules and regulations of the Defense Information School. "Essentially, you want to take a seasoned public affairs officer…and prepare them to teach what they have already been trained to execute" in the field, said former instructor US Navy Lt. Cdr. Bashon Mann (Ret).[6]

Lesson: This was not a drill.

Mann knows what it's like to live through a real crisis. In 2013 he was the deputy public affairs officer for Adm. Jonathan Greenert, the chief of naval operations. Mann received a phone call in his office at the Pentagon that there was an active shooter situation at the nearby Washington Navy Yard. Greenert happened to be at the Navy Yard at the time of the shooting.[7]

It was a day of panic, confusion, and death. As reported by the *New York Times*, shortly after 8:00 a.m. a former navy reservist opened fire in one of the buildings of the secure military facility. "I heard three gunshots, pow, pow, pow, straight in a row," said Patricia Ward, a logistics management specialist from Woodbridge [Virginia], who was in the cafeteria on the first floor when the shooting started. "About three seconds later, there were four more gunshots, and all of the people in the cafeteria were panicking, trying to figure out which way we were going to run out."[8]

By the time the incident ended, 13 people, including the shooter, were dead.[9]

Mann recalled what he did as soon as he learned about the crisis. "I immediately reached out to my personnel on the ground at the Navy Yard to ensure their safety and gain more first-hand information." His most pressing concern was for the safety and security of his six staff people who were producing a video at the Navy Yard. "Along with NCIS [Naval Criminal Investigative Service], we coordinated a plan to ensure our team was collected, informed, and removed from any harm."

After he found out where his people were and that they were safe, he stayed in touch with them. "We actually were in constant contact [via cell phone and email] throughout [the incident] without any interruptions, which was incredible given the circumstances." Mann reached out to the navy's Office of Information, which was also located in the Pentagon, to coordinate the release of details about the crisis as it happened and find out when the details would be released and who would release them. The information office was already up to speed about the shooting; the office and Mann were soon receiving updates from an operations center at the Pentagon.

"An hour did not go by without some form of communications," he recalled. "Our social media team was at the forefront of our communications quite quickly with an [initial] statement and hashtag for the public to follow."

Later Mann, the chief of naval operations, and the secretary of the navy traveled to a local hospital to meet with injured victims and the press.

Lesson: Have a plan and modify it as necessary.

Mann said the mass shooting was a master class in crisis management. "We were able to witness close up how our response strategy would unfold when the screws tightened and how 'water-tight' our processes were to effectively engage and execute in a crisis scenario. There were lessons learned, but overall, we reacted in real time to a life-and-death scenario and performed well, given the loss of 13 shipmates."

He said the most important crisis management lesson learned from the Navy Yard shooting was to "follow your prepared strategy. Have a plan. Without a plan, you are walking in the dark. We did have a plan for an active shooter scenario, but ironically, not one where we were in a support role" as they were that day.

Before the shooting at the Navy Yard, the crisis plan was based on the assumption that an active shooter event would take place inside the Pentagon. The plan was updated afterward to specify who would be solely responsible for releasing information about a crisis and who would take charge if the incident occurred outside of the Pentagon. Mann said another lesson learned was the importance of speaking with one voice in a crisis.

Groundhog Day

As Mann and his colleagues found out, a crisis drill is one thing. But there is nothing like an actual crisis to put a plan to the ultimate test. That's when you know for sure what works, what doesn't, and what needs to be strengthened or improved.

CSX Transportation is a railroad freight shipping company that has had more opportunities than most organizations to react to crisis situations and update and refine their plans and responses, strategies, tactics, and techniques as needed. Working in a highly regulated industry, the company is under constant scrutiny as it operates trains on 21,000 miles of track in 23 states, the District of Columbia, and Canada.[10] Rob Doolittle is a former director of communications and media relations for CSX. He shared with me the following insights and lessons about responding to crisis situations that are not covered elsewhere in this book.[11]

Lesson: Know how newsworthy your crisis can be.

Accidents can make great visuals for television cameras, and train accidents are no exception. Doolittle recalled: "Burning tank cars, 60-foot-long rail cars upended or overturned in a giant pile, steel rails and wooden rail ties lifted off the ground and twisted into unrecognizable shapes—these are all exciting images to splash on a TV screen, and they attract swarms of cameras to events that might actually have very little impact on the public."

Lesson: Do the right thing and do things right.

The mandate from CSX's senior leadership was to "do the right thing" when one of its trains is in an accident. Doing the right thing meant:

- Helping people who were affected by an event
- Cleaning up any environmental impact
- Restoring property to its preaccident condition
- Investigating incidents to determine the root cause and then using that information to improve procedures to help prevent similar accidents

Lesson: Make sure everyone knows what to do when the media calls.

All CSX employees understood that media queries were to be referred to the company's media relations department. CSX maintained a media hotline that was monitored 24/7. The hotline phone number was widely publicized so that employees who interacted regularly with the public and might find themselves at the scene of an incident knew how to refer inquiries to the media team.

Lesson: Know what decisions will have to be made and when.

Initial decisions that had to be made about each CSX accident included whether to manage the situation remotely or on site, what effect having representatives on the scene would have on the news coverage, who would handle press inquiries if a company spokesperson was traveling to the site, and whether additional help from an outside public relations agency was necessary.

Lesson: It's just as important to know what you can't say as what you can.

Major details about accidents were quickly released by the company to ensure the public had relevant information and that CSX was seen as a concerned, responsive organization. The information included the type of train that was involved, its origin and destination, and what it was carrying.

But there were limits to what could be divulged to the public. Because major accidents were frequently investigated by one or more federal authorities, the company was prohibited from sharing some details about serious incidents until after official investigations were complete, Doolittle said.

Lesson: Be consistent.

To ensure that the company's messages to the media and public were consistent, the media relations teams used a library of preapproved statements and talking points that were customized for each accident.

Lesson: Notify key audiences.

The company notified customers about accidents that were expected to impact or delay their shipments by sending messages through the sales and marketing team to customer contacts and by posting messages on customer-focused web pages. "CSX went to great lengths to limit the impact of major events on customers to the extent possible by re-routing trains around portions of the railroad that were affected when delays were expected to be significant," Doolittle recalled.

Lesson: Keep people informed.

The number of statements that were issued depended on how disruptive the accident was to a community, safety risks, and the attention it received by the media. Statements were also used as the basis for press interviews and responding to questions from reporters.

To help keep everyone in the loop, the statements were shared with CSX teams who were responsible for communicating with investors, government officials, employees, and others.

Lesson: Monitor social media.

CSX closely monitored social media and news coverage, especially during major incidents. "The social media conversations were very helpful in understanding what issues were of primary concern to the public, whether company messages were reaching the intended audiences, and whether there were factual errors in circulation that needed to be addressed or corrected," Doolittle said.

Lesson: Pay attention to mainstream news organizations.

Doolittle's team also followed other news organizations to monitor the tone and substance of their stories, spot any reporting errors that needed to be corrected, and make sure the news outlets received and used the company's updates about accidents.

Lesson: Keep calm and carry on.

Doolittle said that reacting calmly, matter-of-factly, and with information about situations that looked like chaos to the casual observer enhanced his ability to communicate the railroad's key messages to the media.

Lesson: Never stop learning.

The communications team evaluated the effectiveness of its response to every major event through after-action reviews to identify opportunities for improvement. They received input from colleagues in other departments (government relations, public safety, etc.) to help ensure they had a balanced perspective.

*   *   *

As others have found out, there are no assurances when it comes to a crisis. Because there are no guarantees that a crisis plan will work as hoped, the more you practice implementing it, the better off you will be when it has to be used in a real crisis situation.

What will you learn from your crisis management practice sessions?

CHAPTER 4
When the Sh*t Hits the Fan: Best Practices

These guidelines will help place you on the right road to address, resolve, and put the crisis behind you as soon as possible.

Be sure to read this chapter if you:

- Are having a crisis right now.
- Don't have time to read any other chapters in this book.
- Don't have a crisis plan.
- Can't find the crisis plan you have.
- Have a crisis plan but don't know the last time it was updated or tested.
- Want to make sure your crisis plan is up-to-date and you have not left anything out.
- Are unfamiliar with basic aspects of public relations, do not have access to a PR consultant or agency, and need help and need it *NOW*.

As you read this chapter, keep this advice in mind:

- Follow the first Law of Holes: When you find yourself in a hole, stop digging. Do not do or say anything that can make matters worse or prolong the crisis.
- Remember the words of former British prime minister Winston Churchill: "If you're going through hell, keep going."
- Although the event that triggers a crisis for you or your organization will vary, the basic rules and guidelines for how you should respond to, manage, and communicate any crisis are basically the same.

After you read this chapter (and time and circumstances permitting), read Chapter 2 about crisis plans, where some of what you'll read below is discussed in depth.

What to Do First

A crisis can be a time of confusion, disorder, distraction, and intense pressure. Here's a list of basic guidelines to help you tackle the challenges you are encountering or will soon face. These guidelines will help place you on the right road to address, resolve, and put the crisis behind you as soon as possible.

Get the Facts

- Get the facts and get them right. Confirm or verify as many details about the crisis or emergency as soon as you can. Don't deny the obvious or accept "alternative facts." Be honest with yourself about what has happened or is happening. It is what it is.

Define Success

- Based on what you know about the situation, how do you define success in dealing with the crisis? How will the issues you are confronting be resolved? How will you know when the crisis is over?

Control

- Take control of the situation.
- Control the crisis instead of letting the crisis control you.
- Demonstrate that you and the company are in charge of or on top of the situation.

Show Concern

- Demonstrate the organization's concern and empathy.
- Put yourself in the shoes of those who are affected by the crisis. If you were in their place, what would you want the company to do or say about the situation?

Communicate

- Provide accurate and up-to-date information to key audiences or stakeholders via Twitter, Facebook, email, websites, etc.
- If there are things you do not or cannot know about the crisis, be prepared to explain why that's the case and when you will have that information available.

Be Careful What You Say

Based on what you know now, notify the appropriate individuals or organizations and keep them informed when it is necessary.

- Always tell the truth.
- Be honest and candid without violating any confidences.
- Do not speculate about:
  - o The cause of the crisis.
  - o Resumption of normal business operations.
  - o Any outside effects of the emergency.
  - o The dollar value of the losses, if any.

Set Priorities

- Set priorities for what has to be done to achieve success and in what order.
- Establish realistic deadlines for dealing with each aspect of the crisis.
- Stay absolutely focused on meeting the priorities, and avoid the temptation to do anything that gets in the way of achieving them.

Take Action

- Don't wait. Once you know what needs to be done, do it. A crisis is not like a bottle of wine—it can get worse, not better, with age.
- The sooner you deal with the crisis, the sooner you will be able to put it behind you and move on—or help prevent a reoccurrence of the same emergency.

Get the Help You Need

- Unless you have no choice or any other options, don't try to carry the entire weight of the crisis on your shoulders. You may have to bring in more people within your organization who can help respond and manage the crisis or retain the services of outside consultants and experts.
- The help you need will depend on the nature of the crisis, where it occurs, and your access to legal, PR, and other necessary help you may need.

- The suggestions for who you may need to contact for each crisis are just that—suggestions. Use your judgment—or ask others for theirs—about whom to contact, when, and why. No single individual is likely to have the knowledge, expertise, or skills that may be needed to navigate their way through a crisis. This, of course, is why I wrote this book. And why you may also need the help and guidance of others to get through your own ordeal.

Follow Up

- Ensure that all deadlines and priorities are being met.

Write It Down

Keep track of what you did, when, why, and how it was done. You can use the notes to ensure that you or your team are not missing or forgetting to do something important. These notes will come in handy when it's time to evaluate your responses to the crisis after it is over and to be better prepared if another crisis strikes.

Next Steps

Now that you know how to approach the crisis, here's what you need to do next. Think of the following guidelines as the best practices you should strive to meet as you deal with your situation.

What you do and when you do it will depend on the nature of your crisis. Some things may have to be done one at a time and in the order in which they are listed below. Others might have to be grouped together and done simultaneously.

Stay Informed

- Obtain the latest accurate information about the crisis and any updates.
- If you can't get the answers to your questions, do your best to get them as soon as you can.
- You or your staff may need to monitor social media platforms and the internet for news or developments.

- In some crisis situations it may be impossible to know everything you need to know when you want to know it. That's not unusual in a crisis. Work around any obstacles the best you can.

Do a Reality Check

Use the following checklist to help ensure you know—or will try your best to know—everything that you should about your crisis. Don't guess or assume anything. Use the Known and Unknown columns to keep track of what you do know now or need to find out as soon as possible.

	Known	Unknown
- What happened	☐	☐
- Were there any deaths or injuries	☐	☐
- If there were injuries, how many and how severe?	☐	☐
- When did it happen	☐	☐
- Where did it happen	☐	☐
- How is it affecting or impacting us	☐	☐
- Who is affected or impacted by it	☐	☐
- Why did it happen	☐	☐
- How did it happen	☐	☐
- Who knows about it	☐	☐
o Staff/employees	☐	☐
o Legal team	☐	☐
o HR department or consultant	☐	☐
o IT	☐	☐
o Public relations department or consultant	☐	☐
o Board of directors	☐	☐
o Vendors	☐	☐
o Clients/customers	☐	☐
o News organizations	☐	☐

- o Public   ☐   ☐
- o Social media   ☐   ☐
- How do they know about it   ☐   ☐
- Where and how can people find more information   ☐   ☐
- What, if anything, has been done about it   ☐   ☐
- How recent is the above information   ☐   ☐
- What else should we know, but don't   ☐   ☐

React Immediately

If you see, hear, read, or are told anything about the crisis that you know to be inaccurate or misleading, take whatever steps are necessary to correct the misinformation. The longer incorrect information is left to stand, the more likely it will spread, become conventional wisdom, and be harder to correct.

Set Priorities and Deadlines

List in order of priority what you will do in response to the crisis and the deadline for completing these tasks.

Priority   Deadline

1.

2.

3.

4.

5.

6.

7.

8.

9.

10.

Cut Red Tape

The larger the organization, the more likely it is that you will encounter some form of bureaucracy that can slow you down or get in the way of doing what needs to be done. Find ways to make things happen as quickly as possible.

Organize Your Thoughts

If you think you will never have to talk about your crisis because no one will ever find out about it, I suggest you think again. News, information, or gossip about a crisis has a way of spreading, even in the most tight-lipped organizations. It's usually not a matter of *if* a crisis will become known, but *when*. That's why it's always best to be prepared and at least have a brief statement that's ready to use.

Before you prepare a statement or say one word about your crisis to anyone—employees, stakeholders, the media, or the public—it is absolutely essential that you know what you are talking about. If you say anything without having at least the bare facts of a situation, you can make things worse, show that you are not in command, and create doubt and uncertainty.

The facts you should have in your statement—or be able to explain why you do not have—are the who, what, when, where, why, and how of your crisis. These are the same categories of information that good journalists include in their stories. It can help to think like a journalist—even if the story about your crisis is never covered by the media. After all, anyone who hears about your crisis—or anyone you want to tell about it—will want to know this basic information about the situation.

Put yourself in the shoes of the journalists who receive your information, and ask yourself this: If I were a reporter, what would I ask about what I just heard? Then carefully review the draft statement and strengthen, revise, or improve it as necessary.

But no matter how strong and ironclad you think your statement is, some reporter, employee, investor, or member of the public may have concerns or issues about it, ask critical questions, or demand more information. Be prepared for what might come.

Whenever you receive new information about the crisis, be sure to update the who, what, where, when, why, and how about the situation.

For more advice on how to work with the media during a crisis, go to Chapter 5.

Be Seen and Heard

Perceptions are as important as reality in a crisis. In addition to doing something about the situation, you should also be *seen* doing something about it. Being seen can help assure people that you are in charge, in control, and on the job. Hiding or staying out of sight in times of crisis will send the message that no one is in charge, no one knows what's happening, no one is doing anything about it, or that no one cares.

There are any number of ways you can be seen and heard:

- Meet with staff and employees.
- Hold a conference call with clients and vendors.
- Post messages on social media to take advantage of the best available communication technologies.
- Talk to the media.

Tell people what you know about the crisis and what you are doing about it and answer their questions as best you can. Be sure to provide information from the viewpoint of the public's interest rather than from the organization's interest.

- Identify and reach out to people who are affected by the crisis or will have an interest in the outcome.
- Release only accurate, confirmed, and verified information.
- When appropriate, refer the media to others for the information they are seeking. For example, in case of an accident or medical-related crisis, it could be more appropriate to refer journalists to a hospital, first responders, or healthcare experts.
- Explain what happened in clear, easy-to-understand language; avoid jargon and technical terms.

- Tell employees what they should say to the media, such as: "I'm sorry, but you will have to talk to (insert name) about that."
- Before releasing any information, notify key officials in your organization about what you are going to say so they are not surprised.

Appoint a Crisis Team

Depending on the size, magnitude, and nature of the crisis, it may be necessary to delegate the management of the crisis to a team, team leader, and spokesperson.

The number of team members and their responsibilities will depend on the size of your organization and the nature of the crisis. Try not to burden any one person with too much to do. You cannot afford to let anything slip through the cracks.

To learn more about assembling a crisis team, go to page 30.

Depending on the nature of your crisis, news organizations may be interested in covering it. To learn about working with the media, go to Chapter 5. To learn how the media relations team at CSX Transportation dealt with news organizations that covered train accidents, go to page 46.

CHAPTER 5
How to Work with the Media during a Crisis

The reality is that you may have no choice about whether you want to deal with the media. They may simply show up at your door without warning.

A cardinal rule of crisis management is to immediately announce the bad news and take steps to put the crisis behind you as soon as possible. Telling news organizations about your situation will certainly help you do that. You will also strengthen your image and reputation by being honest and transparent about the crisis.

Yes, I know what you may be thinking if you are in the middle of a crisis right now: "I have a very full plate and don't have time to worry about the media." Fair enough. If you are unable or unwilling to personally work with news organizations at this moment, then delegate this important responsibility to an appropriate member of your staff or retain the services of a PR consultant or company.

The reality is that you may have no choice about whether you want to deal with the media. They may simply show up at your door without warning. Depending on the type of crisis you are going through, word may spread about your situation, and you may be contacted by journalists and news organizations who will want to know about it. Once they learn the details, they may just go ahead and do stories about the crisis, with or without your input.

"Mike Wallace Is Here"

Mike Wallace was a hard-hitting and no-nonsense newsman. You knew you were going to have a bad day when he showed up to interview you for one of his investigative stories for the *60 Minutes* television show. If you were not having a crisis before he arrived, you likely had one by the time he left. Many of the people Wallace interviewed found out the hard way that you may be able to run from the press, but you cannot hide.[1]

There is no shortage today of reporters who make it their job to ask tough, embarrassing, and penetrating questions and keep digging into stories to see where the facts take them. It should be your job, then, to be as prepared as possible to answer their questions about your crisis and tell your side of the story as best you can.

Some Truths about the Media

Refusing to acknowledge that you have or had a crisis or ignoring inquiries from reporters will not make them go away. The media will jump to the conclusion—rightly or wrongly—that you are trying to hide something, which would only make matters worse for you. Rather than putting them off, your refusal to talk to reporters will likely encourage them to dig in and redouble their efforts to find out what's happening at—or to—your organization.

The good news is that, like the public, news organizations usually have short attention spans and, after an initial round of headlines and stories, will be ready to move on to the next "big story"—which will be another step in helping you put the crisis behind you as quickly as possible.

If your company has little or no experience dealing with the media, then your emergency will provide you with a crash course in media relations. This is all the more reason why it's important to understand reporters and how to get along with the media—which is what this chapter is all about. If you have the time now, keep reading. Otherwise, come back here when you can.

Reporters

From my perspective, journalists are neither your friends nor enemies. They are professionals who are trying to do their jobs the best way they can.

First and foremost, reporters are looking to satisfy their own needs, not yours. They are surrogates for their readers and viewers. Their task is to gather as much information as possible and produce a story that will hold an audience's attention. They are storytellers. They will be looking for stories, anecdotes, and simple explanations about your crisis. And they will not have a lot of time or space to tell the story—about 90 seconds for a TV story, less than a minute for radio, only a few hundred words for print or online stories—and only 280 characters per tweet.

Don't say or do anything that would put you in a bad light. A good example is former BP CEO Tony Hayward, who told news organizations during the company's massive oil spill after a rig exploded in the Gulf of Mexico, "I want my life back." The accident killed 11 workers and created the worst oil spill in US history.[2]

Reuters reported that Hayward was appalled when he read what he had said. "I made a hurtful and thoughtless comment," he said in a statement. "I apologize, especially to the families of the 11 men who lost their lives in this tragic accident. Those words don't represent how I feel about this tragedy." [3]

Immediately respond to all calls, texts, or emails from reporters. In this day of never-ending news cycles, deadlines can be fluid and journalists often post their reports and updates on social media platforms as soon as they are ready.

- Remember that you and the media could both be under a lot of pressure. You are trying to deal with a crisis, and reporters are trying to cover it and meet their own deadlines.
- Reporters are not perfect—who is?—and may make mistakes like anyone else. You will need to monitor their stories to make sure they don't get anything wrong and take steps to correct a story as soon as possible. See the section later in this chapter, "When News Organizations Get the Facts Wrong."

When it comes to making mistakes, a company in crisis can make them just as easily as the reporters who cover it. If not properly prepared, corporate officials can make a crisis worse or drag on longer than necessary by what they say to reporters and how they say it.

There are many different communication tools you can use to help tell your side of the story, including your website, social media posts, emails, text messaging, and news releases. For the latest examples of these and other crisis communication tools, go to my website at PublicRelations.com, then click on the Crisis Press Materials page and enter this case-sensitive password (do not include the period): CrisisPressMaterials2020.

Visuals

Depending on the nature of your crisis, it can be important to provide visuals that will help tell the story about what has happened. Television and websites are obviously visual mediums. If TV stations decide to cover your crisis, they will want pictures to go along with their story. And if you cannot provide the pictures, they will find them, whether it's from your website or elsewhere.

Unfortunately, the pictures the media finds may not be the ones you would have preferred or given to them, whether it's a chart, graph, logo, Instagram photo, YouTube video, or picture from your website.

Then again, your crisis may not lend itself to visuals, or it could be one in which the visuals are obvious and easily available, such as the aftermath of a fire, flood, or explosion. The other reality is that you and your staff may be too busy to worry about pictures and will have to spend every second and ounce of energy dealing with the immediate issues in front of you.

Media Interview Checklist

There is no such thing as being too prepared for a media interview. Use the following guidelines to help ensure that you are ready to talk to the media about your crisis.

Topic

- Is there a particular aspect of your crisis that the reporter wants to discuss?

Your Message

- What is the overarching message you want to communicate in the interview?
- What are the three to four most important points you want to make? The more points you make, the less likely it is that the media will include all of them in their stories.

On the Record

- Assume that everything you tell a reporter is on the record and may be used in their story.

Questions

- Anticipate all questions that the reporter might ask about your crisis.
- Put yourself in the shoes of the reporter. If you were the journalist, what questions would you ask?

When You Don't Know

If you don't know the answer to a reporter's question, say so. Then tell them you will find out the answer and get back to them right away. Otherwise, you run the risk that the journalist will try to get the information from somewhere else—and get it wrong.

Deadline

- When does the reporter want to do the interview?
- Can you call them back later for the interview, and what is the best way to contact them?

The Journalist

- What news organization does the reporter work for?
- Who is their audience?
- How much time does the reporter want for the interview?
- Where do they want to conduct the interview?
- Who else is the reporter talking to for the story?
- If feasible, can you research other stories the reporter has done before you do the interview?

Information

- Do you have the latest accurate information about all aspects of your crisis?

Practice

- Have you practiced your answers? By rehearsing (not memorizing) your responses, you can guard against being surprised by something you say.

Visuals

- What visuals can you use to help tell the story about your crisis? (See page 63.)

Length

- Set a time limit of 15–20 minutes for most interviews. Remember, you still have a crisis to manage.
- Keep your answers short: 20–30 seconds for print interviews, 10–20 seconds for radio and television. (See page 69 for information about sound bites and ink bites.)

Setting

- If the interview will be held in your office, make sure any papers or information you don't want the reporter to see have been safely put away. Let your colleagues know that a reporter will be in the office so they are on notice not to do or say anything embarrassing or that could make the crisis worse.
- When the interview will be conducted online or on the phone, ensure that there are no distracting noises that will break your concentration or may be picked up by a microphone or phone. Be sure that your cell phone is turned off. (See page 76 for information about Skype and satellite media tours.)
- If the interview will be done online through a series of exchange emails or text messages, be sure to read out loud the questions and your responses before hitting the Send button. Also, run a spell check on your responses. Consider asking a trusted colleague to review the copy as well. A second pair of eyes might pick up errors or issues that escaped your notice.

Answering Questions

- Have immediate access to all the information you'll need to answer the questions.
- Have an appropriate answer ready for each possible question.
- As necessary, customize your answers for the audience of the news organization.
- Tell the truth and keep your answers consistent, no matter how many times you are interviewed or asked the same or a similar question.
- Find ways to repeat your key points throughout the interview.
- And again, assume *everything* you tell the reporter is on the record.
- Be prepared to cite the source of any studies, statistics, etc., that you use in your answers.
- If you don't know the answer to a question, say so. Then tell the reporter you will have to call them back with an answer.
- Use bridging techniques to avoid giving a direct answer to a question you don't want to answer. Jump from the question the reporter asks to the one you want to answer by saying: "That's an interesting question, but a more important question is..." Then ask and answer your own question.
- Rather than saying "No comment" in response to a question (which can make you sound as if you are trying to cover something up), patiently explain why you can't provide the information the reporter is seeking. Alternative answers could

include: "I'd like to answer that, but the situation is just too fluid right now." Or: "I wish I could tell you, but there are some things that we just don't know, and that's one of them."

- Don't repeat a reporter's negative questions in your answer.

For more advice about answering questions, see the "Sound Bites and Ink Bites" section later in this chapter.

Listen

- Be a good listener. Pay attention to what the reporter is saying and how they are reacting to your answers.
- Don't assume you know what the reporter is asking before they finish the question. Be sure you listen and fully understand the question before responding.

Voice

- Use a conversational tone—don't give a speech.
- Avoid speaking in a monotone.

Dress for the Press (for in-person interviews and news conferences)

- Depending on how much time you have before meeting with reporters, try to dress as appropriately as you can for the interview, especially if it will be on television.
- How you look can send an important message about you. People who wear jeans and T-shirts to an interview send one message (lax, not in charge); men who wear a suit, tie, or sports coat and women who wear a pantsuit or dress send another (professional, in command).
- People who are on TV for a living—news anchors, reporters, and talk show pundits—provide important lessons about what you should or should not wear when meeting with news organizations. Those lessons include wearing solid blue and gray colors, avoiding small tight patterns that will produce a strobe effect on camera, avoiding clothing with big bold prints, and staying away from large or distracting jewelry.
- The bottom line is this: Don't wear anything that distracts people from paying attention to what you have to say about your crisis.

Body Language (for in-person interviews)

- Maintain good posture.
- Use appropriate hand gestures and facial expressions.
- Maintain eye contact with the reporter.
- Don't fidget or do anything that will distract a reporter from your answer.

Feedback

- Record your answers for later reference and evaluation and in case you are mis-quoted. Don't record the reporter without his/her consent.

Attitude

- Be confident and authoritative in your answers and demeanor.
- Be yourself as much as you can. Project self-confidence in the way you dress, your body language, and the tone and manner of your voice.

Interview Pitfalls to Avoid

- Placing blame
- Getting mad, defensive, or arguing with the reporter
- Minimizing the problem
- Saying or doing anything that could create legal risk or liability; consult with an attorney if necessary
- Releasing information about people if it will violate their privacy or legal rights
- Saying "No comment." (See page 66.)
- Answering a question unless you understand what is being asked. If necessary, ask the reporter to repeat or explain the question, or rephrase the question in your own words
- Expecting the reporter to ask you the questions you want to answer. Look for ways to include in your answer the points you want to make
- Responding to hypothetical questions
- Talking longer than you must to respond to a question
- Using lots of numbers or statistics in your answers; use them sparingly to make your point
- Agreeing to talk "off the record"
- Using jargon, technical terms, or acronyms in your answers.

- Feeling compelled to fill a void in a conversation with a reporter. If you have nothing to say, don't say anything.

Sound Bites and Ink Bites

Can you talk about your crisis in seven seconds or less? That's often all the time a television or radio station will give you in an edited on-air story to talk about your crisis.

Seven seconds is not a lot of time. (How long is it? Count out loud from 1,001 to 1,007 to see for yourself, or time yourself against a clock or watch.)

These all-too-brief remarks are known as sound bites—small portions or "bites" from interviews that are inserted in news stories to help enliven, tell, or illustrate news reports. Ink bites, the printed version of sound bites, can range from five to 50 words long. In most cases, if your response to a reporter's question runs longer than the time it takes to read this sentence aloud, most reporters won't use your quote in their stories. Instead, they will condense, paraphrase, summarize, or ignore your answer.

Here are three examples of quotes that news outlets used about different crisis situations:

When it was announced that Philadelphia had made $1 billion in accounting and bookkeeping errors:

"Taxpayers deserve more than this. It's time for the city to treat taxpayer money with the respect that it deserves and government needs to work better," said city controller Rebecca Rhynhart.[4]

For information about this crisis, go to page 89.

After a hostage situation at a UPS facility in New Jersey:

"According to the preliminary investigation, the shooting occurred after the gunman and hostages had exited the building," the attorney general's office said.[5]

For information about this crisis, go to page 161.

After an active shooter crisis ended at a manufacturing company in Illinois:

"I hate that we have to use the term classic workplace shooting, that pains me to do so, at this time I don't know. Again, we can only surmise that with a gentleman who's being terminated that this was something he intended to do," police chief Kristen Ziman said.[6]

For information about this crisis, go to page 92.

Any sound bite or ink bite is a good one since it means you said something interesting and short enough to be included in a reporter's story. But I don't think that good is good enough. Your comments should:

- Accurately capture the essence of what you want to say about the crisis.
- Convey the message you want to send to the public about your crisis.
- Feel right or comfortable for you to say.
- Offend no one.
- Be credible and believable.

An effective way to learn how to prepare and deliver sound bites is to pay attention to how news organizations report what others in the news are saying about their own crisis.

Television and radio news broadcasts and newspaper and magazine articles are full of sound bites and ink bites from people in different professions and walks of life. Studying what these newsmakers say and how they say it is one of the best continuing educations you can obtain in the art of preparing and delivering sound bites and ink bites.

After preparing hundreds of quotes for clients and studying thousands of sound bites over the years, I've concluded that effective sound bites are like sandwiches: there are thousands of ways to make them according to your own tastes and preferences. I think the most effective quotes are those that contain at least one of the following characteristics:

- Clichés   "We find ourselves between a rock and a hard place."

- Absolutes   "This is the worst thing to ever happen at our company."

- Analogies   "It feels like we have been tackled and knocked to the ground. But I know we will get back up and keep trying."

- Firsthand experiences "This crisis reminds me of the time when…"

- Predictions   "We should recover our losses within the next 18 months."

- Warnings   "If we don't solve this problem now, we never will."

- Rhetorical questions "Who could have seen this coming?"

Exercise: Write Your Own Sound Bite

It is usually difficult for most people to come up with the perfect sound bite without some degree of preparation and practice. So before you have to deliver a sound bite about your crisis, take a few minutes to go through the following exercise.

- Describe your crisis in about 100 words.
- Review what you just wrote and eliminate any jargon or other language that may be unfamiliar or confusing to the public; keep the copy simple and basic. Take a look at the list of ingredients for effective sound bites earlier in this chapter and use at least one of them in your description.
- Reduce your comments to a manageable sound bite length—about 7 seconds. Rewrite the copy one more time but keep the length to no more than 50 words.
- We're almost done. Now try to say the same thing in 25 words or less.
- Ask a colleague or friend to play the role of a journalist to ask you this question: "Tell me what happened today at your company."
- Give them your sound bite.
- Finally, ask the "reporter" what they thought of your answer. Was it short enough? Did it effectively convey your key messages or information about the crisis? If not, go back and read this chapter again and try this exercise one more time.

News Releases

In addition to posting information about your crisis on your website and social media platforms, distributing a news release to editors and reporters can be another effective and efficient way to provide information to the media and the public.

These 250- to 600-word documents tell what happened, when it happened, where it happened, who was affected, and how it happened—or as much as you know when you write the news release.

The news release should:

- Summarize the crisis with an appropriate headline.
- Present the information as if it were a pyramid, with the most critical information at the top and the least important at the bottom.
- Have a succinct opening paragraph that captures the who, what, when, where, why, and how of the crisis.
- Include relevant facts, figures, and background information about the crisis.
- Have short sentences and paragraphs with one or two sentences each.
- Include your name, daytime and evening phone numbers, and email and website addresses at the top of the first page.
- Include basic information about your company or organization at the end of the release.
- Follow the same rules for grammar and punctuation that reporters adhere to when they write their articles. It's all laid out for you in *The Associated Press Stylebook*, which can be found online and at many libraries and bookstores.

I've posted links to sample news releases and other press materials on my website at PublicRelations.com which you can access on the Crisis Press Materials page by entering this case-sensitive password (do not include the period): CrisisPressMaterials2020.

There can be obvious and major differences between the news release you send out about your crisis and how news organizations report it. Keep this in mind if and when your crisis is covered by news organizations: news outlets may not report it the way you want or prefer. The most you can hope and work for is that they get the facts right and include your side of the story.

There are links on my website to the stories that news organizations have done about various crisis situations. You can access the links by going to the Crisis Updates page on PublicRelations.com, and then enter this case-sensitive password (do not include the period): CrisisAheadUpdates2020.

While it's impossible to predict whether or how your news release will be used by the media, you can ensure the best possible outcome by:

- Returning calls, emails, or text messages from the media as soon as possible.
- Sending the release to a current and accurate list of news outlets.
- Being prepared to answer any questions reporters may have about the information in the release.

If reporters are interested in doing a story based on the news release, they may call you for an interview or to ask for clarification or more information. Then again, they may not call at all and write their stories based on the information you've included in the release or they've obtained elsewhere.

News Conference Checklist

Depending on how much media interest there is about your crisis, it may make sense to hold a news conference about it. Be aware, however, that other late-breaking or important stories may prevent reporters from attending.

Of all the ways that you provide the media and public with information about your crisis, a news conference will require the most time, resources, and planning, with no guarantee of the results you want. But if holding a news conference makes sense, here's a checklist I use when I plan and organize them for clients:

- Decide on the date, time, and location.
- Decide and finalize the information and messages.
- Finalize/approve a list of participants and speakers.
- Prepare draft press materials, including:
  - News advisory
  - News release
  - Fact sheet
  - Backgrounder
  - Press kit
- Draft suggested sound bites for speakers.
- Research/obtain media lists.
- Script event (who will say what, where they will stand, etc.).
- Issue invitations to participants and speakers.
- Finalize/approve draft press materials.
- Distribute news release.
- Finalize/approve script of event.
- Prepare/finalize remarks for participants.
- Place follow-up calls to selected editors and reporters to encourage them to attend.
- Retain print and TV media monitoring services.
- Retain a photographer to document the event.
- Confirm physical arrangements (podium, PA system, signs, etc.).
- Finalize staging and visuals.
- Hold news conference.

Newspaper Interviews

Many TV and radio stations rely on newspaper articles as "tip sheets" for their own story ideas and often quote or refer to those stories in their newscasts. Why? Because the stations' news staffs are often too small or too busy to report or research the stories themselves.

More so than other news organizations, newspapers and magazines tend to deal with topics in greater depth and detail; it is not unusual for them to publish several thousand words or run a series of articles over a period of days about a topic.

Be sure to keep the following four points in mind:

- Newspaper reporters can do more than simply report what you said. As trained observers, they can also convey to readers your demeanor and mannerisms during the interview, how you talked, how you dressed, and how you answered (or evaded) their questions. Just as you'd be on your best behavior for a television interview, realize that everything you say or do during a print interview could be mentioned or reported in the story.
- Don't be lulled into a false sense of security or complacency. To help "loosen you up," the journalist may start the interview by talking about a completely different subject, and then slowly start discussing the matter at hand. Always keep in mind the three major points you want to make during the interview and try not to let the reporter get you off track.
- Reporters can have roving eyes. If they will be coming to your home or office for the interview, make sure that you haven't left any important or embarrassing documents or other materials where the reporter can see them.
- Don't assume that reporters can't read upside down, as happened to one of my PR clients. After an in-office interview with a reporter, the client was surprised to read in the next day's paper excerpts from a confidential memo on the corner of his desk that he assumed the reporter could not read.

Television Interviews

- If you will be interviewed in a studio, arrive early so you can meet the production staff, look at the set, make sure you are comfortable in the chair you'll be sitting in, etc.

- Know the three to four points you want to make during the interview and find ways to return to these points throughout the interview.
- Look at the reporter during the interview, not at the camera.
- Don't fidget, wiggle in your chair, or do anything that will detract viewers from your message.
- Glance at a mirror before the interview to make sure you look the way you want.
- Use appropriate, but not excessive, gestures and facial expressions to help make or emphasize your points.
- Be authoritative and confident in your answers, manner, and demeanor.
- Keep your answers short, usually 20–30 seconds.
- Avoid speaking in a monotone or speaking too fast; vary your voice pitch and tone to help make or emphasize your points and message.

Radio Interviews

Radio interviews can be one of the easiest types of interviews to do for most people. That's because:

- Most radio interviews are done by phone, so you can talk to the reporter on a cell phone or landline.
- You can have as much background information as you need in front of you during the interview, and you can refer to it as often as you need to.
- Radio interviews are often recorded, so if you don't like an answer you gave or flubbed a response, simply tell the reporter that you want to give your answer over again.

To ensure that your radio interviews go as smoothly as possible:

- Make sure there are no distractions in the room you will call from and no street noises, barking dogs, etc., that will be picked up by the phone.
- Jot down the three to four points you want to cover during the interview and check them off as you make them during the interview.
- Speak in a conversational tone.
- Stand up when you speak (your voice will be stronger and deeper than when sitting down).
- Smile when you talk (it helps make you sound more pleasant, relaxed, and energetic).

- Practice what you want to say ahead of time so your answers are no longer than 30 seconds or so.
- Organize any reference materials before the interview so you won't have to shuffle through papers to find the information you need.
- Find out from the reporter whether you are to call them or they are to call you.
- Make sure you have a phone number or email address where you can reach the reporter before the interview. If the reporter will call you for the interview, be sure to keep your line clear as much as possible prior to the time of the interview.

Finally, record and practice delivering your answers; ask a friend, family member, or colleague to "play reporter" and ask you a combination of easy and tough questions.

Make arrangements beforehand to record your radio interview so you can listen to how you did. What would you like to do differently or better the next time?

Satellite and Skype Media Tours

When a crisis attracts the interest of news organizations in multiple cities, it may make sense to conduct a satellite media tour—a series of one-on-one interviews with television reporters or news anchors that will be broadcast live or recorded for use in a news story later on. These tours make it possible to be interviewed by dozens of TV stations within a few hours.

Satellite media tour services are often provided by video production companies and can be expensive. An acceptable and much more affordable alternative is to do a succession of live or recorded video interviews using your computer, mobile device, or smartphone.

Thanks to Skype and other platforms, it's very easy to conduct TV interviews from the comfort of your home or other convenient locations. It's important, however, that you find a place that is quiet and secluded so there are no distractions or disruptions during the interview.

Robert Kelly, an American expert on Korean politics, learned this the hard way. Kelly was doing an interview with the BBC from the study in his apartment when one of his small children managed to open the door, enter the room, and approach her father. A second toddler soon came through the doorway, followed by their mother who grabbed both children and frantically closed the door so her husband could continue the conversation with the BBC.[7]

The video of the interview went viral. Kelly said later that he thought the embarrassing incident meant his "career as a talking head was over."[8]

Op-Eds and Bylined Articles

Op-eds and bylined articles are opinion pieces published by newspapers and magazines that explain and discuss an individual's viewpoints or experiences. They can also be used to help explain what happened in a crisis, the steps an organization took to deal with the crisis, and how the company will make sure that nothing like it happens again.

In general, op-eds:

- Provide readers with a new, interesting, or unusual perspective on an issue, cause, or topic.
- Help educate or inform the reader about a topic that concerns them.
- Provide readers with information or lessons they probably would not receive anywhere else.
- Are based on your experience or expertise.
- Are usually 500–1,500 words in length (depends on the publication).

The benefit in writing an op-ed or bylined article is that you are taking your message directly to the public. The bad news is that most local newspapers will accept submissions only from those in their readership area, reserve limited space for these articles, can take days or weeks to publish the article, and can be subject to editing and condensing with or without your approval.

Before writing an op-ed about some aspect of your crisis, I suggest you read several issues of the publication to get a feel for the style and topics they prefer and request a copy of their guidelines.

Letters to the Editor

Like op-eds, letters to the editor can be effective by bypassing the media's filter so you can tell your side of the story about a crisis directly to the public. The bad news again is that whatever you say can be shortened and edited, and there is no guarantee if or when it will be published. Check with each publication about its policy for accepting and publishing letters to the editor.

Online Pressrooms

No matter what information you share with the public and the media about your crisis, you should make it as easy as possible for them to find and use it. That means having and updating a clearly marked pressroom or media page on your website with working links to the news releases and news stories about the crisis.

For examples of online pressrooms, go to the Crisis Press Materials page at PublicRelations.com and enter this case-senstive password (do not include the period): CrisisPressMaterials2020.

When News Organizations Get the Facts Wrong

Reporters produce anywhere from a handful to hundreds of stories every year, so it may be inevitable that they occasionally get something wrong in their stories. But even if journalists make mistakes less than 1 percent of the time, think of all the stories that are wrong in some way. All facts matter. Unless errors are corrected, they will become part of the history and news coverage of the crisis and the "official" record of what happened.

Because of the increased reliance on technology, it is more important than ever to be alert for any mistakes, misinformation, or disinformation that might make it into a story about your crisis.

The fire that devastated the Notre Dame Cathedral in Paris is a case in point. As noted on page 177, an algorithm used by YouTube mistakenly linked a video of the fire to information about 9/11, misleading viewers into thinking there was a link between the two events. The staff at YouTube had to step in to eliminate the misinformation.[9]

While it's impossible to unring a bell that has been rung, it is possible—and important—that you take steps to have an error in a story corrected as soon as possible.

When the media makes a mistake, you should:

- Contact the reporter who did the story and explain the error.
- If you can't reach the reporter right away, ask to speak to an editor about the matter.
- Ask that a correction be made as soon as possible.
- Monitor the news organization to make sure they make the correction.

When called to their attention, newspapers will usually print a correction the next day and immediately run a corrected version of the article online; magazines may run a clarification in their next issue. Some news outlets include on their website information on how to contact them about mistakes in their news coverage and their process for making corrections.

You must act fast, however, if the mistake is broadcast on television or radio. If you contact the station immediately, sometimes they will announce the correction during the same newscast or make note of it on the next broadcast.

Exercise: Play Reporter

Before you are interviewed by a reporter about your crisis, take the time to ask questions by the toughest journalist in the world: you. Since you are (or should be) intimately familiar with every detail and nuance of your crisis, scandal, or emergency, you are also in the best position to come up with the most difficult or embarrassing questions a reporter might ask.

In this exercise, you'll put yourself in the shoes of the journalist and ask yourself all the possible questions they might pose to you in an interview about your crisis.

To help get you started in the right direction, review the following sample scenario along with some of the questions a reporter could ask about it. You're on your own to answer the questions for which no information has been provided in the scenario.

Scenario: The building in which your company is headquartered was destroyed by a fire. At the time of the fire there were 75 employees in your offices, but you do not know yet how many of them escaped, died, or were injured. The fire occurred at 10:00 a.m. today.

> Reporter: I understand that a fire has seriously damaged your offices. What can you tell me about what happened?
>
> Your response:
>
>
> Reporter: Were there any casualties?
>
> Your response:

Reporter: Do you know what caused the fire? Are there any suspects?

Your response:

Reporter: How much damage did the fire cause?

Your response:

Reporter: How will the fire affect the operations of your company?

Your response:

Reporter: What else should the public know about what happened?

Your response:

Reporter: Tell me about the company and what it does.

Your response:

Now read your responses out loud to hear how they sound and make sure you are pleased with the answers. You can use the dozens of scenarios in Chapter 1 as the basis of additional exercises.

CHAPTER 6
Learn from the Successes and Mistakes of Others

The crisis triggers run the gamut from A to Z—starting with accidents and ending with zombies

This is the chapter where you can find out how others responded to their own crisis situation. It's always better, of course, to profit from the terrible experiences of companies, organizations, and individuals who went through hell instead of suffering through similar incidents yourself.

Don't make the mistake of believing that a crisis will never happen to you. Too many organizations have found out the hard way that the crisis scenarios they had dismissed as unlikely one day were the same ones they had to deal with the next.

The examples below reinforce the importance of having a crisis management and communication plan. If you already have a plan in place, then the case studies in this chapter should remind you to review and update your plan every year and conduct regularly scheduled drills and exercises to help ensure the plan will work for different crisis scenarios. See Chapter 3 for more information and anecdotes about crisis exercises.

What Is a Crisis?

I define a crisis as any internal or external event that can impact the image, reputation, activity, bottom line, or future of an organization or disrupt or prevent normal operations. A crisis can hurt the recruitment and retention of employees, diminish staff morale, and expose the company to legal risks. Some corporate emergencies may never become known to the public, while others can be the fodder of news reports, international headlines, and social media posts. One crisis may blow over in a day, while another could drag on for days, weeks, or months.

No matter what the crisis is or how it impacts your organization, it is absolutely essential to put it behind you and get back to normal as quickly as possible.

Crisis Triggers

I've identified scores of events, situations, and activities that triggered a crisis for companies and individuals. They are presented below as case studies that I prepared on the basis of the news coverage about the crisis and the best practices that were used to respond to the situation. The crisis triggers run the gamut from A to Z, starting with accidents and ending with zombies (different crises that return to attack the same company). They are presented below as case studies in alphabetical order.

The case studies list the type of crisis; industry or other appropriate category; country; and the name of the company, organization, or individual, followed by a brief description of what happened as reported by news organizations and websites. The description is followed by "Edward's Take"—my analysis of how well or poorly the company, organization, or individual did in responding to—or in some cases creating—a crisis. This is in keeping with the purpose of this book: to provide advice and counsel to those who want to prevent a crisis from happening, are having a crisis *right now*, or are seeking a quick read on how others reacted to a crisis.

The best practices are clearly labeled in each case study and show how those who were going through a crisis adhered to those standards. Other than expressing my views on how others responded to a crisis, I have no opinions about, do not endorse, and make no recommendations concerning the services, expertise, or products of any individual, company, or organization mentioned in this book. The only reason they are included is because their role or involvement in a crisis or training exercise was reported by a news organization or website or, as in the case of the Defense Department, I observed their crisis management training session. The news coverage and websites are listed in the Notes section, which also documents the sources of information for every crisis example in this book and any statements, observations, and opinions that are not my own.

At the end of this chapter there is a summary of what I consider to be the best ways to prevent, prepare for, respond to, manage, and bounce back from a crisis.

Spoiler alert: My analyses do not provide step-by-step or detailed case studies or timelines from the time a crisis was triggered to when it was resolved. Those would fill a book (or more) all by themselves. For updates about a crisis, go to the Crisis Updates page on my website at PublicRelations.com and enter this case-sensitive password (do not include the period): CrisisAheadUpdates2020.

Of course, if you are having a crisis at this moment or expect to have one soon, I doubt that you would have the time or patience to read anything other than this book anyway.

For your convenience, here's a list of the crisis triggers and where you can read how a corporation, organization, or individual responded to them.

If you'd like to learn more about the following case studies, visit my website at PublicRelations.com. On the password-protected Crisis Updates page you will find links to updates about the crisis. Use this case-sensitive password to access the page (do not include the period): CrisisAheadUpdates2020.

Finally, if you'd like to put yourself in the shoes of someone who was having a similar crisis and game-play how you would respond, check out the dozens of scenarios that begin on page 11 (What Would You Do If…), many of which were the basis of real crisis situations.

Crisis Case Studies

PREVENTABLE?

Crisis Trigger: Accidents

Categories: Airlines, Airplane Manufacturing

Country: United States

Company: Boeing

Reality Check:

Accidents can happen anytime, to anyone and any organization anywhere in the world. Although most accidents never result in local, national, or international headlines, those that do usually affect many people, high-profile companies or individuals, or involve unusual circumstances or situations.

What Happened:

Two jetliners manufactured by the Boeing Company crashed within months of each other.[1] According to news reports, Boeing had known about a software problem that was later linked to the crashes. The Federal Aviation Administration appeared to partially blame Boeing for the accident.[1] Boeing[1] and even a member of Congress implied that the pilots were somehow at fault.[1]

Edward's Take:

Boeing's actions before and after the two accidents became a textbook example of what not to do in preventing and responding to a crisis.

Best Practice: Be aggressive in identifying and addressing problems that can lead to a crisis.

If Boeing had been more aggressive in addressing the problem that caused the accidents, the two horrific tragedies might have been prevented.

Best Practice: When you know something is wrong, say something and do something about it.

Don't remain quiet after you become aware of a problem that could endanger the safety of people. Once the truth emerges, the failure to notify authorities and the public about the problem can only make a bad situation worse.

Best Practice: Don't blame or imply that you are blaming others for your mistakes.

Blaming others or being perceived as blaming others is never a good move—especially before a full and complete investigation into a crisis has been completed. But as noted above, Boeing and government officials appeared to do just that in the wake of the crashes.[1]

Best Practice: If you are not at fault, say so.

The union that represents airline pilots said the pilots were not to blame for these accidents.[1]

Best Practice: Don't delay in apologizing.

After the crash of the second plane, it took the company *26 days* to issue a video apology for the accident.[1]

MORE THAN JUST A ROUNDING ERROR

Crisis Trigger:	Accounting Mistakes
Category:	Accounting
Country:	United States
Organization:	City of Philadelphia

Reality Check:

Organizations should be prepared when their "bean counters" come up with the wrong number of beans. Fortunately, mistakes by accountants and bookkeepers do not happen that often. But when they do, they can create news about and a crisis for the organization.

What Happened:

An internal audit found that the City of Philadelphia made a series of accounting mistakes totaling more than $900 million.[2]

Edward's Take:

Philadelphia's response to their crisis pulled no punches. It was open, honest, and transparent.

Best Practice: Be transparent.

Speaking at a news conference,[2] a city official was up-front about the accounting errors and the steps she was taking to address the embarrassing situation. The mistakes were found because of an internal audit,[2] which, from a PR perspective, was preferable to having an outside agency or authority find the errors. It's always better that you find the problem instead of someone else.

Best Practice: As soon as you know something, say something.

City Controller Rebecca Rhynhart issued a news release with this headline: "Office of the City Controller Finds Serious Issues with City's Financial Management; Recommends Urgency in Addressing Findings."[2] In addition to the news release, Rhynhart held a news conference and answered reporters' questions about the findings.[2]

Best Practice: Provide full disclosure.

Rhynhart made public an audit report with an executive summary and details about the internal audit that had discovered the accounting errors.[2]

Best Practice: Don't varnish the truth.

Finding a problem is one thing but making sure the problem will be solved is something else. Rhynhart did the right thing when she said, "If these deficiencies continue to go unaddressed, this could result in the city's financial statements being considered an inefficient tool for assessing the city's financial health."[2]

Best Practice: Manage expectations.

A spokesperson for the mayor said, "We share [Rhynhart's] sense of urgency and have taken the appropriate steps to resolve it. We obviously wish this could be fixed overnight, but a problem like this requires time to be fully resolved responsibly. We look forward to completing this process by year's end."[2]

POINTING FINGERS

Crisis Trigger:	Accusations
Category:	Entertainment
Country:	United States
Individual:	Kevin Spacey

Reality Check:

It is easy to be dragged into the court of public opinion. All that's needed is for someone to make an accusation against your company or organization or you personally.

What Happened:

More than 30 people accused actor Kevin Spacey of sexual assault, including one young actor who was 14 at the time.[3]

Edward's Take:

The impact of accusations can be immediate and long-lasting. Individuals who are accused of wrongdoing are not the only ones who can be thrust into the public spotlight—so too can those for whom that person works or with whom they are associated.

Best Practice: Tell your side of the story.

In response to the allegation that he sexually assaulted a 14-year-old, Spacey tweeted, "I honestly do not remember the encounter; it would have been over 30 years ago. But if I did behave then as he describes, I owe him the sincerest apology for what would have been deeply inappropriate drunken behavior, and I am sorry for the feelings he describes having carried with him all these years."[3]

Best Practice: Don't confuse the issue.

In that same tweet, the actor said, "I choose now to live as a gay man. I want to deal with this honestly and openly and that starts with examining my own behavior."[3] The actor was criticized for linking his apology concerning allegations of abuse with his announcement that he was gay.[3]

Best Practice: Take steps to protect your image and reputation.

In the aftermath of the accusations, some people and organizations chose to distance themselves from the actor. The International Academy of Television Arts and Sciences said it would not present Spacey with a special Emmy, and Netflix announced it would end its popular *House of Cards* TV series, which starred Spacey.[3]

Spacey was fired from the movie *All the Money in the World*, which had already been filmed and was less than two months away from being released. The producers deleted Spacey from all scenes in the movie and hired another actor to reshoot those scenes. These actions, observed online news site Vox, underlined "how seriously Hollywood is taking the allegations of sexual assault that have been levied against [Spacey]—or at least how desperate many people in the entertainment industry are to distance themselves from a man whose behavior was allegedly a longstanding open secret."[3]

TAKE COVER!

Crisis Trigger:	Active Shooter
Category:	Manufacturing
Country:	United States
Company:	Henry Pratt Co.

Reality Check:

Anyone with a gun can walk into a business or school and start shooting. Sometimes there is a reason behind the madness—such as a grudge—and sometimes no reason can be found or determined. Active shooter situations create panic, confusion, and news.

What Happened:

A 15-year employee of the Henry Pratt manufacturing company in suburban Chicago opened fire on his colleagues. The gunman killed five coworkers and wounded five police officers before he was fatally shot.[4]

Edward's Take:

The sequence of events that played out that day was all too familiar. Police were called and arrived within minutes to deal with another mass shooting incident.

Best Practice: Show sympathy.

Appropriate expressions of grief, sorrow, and condolences were issued by the company and its parent organization, Mueller Water Products, which posted this message on their website and social media platforms: "Mueller Water Products is shocked and deeply saddened by the horrific tragedy that occurred today at our Henry Pratt facility in Aurora, Illinois. Our hearts are with the victims and their loved ones, the first responders, the Aurora community and the entire Mueller family during this extremely difficult time."[4]

Best Practice: Show that you care.

The company announced that it had created a survivors' fund to provide financial support to the families of the employees who were killed and the employees who were injured or traumatized by the shooting.[4]

Mueller Water Products issued a statement that said, "Our entire focus is on the health and well-being of our colleagues, and we are committed to providing any and all support to them and their families. We continue to work closely with law enforcement, with whom we share our deepest gratitude for their support. We will provide updates as we learn more."[4]

See page 44 for another perspective on how people responded to a mass shooting at a military facility in Washington, DC.

WHAT WERE THEY THINKING?

Crisis Trigger:	Advertising/Marketing
Category:	Cosmetics
Countries:	England, Scotland, Wales, Northern Ireland
Company:	Avon

Reality Check:

Making people feel ashamed about how they look seems like one of the worst ways to sell a product. But that does not stop some companies from using the tactic anyway, with predictable blowback from the public and news organizations.

What Happened:

In the United Kingdom, Avon tweeted a page from an ad for an anticellulite product that showed the photo of a woman along with the message that dimples on thighs are not "cute."[5] Critics accused the beauty company of shaming women. After being criticized, the company withdrew the ad and apologized for it.[5]

Edward's Take:

Being creative is one thing, but offending people with your creativity is something else. If anyone thought that these ads were a bad idea, they apparently never spoke up or were ignored or overruled. What's worse: not knowing you will offend people with an ad, or knowing and not caring?

Best Practice: Test your messages out on others first.

Carefully consider the consequences and impact of what you say in your advertisements, how you say it, and why you are saying it. Do your research. Seek and listen to as many different opinions as possible and take to heart what you are told or learn—before it's too late. Thanks to social media, the public's reaction to anything you do or say can be immediate and devastating. Do not dig yourself deeper into a hole by ignoring their important and valuable feedback.

Best Practice: Respond quickly to criticism.

Avon wasted no time in responding to criticisms that were posted on Twitter by body positive activist Jameela Jamil, who said, "Everyone has dimples on their thighs. I do, you do, and the clowns at @Avon_UK certainly do. Stop shaming women about age, gravity, and cellulite. They're inevitable, completely normal things. To make us fear them and try to 'fix' them is to literally set us up for failure."[5]

Best Practice: When you are wrong, say so.

Although claiming that the ad "was intended to be light-hearted and fun," Avon admitted it had made a mistake, saying "We messed up" and "We realize we missed the mark." They pulled the offending advertisement.[5]

Avon likely scored points with the public for at least admitting their mistakes, removing the ads, and showing that, at least in this case, they listen to and act on feedback from consumers.[5]

NOTHING PLATONIC ABOUT IT

Crisis Trigger:	Affairs (romantic)
Category:	Entertainment
Country:	United States
Company:	Warner Brothers
Individual:	Kevin Tsujihara

Reality Check:

It is human nature to become attracted to another person. That attraction can lead to romantic affairs and even marriage. In the business world, however, those affairs can create problems for one or both people, especially if one of them is in a position of power or authority. When those relationships become public, the affairs can create issues that put people and the companies they work for into the public spotlight.

What Happened:

Warner Brothers chairman Kevin Tsujihara resigned after it was confirmed that he had an affair with actress Charlotte Kirk and allegedly used his influence to help her land acting jobs at the studio.[6]

Edward's Take:

The sudden and unexpected resignations of CEOs or other top corporate officials can create concern and panic within organizations.

Best Practice: As soon as you know something, do something.

Warner Media CEO John Stankey put the best possible face on the situation when he issued this statement: "It is in the best interest of Warner Media, Warner Bros., our employees and our partners for Kevin to step down as Chairman and CEO of Warner Bros."[6]

Best Practice: Limit any disruptions to your business as much as possible.

Stankey, in a memo to Warner Media staffers, said he would try to limit the disruption that the resignation had on the company. "You have my commitment to work diligently and quickly to minimize any disruption in the day-to-day operations of the studio as a result of this leadership transition. I will share an interim leadership structure with all of you tomorrow."[6]

Best Practice: Express appreciation and help bolster morale.

Stankey expressed his appreciation to the staff. "I also want to thank all of our employees, particularly the teams at Warner Bros., for your patience and honesty, and we will continue to lean on your collective resiliency, dedication and professionalism as we chart a new path for our company together."[6]

MEA CULPA

Crisis Trigger:	Apology (the need to make one)
Category:	Entertainers
Country:	United States
Individual:	Barbra Streisand

Reality Check:

Organizations and high-profile individuals can get themselves into a lot of trouble by saying or doing things that must have sounded like a good idea at the time, only to have to apologize to the world for their actions or words.

What Happened:

Actress/singer/director Barbra Streisand told *The Times of London* that two men who accused singer Michael Jackson of molesting them when they were children were "thrilled to be there" during the alleged abuse, which "didn't kill them." She later apologized for her comments.[7]

Edward's Take:

Although it is impossible to unring a bell, people can wish that they had never rung the bell in the first place.

Best Practice: When you are wrong, say so.

Streisand was roundly criticized on social media for her remarks about Jackson's accusers.[7] After contacting the Associated Press to clarify her comments, she posted the following full-throated apology online: "I am profoundly sorry for any pain or misunderstanding I caused by not choosing my words more carefully about Michael Jackson and his victims," she wrote. "I didn't mean to dismiss the trauma these boys experienced in any way. Like all survivors of sexual assault, they will have to carry this for the rest of their lives. I feel deep remorse and I hope that James and Wade know that I truly respect and admire them for speaking their truth."[7]

Streisand was hardly the first celebrity who had to apologize for something they said or did. Comedian Kathy Griffin quickly went into apology mode after posting what was supposed to be a humorous photograph of her holding what appeared to be the severed bloody head of President Donald Trump. She admitted that she had crossed the line and the photograph was not funny at all.[7]

Best Practice: Think twice before saying a single word.

Think about what you want to say before you share your thoughts with the world. Why do you want to say it? How might others react when they hear it? If what you say causes a commotion or backlash, why would you say it in the first place?

IN CUSTODY

Crisis Trigger:	Arrests
Category:	Airlines
Country:	United States
Company:	Delta Air Lines

Reality Check:

Of all the ways you do not want to see the leaders or employees of your company make news, being arrested is probably right at the top of the list. It's never good when there are headlines about employees or company officials being led away in handcuffs, being forced to do the "perp walk" at a police station, jail, or courthouse, and trying unsuccessfully to hide their face.

What Happened:

At John F. Kennedy International Airport, an employee of Delta Air Lines was arrested for stealing a bag containing about $250,000 in cash that he was supposed to have loaded onto a plane headed to Miami, Florida.[8]

Edward's Take:

The arrest of a company employee or official and the reason behind it should be dealt with quickly and effectively by the company as it tries to put the matter behind it and get back to business.

Best Practice: Tell people what you think about what happened.

Delta made it clear what it thought about the situation, saying, "The alleged actions of this employee are unacceptable and in no way reflect the professionalism and values we expect from Delta team members."[8]

Best Practice: Tell people what you are doing about the situation.

A Delta spokesperson told ABC News, "We are taking this situation very seriously and working directly with authorities on their investigation as well as conducting an internal investigation of our own." [8]

OOPS!

Crisis Trigger:	Attention to Detail
Category:	Retailers
Country:	New Zealand
Company:	IKEA

Reality Check:

If the devil is in the details, then there can be hell to pay when there is something wrong with the details or something important is missing. The failure to check on every detail of a project, product, or activity can create embarrassing situations for companies.

What Happened:

How do you lose an entire country? IKEA managed to do just that when they marketed a global map that did not include New Zealand.[9] A sharp-eyed customer in Washington, DC, noticed the omission and posted a photo of the map on the website Reddit.[9]

Edward's Take:

You can learn from IKEA's mistake by having other people closely review your work, projects, plans, or activities with a critical eye; putting ego and pride aside and being open to comments, observations, recommendations, or suggestions; and asking yourself and others what could possibly go wrong with what you want to do, are doing, or will do.

Don't hesitate to second-guess past successes or failures: what could have gone wrong or did go wrong? Were you good, or just lucky—or unlucky? What could you do differently or better the next time to ensure the best possible outcome—and the least possible risk?

Best Practice: Take ownership of the problem.

IKEA said they would take steps to address the snafu. "IKEA is responsible for securing correct and compliant motifs on all our products. We can see that the process has failed regarding the product BJÖRKSTA world map. We will take necessary actions and the product is now being phased out from our stores. We regret this mistake and apologize."[9]

Best Practice: The sooner you fix the problem, the better.

The timing of this episode was especially embarrassing because the Swedish home goods chain had previously announced that it would open stores in New Zealand. Noting this, a Twitter user posted: "Hopefully IKEA won't be using their own map to find us when they open their first store in New Zealand."[9]

PUSHBACK

Crisis Trigger:	Backlash
Category:	Automobiles
Continent:	Asia
Company:	Tesla

Reality Check:

You'd think that people would be happy to learn that a company had reduced the price of a popular product. But try telling someone who had recently paid full price that it would soon be cheaper for *other* people to buy the same product.

What Happened:

Tesla owners in Asia staged protests to express their unhappiness with the electric car maker's decision to reduce the price of selected models.[10] Some customers had paid much more for the car before the price rollback.[10]

Edward's Take:

Tesla found itself between a rock and a hard place when it reduced the price of some models.

Best Practice: Explain and justify your actions and decisions.

Tesla said the price reductions were the result of cost savings associated with its shift from in-store to online sales.[10]

Best Practice: Anticipate how others will react to your decisions.

Tesla should have seen this crisis coming a mile away. The following online post by a customer in Asia was typical:

"I received Tesla's Model X on February 25, and I only drove this car for five days before Tesla announced a price reduction of 174,300 yuan ($25,989.87)," wrote Weibo user Luweijuzi, according to a report by *Global Times*. "I'm probably the most unlucky new buyer."[10]

Best Practice: Do what you need to do to fix the problem.

It did not take long for Tesla to reconsider its pricing and sales strategies. A few days later it announced that it was changing course again because it would keep more stores open than previously announced, so the price reductions would not be as much.[10]

THE LAST PENNY

Crisis Trigger:	Bankruptcy
Category:	Retailers
Country:	United States
Company:	Sears

Reality Check:

It can take a lot of time, money, and effort to start a business and stay in business. Too often, those efforts fall short and it becomes necessary to gain some extra time to keep the enterprise going, stave off creditors, and give the business as much chance as possible to succeed.

What Happened:

The Sears retail chain filed for bankruptcy.[11]

Edward's Take:

News coverage about the challenges facing Sears often made it appear that the iconic retailer was ready to join the list of brick-and-mortar stores that could not survive in the age of online shopping.

Best Practice: Make the best of a bad situation.

The bad news is that bankruptcy is a signal to the world that your company is in crisis, could be on life support, and may not survive. But the good news is that declaring bankruptcy enables companies to reorganize their finances and find ways to get back on their feet. That's exactly what Sears appeared to do, sending an important message that it was doing what it could to recover by using all of the appropriate tools at its disposal.

Best Practice: Don't give up.

Sometimes the obituaries turn out to be premature when a white knight appears to rescue the company from bankruptcy. Or, as was the case with Sears, it may emerge from bankruptcy as a shadow of its former self as reported in this 2019 news story:

"Sears has gotten its second chance, and the department store giant is going lower case. Sears Holdings has opened the first three locations for its new Sears Home & Life stores in Overland Park, Kansas, Lafayette, Louisiana, and Anchorage, Alaska, CNBC reports. The new format will boast new branding, average 12,500 SF and focus on mattresses, appliances, tools and smart home services."[11]

Best Practice: Keep key audiences posted about your progress in recovering from a crisis.

I have no doubt that Sears' efforts to make a comeback will continue to attract the interest of news organizations. But will the stories be about the death of the company or its successful rebirth? As reporters often say about an unresolved situation, "That remains to be seen. Time will tell."

NOT WELCOMED HERE

Crisis Trigger:	Banning Products
Categories:	Plastics, Theme Parks
Country:	United States
Company:	The Walt Disney Company

Reality Check:

What's in today can be out tomorrow.

What Happened:

In 2018, Walt Disney banned all single-use plastic straws and stirrers from its locations around the world.[12]

Edward's Take:

Pay attention to trends, developments, and changing priorities and tastes so you will not be surprised if and when your product is no longer looked upon with favor. And be prepared to act when necessary.

The growing trend of eliminating the use of plastics is a case in point.

Best Practice: Keep an eye on trends and developments that can affect your image and reputation.

There's no doubt about the impact of plastics on the environment. About 80 percent of all the litter in all the oceans is plastic. More than 60 countries have banned single-use plastic items.[12]

Best Practice: Make it clear what you are doing and why you are doing it.

A Disney official did an excellent job explaining the company's decision: "Eliminating plastic straws and other plastic items are meaningful steps in our long-standing commitment to environmental stewardship," said Bob Chapek, chairman, Disney Parks, Experiences, and Consumer Products. "These new global efforts help to reduce our environmental footprint and advance our long-term sustainability goals."[12]

Best Practice: Time announcements to ensure maximum impact.

Disney picked a good day to make their announcement about banning plastics: right before Earth Day 2019.[12]

Best Practice: Explain the impact that your actions or decisions will have.

Disney said the ban would reduce the use of more than 175 million straws and 13 million stirrers each year. The plastic straws were replaced with paper ones.[12]

Best Practice: Tell people what the next steps will be.

In addition to banning plastic straws, Disney said it would transition to refillable in-room amenities in their hotels and on their cruise ships and reduce plastics in guest rooms by 80 percent. They also planned to cut back on the number of plastic shopping bags in parks and on their cruise lines and eliminate the use of all of their polystyrene cups.[12]

SHIRKING RESPONSIBILITY

Crisis Trigger:	Blaming Others/Scapegoating
Category:	Banks
Country:	United States
Company:	Wells Fargo

Reality Check:

Some people—and organizations—will not admit when they make a mistake. For them it's much easier to blame others. It is bad PR for companies to make people scapegoats for the problems or issues that got them into hot water in the first place.

What Happened:

Wells Fargo executives blamed low-level bank employees for the illegal sales practices of the company.[13] But the employees had a different story to tell about the crisis.[13]

Edward's Take:

Those who pass the buck often create a bigger hole from which they must escape. It's always wrong when someone blames others for their own mistakes or errors in judgment. Companies, organizations, and individuals who find that they have become scapegoats need to respond immediately, fight back, and defend themselves. Otherwise, people will assume that the blame is justified.

Best Practice: Tell your side of the story.

I was glad to see that former employees at Wells Fargo took steps to get their side of the story out to the public and the media. Several former workers at the bank told CNN about the pressure they were under from managers to meet sales goals. But "the same managers turned a blind eye when ethical and even legal lines were crossed," according to the CNN story.[13]

Best Practice: Make your point with anecdotes about your experience.

Sabrina Bertrand, who had worked at Wells Fargo, recalled, "I had managers in my face yelling at me. They wanted you to open up [multiple] checking accounts for people that couldn't even manage their original checking account. The sales pressure from management was unbearable."[13]

WHAT'S IT WORTH TO YOU?

Crisis Trigger:	Bribery
Category:	Education
Country:	United States
Organization:	University of Southern California

Reality Check:

When merit or achievement are not enough for people to get what they want, they sometimes resort to desperate and illegal ways to accomplish their goals. Those extreme efforts can put them, and the people around them, into hot water.

What Happened:

Dozens of wealthy parents were accused by the FBI of using illegal methods to get their children accepted into some of the most prestigious schools in the United States, including the University of Southern California (USC).[14]

Edward's Take:

When laws, rules, and regulations are broken, it is important to move quickly—and to be seen moving quickly. USC officials said and did the right things to address the crisis expeditiously.

Best Practice: Move quickly.

The day after federal charges were filed against the parents, the University of Southern California announced that all students connected with the cheating scandal would be denied admission.[14]

Best Practice: Do your homework.

USC said it would conduct case-by-case reviews of students already enrolled at the university who may have ties to the scandal. A spokesperson said USC would "make informed, appropriate decisions once those reviews have been completed. Some of these individuals may have been minors at the time of their application process."[14]

Best Practice: Investigate.

The university said it would launch an internal investigation into the situation.[14]

Best Practice: Take appropriate action.

USC said it would review the process by which students are considered for admission, and the school fired two employees who had been charged by federal officials for their roles in the scandal.[14]

YOU CAN'T GET THERE FROM HERE RIGHT NOW

Crisis Trigger:	Bridge Collapse
Category:	Infrastructure
Country:	United States
Organizations:	Florida International University, National Transportation Safety Board

Reality Check:

It is no longer news that the infrastructure of some countries—their bridges, highways, and roads—is in bad shape and needs immediate repair or replacement. It is news, however, when a new addition to the infrastructure falls down.

What Happened:

A new pedestrian bridge collapsed at Florida International University in Miami, Florida, killing six people and sending 10 others to the hospital.[15]

Edward's Take:

The newly built pedestrian bridge had been open for less than a week and received a clean bill of health that very morning by the company that designed it.[15] No one would have thought that a brand-new structure would collapse the way it did.

Best Practice: Defer to the appropriate authorities and experts.

Know when it is your responsibility to investigate the reasons behind a crisis and when it is not. In the United States, bridge accidents are investigated by the National Transportation Safety Board,[15] which immediately looked into this accident.[15]

Best Practice: Keep people posted about the progress in investigating a crisis.

The National Transportation Safety Board (NTSB) kept the media and the public appropriately informed about its work as developments warranted. In their first report about the bridge collapse, the government agency noted that "the information in this report is preliminary and will be supplemented or corrected during the course of the investigation."[15]

The NTSB's "just-the-facts" approach to the investigation was right on target and provided vital details of what was known at the time. The agency included key information about the purpose and history of the bridge, when it was to be completed, and how it was being built. The agency ended the report with information about the next steps in their investigation and who would be assisting in the effort.[15]

UNFAIR ADVANTAGE

Crisis Trigger:	Cheating
Category:	Online Gaming
Country:	United States
Company:	Fortnite

Reality Check:

The drive to win helps people and companies achieve important goals and objectives. When taken to the extreme, however, the determination to succeed at any cost can cross the line, resulting in a reputation that no one wants and forcing an organization to act to protect its image and integrity.

What Happened:

People were caught cheating as they played in the Fortnite World Cup Online Open, an online gaming competition.[16] Among other things, the offenders colluded with each other to boost their scores[16] and gained unfair advantage by violating contest rules.[16]

Edward's Take:

Ethics should be a top priority for any company or organization, no matter what industry or profession they are in. Letting people know what you have done to address a cheating or comparable situation will help strengthen your image and reputation and put people on notice that they need to follow the rules or face consequences.

In the aftermath of its investigation into alleged cheating by players of its popular online game, Epic Games took the appropriate steps in dealing with the guilty parties.

Best Practice: Take action.

After investigating allegations of cheating, Epic Games disqualified hundreds of accounts and canceled the cash prizes that more than 200 people had won by cheating.[16]

Best Practice: Be transparent.

In an effort to assure players and nonplayers alike about the integrity of the game, the company posted information online about how it monitors competitive play, how it vets and verifies winners and assures that people played by the rules, and what would happen to those caught breaking the rules.[16]

Best Practice: Provide full disclosure.

The gaming company announced how many accounts had been banned, for how long, and how many prize winners had their winnings forfeited. The company provided a link so that people could read the rules for themselves. People were invited to report suspicious activity for the company to investigate.[16]

Best Practice: Reinforce your core values.

The company made it clear on their website the values that it considers important when it posted this message: "Our primary goal is to support competition that is fun, inclusive, and in line with the overall spirit of Fortnite. Unsportsmanlike conduct from participants is not within that spirit and will not be tolerated in Fortnite competition."[16]

SINFUL

Crisis Trigger:	Child Abuse
Category:	Religion
Country:	Vatican City
Organization:	Catholic Church
Individual:	Pope Francis

Reality Check:

The sexual abuse of children by priests has been a decades-old problem in the Catholic Church.[17]

What Happened:

In his annual Christmas speech to Vatican officials in 2018, Pope Francis said priests who raped and molested children should turn themselves in to authorities and that the Catholic Church would no longer hide their crimes.[17]

Edward's Take:

The longer a crisis is not addressed or resolved, the worse it is likely to get. A case in point is the child sexual abuse scandals that have plagued the Catholic Church for decades. Headlines, investigations, arrests, and lawsuits can focus public attention on a crisis. But it takes leadership, determination, and commitment to address and resolve it, which, until recently, were sadly lacking in this sordid scandal.

There is a lot at stake: the lives of innocent children, the reputation of a religion with 1.3 billion followers,[17] and the credibility of its leaders.

Best Practice: Acknowledge there is a problem.

Pope Francis admitted that the church had a history of not taking the abuse scandal seriously. He blamed inexperienced or shortsighted church leaders who acted "irresponsibly" by refusing to believe victims.[17]

Best Practice: Take a stand and commit to addressing the problem.

Pope Francis said that going forward, "the church will spare no effort to do all that is necessary to bring to justice whosoever has committed such crimes."[17] He said an international summit would be held at which church leaders would discuss preventing sexual abuse.[17]

Best Practice: Issue a call for action, part 1.

Pope Francis urged victims to come forward, thanked the media for giving them voice, and told abusers to "convert and hand yourself over to human justice, and prepare for divine justice."[17]

Best Practice: Issue a call for action, part 2.

The Pope urged those who have been victims of sexual abuse, abuse of power, and abuse of conscience to speak out. "The greater scandal in this matter is that of cloaking the truth," he said.[17]

Best Practice: Manage expectations.

Francis said that addressing the scandal "is no easy task, since the guilty are capable of skillfully covering their track." He noted that they are careful about choosing victims and look for those who will stay silent and live in "fear of shame and the terror of rejection."[17]

Best Practice: Be realistic.

Don't make statements or promises that you can't back up or are unbelievable. Anne Barrett Doyle of the online resource BishopAccountability said it was fantasy to believe that abusive priests would surrender themselves to authorities, when the Vatican itself has blocked bishops from adopting mandatory reporting protocols.[17]

Doyle said, "[Francis] minimizes and mischaracterizes the protection of abusers by church leaders, chalking it up to lack of training or awareness, rather than a deliberate choice to conceal and deceive." She challenged his statement that the cover-up was a thing of the past.[17]

EXTRA INGREDIENTS

Crisis Trigger:	Contamination
Categories:	Agriculture, Food
Country:	United States
Company:	Growers Express

Reality Check:

When necessary, companies and government agencies will alert the public about issues related to the safety of the food that is sold in stores and other locations.

What Happened:

Citing concerns over the potential risk of listeria, a recall notice was issued by Growers Express.[18] The company, which provides a variety of vegetables for the Green Giant brand, said the recall covered some fresh vegetables that were sold under the Green Giant, Trader Joe's, and Signature Farms labels.[18]

Edward's Take:

Contaminated meats, vegetables, and other items can be hazardous to the health of consumers—and damage the image, reputation, and bottom line of the companies that grow, process, and sell the food.

Best Practice: Explain how you discovered the problem.

Tom Byrne, president of Growers Express, explained that the company "stopped production immediately after being notified of a single positive sample by the Massachusetts Department of Health."[18]

Best Practice: Tell people how you are addressing the crisis.

"The safety of our consumers is our first priority," the company said. "We are deep sanitizing the entire facility and our line equipment, as well as conducting continued testing on top of our usual battery of sanitation and quality and safety tests before resuming production."[18]

NO SIGN OF WRONGDOING...YET

Crisis Trigger:	Cover-Ups
Category:	Ride-hailing
Country:	United States
Company:	Uber

Reality Check:

Being reluctant to share sensitive, confidential, or embarrassing information with the media and the public is one thing. But covering it up to help ensure that it never sees the light of day is something else—and could be construed as a criminal act.

What Happened:

Ride-hailing company Uber paid $148 million to settle claims that they covered up a data breach in which hackers stole the confidential information of about 25 million people.[19]

Edward's Take:

A cover-up can be just as bad or worse than the thing that is being covered up. Don't compound the error by trying to sweep things under the rug. Own up to what happened and move on. Companies such as Uber that would rather hide a crisis than disclose it to the public are simply making matters worse. They obviously never heard of the First Law of Holes on page 51: When you find yourself in a hole, stop digging. Uber kept on digging themselves into a deeper hole.

Best Practice: Know what's happening in your company or organization.

In November 2017, Uber CEO Dara Khosrowshahi said he had "recently learned that in late 2016 we became aware that two individuals outside the company had inappropriately accessed user data stored on a third-party cloud-based service that we use."[19]

Best Practice: Don't make excuses.

The Uber CEO went on to say, "None of this should have happened, and I will not make excuses for it."[19]

Best Practice: Tell people what you have done or will do to address the crisis.

In that same statement he said, "While I can't erase the past, I can commit on behalf of every Uber employee that we will learn from our mistakes. We are changing the way we do business, putting integrity at the core of every decision we make and working hard to earn the trust of our customers."[19]

POOR TREATMENT

Crisis Trigger:	Customer Complaints
Category:	Railroads
Country:	United States
Organization:	New Jersey Transit

Reality Check:

The longer you take to address a problem, the longer it will take to fix it.

What Happened:

Commuters complained about the poor service provided by the New Jersey Transit system.[20]

Edward's Take:

Every business depends on others to buy their products or services. It's a simple equation: No customers equals no business. That is why it is so puzzling when companies or their employees do things that alienate people and encourage them to take their business elsewhere. The damage is compounded when news organizations and the public find out about the incidents. In these cases, the maxim that "there is no such thing as bad publicity" simply is not true.

Best Practice: Acknowledge that there is a problem.

The first step in dealing with a crisis is to admit that, well, there is a problem. Kevin Corbett, the executive director of New Jersey Transit, did just that when he told the organization's board of directors, "Over the past week or so, we have not been able to dependably offer the level of service that we hoped for."[20]

Best Practice: Take action.

The transit agency's board of directors approved a new operating budget to provide additional resources to improve train service and reduce delays.[20]

Best Practice: Tell people what you're doing to address the problem.

New Jersey governor Phil Murphy held a news conference at one of the train stations to announce a series of improvements and reforms designed to make things better for commuters. This included new rail cars, more buses, an improved mobile app, and more reliable and faster information about train delays.[20]

Best Practice: Manage expectations.

Corbett told the board, "Although I hate to say it, these are issues that won't be solved overnight."[20]

ALL SYSTEMS DOWN

Crisis Trigger:	Cyberattacks
Category:	Manufacturing
Country:	Norway
Company:	Norsk Hydro

Reality Check:

Computers and software programs have become the lifeblood of businesses and organizations around the world. When hackers introduce a deadly virus into that bloodstream or completely take over the computers, then all business can grind to an immediate and unexpected halt. The ability to prevent or respond to cyberattacks has quickly become an important survival tool.

What Happened:

Hydro, one of the world's largest aluminum manufacturers, experienced a cyberattack.[21]

Edward's Take:

Hydro appeared to be well prepared when it had to deal with a cyberattack.

Best Practice: Overcome obstacles.

Although the cyberattack shut down the aluminum manufacturer's website, the company found a work-around by posting updates on Facebook and placing information at some of the entrances of their building. Workers reverted to using their smartphones to check for email. Norsk Hydro had taken the precaution of backing up all of their data, which they would later use to restore their systems when it was safe to do so.[21]

Best Practice: Do not speculate.

If you don't know who or what is behind the crisis, do not guess or speculate. According to one news report, a Hydro spokesperson was quoted as saying that he could not yet confirm who was behind the attack.[21]

Best Practice: Get the help you need.

Norway's state cybersecurity agency helped Hydro respond to the cyberattack and get through the crisis.[21]

BREAKING POINT

Crisis Trigger:	Dam Collapse
Category:	Infrastructure
Country:	Brazil
Company:	Vale S.A.

Reality Check:

Responses to large-scale disasters that result in injuries, death, and destruction often follow a familiar script.

What Happened:

Dozens of people died and hundreds were reported missing after a dam collapsed at an iron mine in Brazil.[22]

Edward's Take:

Company and government officials responded quickly to the disaster.

Best Practice: Keep people posted.

Vale, the company that managed the mine, provided online updates with the names of people who were reported missing; government officials briefed the media about various aspects of the disaster and the steps they were taking to help victims and their families, locate the missing, provide assistance to victims, and monitor and contain the damage.[22]

Best Practice: Show people you care about what happened.

The president of Brazil flew over the site to inspect the damage and later posted the following tweet: "It is hard to witness this whole scenario and not be emotional. We will do everything in our reach to help the victims, minimize damage, investigate the facts, claim justice, and prevent new tragedies like the ones in Mariana and Brumadinho for the well-being of Brazilians and the environment."[22]

Best Practice: Show sympathy.

Government officials declared a period of mourning for the victims.[22]

Best Practice: Apologize.

CNN reported, "In a company video over the weekend, Vale chief Fabio Schvartsman called the Brumadinho dam break 'inexcusable' and asked the Brazilian public for forgiveness. He said the company will aid victims and noted that Vale put 'immense effort' into improving its dams after the disaster in Mariana."[22]

Best Practice: Ensure that a similar crisis does not happen again.

Vale, the Brazilian mining company, was linked to a similar deadly dam disaster that killed 19 people in 2015.[22]

FOR ALL THE WORLD TO SEE

Crisis Trigger:	Data Breaches and Security
Category:	Credit Scores
Country:	United States
Company:	Equifax

Reality Check:

We have come to depend on those with whom we share private and confidential information to keep it private and confidential.

What Happened:

Equifax, a major consumer credit reporting company, announced that hackers had accessed its computers and obtained the confidential information of 143 million Americans. Although the data breach occurred in July 2017, the company did not announce it until several months later.[23]

Edward's Take:

The theft of data calls into question the safeguards that companies have put into place to protect names, addresses, credit card information, and other details of our lives. It also calls into question whether those companies can ever be trusted again.

Best Practice: Promptly announce bad news.

Instead of announcing it immediately, Equifax waited six weeks before admitting it had been hacked.[23] This was a mistake. Consumers have a right to know as soon as their confidential information has been stolen or compromised. The company made a bad situation worse by failing to quickly disclose what happened.

Best Practice: Apologize.

Richard F. Smith, the CEO of Equifax, wrote an op-ed for *USA Today* in which he apologized for the cybersecurity breach and discussed the steps the company had taken and would take to address the crisis. "We apologize to everyone affected. This is the most humbling moment in our 118-year history," he said.[23]

Best Practice: Explain why there was a delay in disclosing the problem.

In the op-ed, Smith wrote:

> Understandably, many people are questioning why it took six weeks to report the incident to the public. Shortly after discovering the intrusion, we engaged a leading cybersecurity firm to conduct an investigation. At the time, we thought the intrusion was limited. The team, working with Equifax Security personnel, devoted thousands of hours during the following weeks to investigate.[23]

FIGHTING BACK

Crisis Trigger:	Deadly Bacterium
Categories:	Agriculture, Olive Oil Industry
Country:	Spain
Organizations:	Spanish Olive Oil Interprofessional Association, Spain's National Institute for Agricultural Research

Reality Check:

Spain leads the world in the production and sales of olive oil; about half of the world's olive oil comes from this one country.[24]

What Happened:

A plant bacterium (*Xylella fastidiosa*) that killed a million olive trees in Italy was discovered to have spread to Spain. The Spanish olive oil industry fought back.[24]

Edward's Take:

Threats to any agricultural crops need to be taken seriously. The Spanish government and the country's olive oil industry took appropriate steps to address the problem and keep people informed about their activities.

Best Practice: When you see something, do something.

The Spanish government was the first to address the spread of the disease that could harm an important part of the country's economy. It called for a research project to investigate and halt the deadly disease.[24]

Best Practice: Investigate.

Spain's National Institute for Agricultural Research launched a three-year program to find ways to stop the spread of the disease; several research centers across the country were to participate in the project.[24]

Best Practice: Get the help you need.

Spain's olive oil trade association partnered with several research institutions to tackle the crisis.[24]

Best Practice: Tell people what you are doing.

"We are setting out different working groups which will specifically focus on how the Xylella affects the olive groves, from risk analysis for the eradication of the bacterium in olive trees to the study of the genetic structure of [the disease]," said Teresa Millán, manager of the Spanish Olive Oil Interprofessional Association.[24]

Best Practice: Provide updates about your progress in addressing the problem.

Millán told a trade publication, "Right now we are studying the budget that we will be able to allocate. These are midterm projects, lasting for several years, and our aim is to support the development of those lines of work for three years."[24]

UNSOLVED

Crisis Trigger:	Death
Category:	Hotels and Resorts
Country:	Dominican Republic
Company:	Hard Rock International

Reality Check:

People die every day for any number of reasons. But when individuals die under mysterious or suspicious circumstances, their demise can put the venues where the death occurred into the public spotlight.

What Happened:

At least nine American tourists died while on vacation in the Dominican Republic within a 12-month period.[25] Two of the deaths occurred at the Hard Rock Hotel & Casino Punta Cana, where dozens of others had also become ill.[25]

As reported by NBC News, "While the causes of death are not clear in all cases, investigators are looking into bootlegged and unregulated alcohol as one of the sources. Toxicology reports are still pending."[25]

Edward's Take:

Tourism creates jobs, and jobs help create strong local and national economies. When anything happens that causes tourists to stay away from a city, country, or destination, then companies and governments need to act quickly to address the problem.

Best Practice: Tell people what you are doing to address the problem.

The resort issued the following statement: "We can assure you, the safety and health of our guests is now, and has always been our highest priority. We currently implement beverage protocols, including purchasing sealed and unopened products from licensed and reputable vendors, as well as daily inspections of all products served throughout the hotel bars and in-room liquor dispensers.

"Additionally, our team members are trained to inspect all supplies, equipment and products that enter the property. Of course, we will continue to evaluate and recalibrate our protocols to strengthen and enhance guest safety."[25]

As an added precaution, the resort announced it was removing liquor bottles from all guest rooms.[25]

Best Practice: Get the additional help you need.

The hotel said it would contract with a healthcare facility in the United States "to provide its guests with more comprehensive medical care."[25]

Best Practice: Express sympathy.

The resort issued the following statement: "Hard Rock Hotel & Casino Punta Cana is deeply saddened by these two unfortunate incidents, and we extend our sincerest sympathy to the families of Mr. Harrison and Mr. Wallace. We are currently waiting for official reports regarding these deaths, which occurred in July of 2018 and April of 2019 respectively."[25]

GONE

Crisis Trigger:	Destruction of Documents
Category:	Government
Country:	Canada
Organization:	Canadian Security Intelligence Service

Reality Check:

Documents that are destroyed—and for which there are no copies—can create serious problems for groups and organizations. This is especially true when the documents were destroyed on purpose.

What Happened:

Canada's spy agency, the Canadian Security Intelligence Service (CSIS), destroyed documents about former prime minister Pierre Trudeau.[26]

Edward's Take:

The intentional destruction of documents or other historical records—as justified as it may be by bureaucrats and other government officials—can feed and reinforce people's paranoia and suspicions.

Best Practice: Have systems in place that can flag a crisis as soon as possible.

The destruction of the files was discovered and reported by news organizations 30 years later.[26]

Best Practice: Defend your actions.

The spy service told one news organization that it could not justify keeping the files.

"CSIS takes privacy considerations related to its work very seriously. We are committed to ensuring that the retention of information continues to be in compliance with all legislation and ministerial direction," the agency said.[26]

Best Practice: Issue a call for action.

"This wanton destruction cries out for parliamentary intervention to ensure that historically significant documents held by government agencies are preserved instead of being made to disappear down an Orwellian memory hole," said Steve Hewitt, a senior lecturer at the University of Birmingham.[26]

YOU ARE NOT WELCOME HERE

Crisis Trigger:	Discrimination
Category:	Restaurants
Country:	United States
Company:	Starbucks

Reality Check:

Companies that discriminate against people for any reason—whether it is the color of their skin or their sexual orientation—quickly learn that discrimination is not good for business.

What Happened:

Two black men were at a Starbucks in Philadelphia for a business meeting. They were arrested when they refused to leave the restaurant.[27]

Edward's Take:

Starbucks went the extra mile in responding and managing the crisis and taking steps to help ensure it was not repeated.

Best Practice: Get the facts.

In a message posted on the company's website, Starbucks CEO Kevin Johnson said, "We have immediately begun a thorough investigation of our practices. In addition to our own review, we will work with outside experts and community leaders to understand and adopt best practices."[27]

Best Practice: Commit to taking action.

In the online post, the CEO promised to "make any necessary changes to our practices that would help prevent such an occurrence from ever happening again.

We also will further train our partners to better know when police assistance is warranted."[27]

Starbucks later closed all of its restaurants for a full day to provide training to employees to help ensure that similar incidents would not happen again.[27] See page 239 to learn why the training was not entirely successful.

Best Practice: Reinforce your commitment to your organization's core values.

Johnson said in his message that "Starbucks stands firmly against discrimination or racial profiling. The video shot by customers is very hard to watch and the actions in it are not representative of our Starbucks mission and values. Creating an environment that is both safe and welcoming for everyone is paramount for every store."[27]

Best Practice: Help prevent a repeat of the problem.

The company also announced a new policy that allows all guests to use the restroom and other facilities of their restaurants even if they do not buy anything.[27]

Best Practice: Apologize.

In an interview on ABC's *Good Morning America*, Johnson said, "The circumstances surrounding the incident and the outcome in our store on Thursday were reprehensible, they were wrong. And for that, I personally apologize to the two gentlemen who visited our store."[27]

TRANSMITTED

Crisis Trigger:	Diseases
Category:	Government
Country:	United States
Organization:	Centers for Disease Control and Prevention

Reality Check:

Although measles was eliminated in the United States in 2000, the disease was reported to be making a comeback because of the refusal of a growing number of people to get their children vaccinated.[28]

What Happened:

The director of the Centers for Disease Control and Prevention urged that all Americans get their children vaccinated against measles.[28]

Edward's Take:

This was a preventable crisis that was caused by people who could have easily protected themselves and their families from a disease that had been declared eliminated.

Best Practice: When you see something, say something.

CDC Director Robert Redfield said, "This current outbreak is deeply troubling, and I call upon all healthcare providers to assure patients about the efficacy and safety of the measles vaccine. And, I encourage all Americans to adhere to CDC vaccine guidelines in order to protect themselves, their families, and their communities from measles and other vaccine preventable diseases. We must work together as a nation to eliminate this disease once and for all."[28]

Best Practice: Cite the source of the problem.

Redfield observed, "A significant factor contributing to the outbreaks in New York is misinformation in the communities about the safety of the measles/mumps/rubella vaccine. Some organizations are deliberately targeting these communities with inaccurate and misleading information about vaccines. CDC continues to encourage parents to speak to their family's healthcare provider about the importance of vaccination. CDC also encourages local leaders to provide accurate, scientific-based information to counter misinformation."[28]

Best Practice: Tell people how serious you are about addressing the problem.

"Stopping these measles outbreaks is a priority for CDC and we are working 24/7 to protect Americans from this contagious disease. Vaccination is the best way to protect against measles," Redfield said in a statement.[28]

Best Practice: Put the problem in perspective.

The CDC director said, "The World Health Organization reported this month that there has been a 300% increase in the number of measles cases worldwide compared with the first 3 months of 2018. That increase is part of a global trend seen over the past few years as other countries struggle with declining vaccination rates and may be exacerbating the situation here."[28]

MISLED

Crisis Trigger:	Disinformation
Categories:	Politicians, Social Media
Country:	United States
Company:	Facebook
Individual:	Nancy Pelosi

Reality Check:

It's hard enough to keep up with what's happening in the world without having to wonder or worry whether the information you are reading is true or not. Disinformation—made-up "information" that is intentionally wrong or misleading in order to create doubt, confusion, or disorder—can have a negative effect on the companies and organizations that allow it to be distributed.

What Happened:

Facebook refused to delete an obviously fake video of US House Speaker Nancy Pelosi that made her appear to be drunk and slurring her words.[29]

Edward's Take:

Facebook created their own PR problem when they claimed that they were combating disinformation but then refused to delete a video that was altered to make it appear that House Speaker Nancy Pelosi was slurring her words. The social media platform's policies do not permit the posting of "misleading and inaccurate" information.[29]

Best Practice: Speak up.

Pelosi did a radio interview in which she criticized Facebook. "We have said all along, poor Facebook, they were unwittingly exploited by the Russians. I think wittingly, because right now they are putting up something that they know is false. I think it's wrong," she said. "I can take it.... But [Facebook is] lying to the public. They have proven—by not taking down something they know is false—that they were willing enablers of the Russian interference in our election."[29]

Best Practice: Respond to questions from the media.

The radio station noted on its website that "Facebook did not immediately respond to a request for comment."[29]

Best Practice: Tell people what you did to address the problem.

Facebook said it limited the distribution of the video after confirming that it had been doctored. The company also utilized tools to prevent content from showing up in its newsfeed and flagged the video with a fact-check box that labels the content as false.[29]

"Speed is critical to this system, and we continue to improve our response," Facebook said after the video surfaced. It noted that "people who see the video in feed, try to share it from feed, or already shared it are alerted that it's false."[29]

DEFENSELESS

Crisis Trigger:	Domestic Violence
Category:	Sports
Country:	United States
Company:	San Francisco Giants
Individuals:	Larry Baer, Pam Baer

Reality Check:

Domestic violence is never acceptable. When such incidents become public, the guilty parties have a lot of explaining to do. Sometimes there can be more to the incidents than first meets the eye.

What Happened:

Larry Baer, owner of the San Francisco Giants baseball team, was captured on video having a physical altercation with his wife, Pam. The couple later explained they were having a family argument.[30]

Edward's Take:

Everyone involved or affected by the incident did the right thing by either providing their versions of the events or issuing statements to the media and the public about the next steps.

Best Practice: Tell your side of the story.

Pam Baer released a statement about the incident in which she said: "My husband and I had an argument in public about which we are quite embarrassed. I took his cellphone. He wanted it back and I did not want to give it back. I started to get up and the chair I was sitting in began to tip. Due to an injury I sustained in my foot three days ago, I lost my balance. I did not sustain any injury based on what happened (Friday). Larry and I always have been and still are happily married."[30]

The couple released a joint statement about the incident: "Regrettably today we had a heated argument in public over a family matter. We are deeply embarrassed by the situation and have resolved the issue."[30]

Larry Baer later released his own statement: "I am truly sorry for the pain that I have brought to my wife, children and to the organization. It is not reflective of the kind of a person that I aspire to be, but it happened, and I will do whatever it takes to make sure that I never behave in such an inappropriate manner again."[30]

Best Practice: Don't say anything until you have the facts.

A spokesman for Major League Baseball said they were "aware of the incident and, just like any other situation like this, will immediately begin to gather the facts. We will have no further comment until this process is completed."[30]

Best Practice: Provide updates about the status of the situation.

Team officials released the following statement: "The Board of Directors of San Francisco Baseball Associates is closely monitoring the matter involving Giants President and CEO Larry Baer. Pursuant to League policy, Major League Baseball is taking the lead in gathering all facts surrounding the situation. The organization is cooperating fully with the process.

"Mr. Baer has acknowledged that his behavior was unacceptable, apologized to the organization and is committed to taking steps to make sure that this never happens again. He has also requested, and the Board has accepted, his request to take personal time away from the Giants beginning today. The Board has asked the Giants executive team to manage the day-to-day operations of the Club during this period, reporting directly to the Board.

"As leaders in the community, we at the Giants hold ourselves to the highest standards and those standards will guide how we consider this matter moving forward. We have no further comment at this time."[30]

SHEDDING MORE THAN JUST POUNDS

Crisis Trigger:	Downsizing
Category:	Restaurants
Country:	United States
Company:	Subway

Reality Check:

To succeed in business, companies need to make sure that as many people as possible can buy their products or services. Some companies do that by opening up more stores in more locations. That kind of expansion is good, of course, as long as there are enough customers to justify the expansion. But what happens when business drops off and the company starts to lose money?

What Happened:

Subway shut down more than 1,000 of its fast food restaurants in the United States, more than it had planned.[31] The chain originally planned to close about 500 locations.[31]

Edward's Take:

Subway made the best of a bad situation by shutting down 1,000 apparently unprofitable stores and focusing on the big picture—generating more traffic and making more money.

Best Practice: Explain your decision.

In a statement, a Subway spokesperson explained the rationale behind the move, saying that, "Our main goals are to drive guest traffic and grow franchise owner profits. Everything we do has to achieve these goals."[31]

Best Practice: Provide context and perspective for your decisions.

Subway said, "As part of the optimization plan we shared last year, to achieve this goal some owners will close, relocate, or remodel their locations and that will result in slightly fewer, but more profitable restaurants."[31]

TOO OLD?

Crisis Trigger:	Drivers (elderly)
Categories:	Automobiles, Government
Country:	Japan
Organization:	Government of Japan

Reality Check:

The older we get, the more difficult—and dangerous—it can be to do certain things, such as driving a car.

What Happened:

A new government survey found that one in four people in Japan who are 80 years or older were still driving cars.[32]

Edward's Take:

Unless they have other transportation options, many elderly people may have no choice but to drive an automobile in order to take care of basic and necessary tasks. But at what point do elderly people become a danger to themselves and others? And how does a government help ensure their safety and that of the public?

Best Practice: Take action.

In response to a series of fatal accidents involving elderly drivers, the Japanese government proposed that drivers 75 years of age or older be tested for their cognitive abilities when they renew their licenses.[32]

The government was also considering a proposal to encourage elderly drivers whose reflexes are not as good as they used to be to drive automobiles with enhanced safety features.[32]

Best Practice: Get the help you need to address the problem.

A government agency consulted experts for their advice and recommendations on how to prevent accidents that are caused by older drivers. One of their recommendations was to establish a new type of driver's license that restricts people to when and where they can drive and which cars they can operate.[32]

HOW MANY FINGERS AM I HOLDING UP?

Crisis Trigger:	DUI/DWI
Category:	Athletes
Country:	United States
Individual:	Tiger Woods

Reality Check:

People who drive after drinking alcohol or taking drugs run the risk of being arrested.

What Happened:

Tiger Woods was arrested for driving under the influence.[33]

Edward's Take:

CEOs and other prominent people who are arrested for driving under the influence can generate embarrassing publicity for themselves and their organizations.

Best Practice: Tell your side of the story.

Woods tried to set the record straight for why he was arrested, claiming in a statement: "I understand the severity of what I did, and I take full responsibility for my actions, I want the public to know that alcohol was not involved. What happened was an unexpected reaction to prescribed medications. I didn't realize the mix of medications had affected me so strongly."[33]

Best Practice: Tell the full story.

The failure to tell the full story about a crisis situation can come back to haunt you later when the entire truth comes out. This was certainly the case when NBC News later reported the results of Woods' toxicology tests, which showed that the golfer had painkillers, sleep drugs, and an ingredient in marijuana in his system when he was arrested.[33]

Best Practice: Apologize.

Woods did the right thing by apologizing for the incident and promising "I will do everything in my power to ensure this never happens again." He even thanked those who arrested him for their professionalism.[33]

SHAKING ALL OVER

Crisis Trigger:	Earthquakes
Category:	Government
Country:	United States
Organization:	Alaska Department of Transportation and Public Facilities

Reality Check:

Earthquakes are not unique to California. Just ask the people in Alaska; Japan; and even Washington, DC. Those who have lived through an earthquake can provide important and valuable lessons to everyone else on how to prepare for, live through, and bounce back from what could be a deadly and devastating crisis.

What Happened:

Two earthquakes created widespread damage to roads and businesses in Anchorage, Alaska. A week later the state's department of transportation had repaired and quickly reopened key roadways.[34]

Edward's Take:

Government agencies are often criticized for how long it takes for them to respond to and help people recovering from natural disasters such as fires and floods. Alaska was a welcome exception. The state received well-earned plaudits for repairing roads that were damaged by an earthquake and making them drivable in record time.[34]

Best Practice: Exceed expectations.

Crews from the state's department of transportation were able to repair most major road damage within four days. As one person noted on social media, "It would take California years to get this done." Said another, "That is unbelievably awesome! Hooray for the Alaskan people! Wish repairs went that fast in Texas."[34]

Best Practice: Overcome challenges and obstacles.

The feat was even more impressive considering the weather conditions at the time—freezing temperatures and rain, snow, and high winds.[34]

Best Practice: Plan ahead for a crisis.

Alaska's ability to open the road only 100 hours after the earthquake was no accident. They had already planned for such an event.[34]

Best Practice: Thank people.

The Alaska Department of Transportation posted before and after photos of the damaged roadway online. They wrote that the pictures "[speak] volumes to the level of work our crews have been putting in 24/7 this past week."[34]

BE CAREFUL WHAT YOU WISH FOR

Crisis Trigger:	Elections
Category:	Government
Country:	England
Organizations:	British Parliament, European Union

Reality Check:

Elections have consequences.

What Happened:

England voted to leave the European Union.[35]

Edward's Take:

It is rare for a ballot measure to be as controversial or have such a long-term impact as the proposal that was approved by England to leave the European Union. The underlying issues the referendum sought to address had polarized the country, and its narrow passage did nothing to heal the rifts. Indeed, it created additional political turmoil and uncertainty that included high-profile resignations from the governments of prime ministers Theresa May[35] and Boris Johnson[35] and the initial failure of the British Parliament to agree on how the country would leave the European Union.[35]

There was no easy solution to a crisis of this magnitude, which was a classic "between a rock and a hard place" situation. Although England finally left the EU in January 2020, the impact of the election will likely be felt for years.

Best Practice: Expect the unexpected.

As noted in the *Harvard Business Review*, "Brexit was also essentially a political shock versus an economic one, and one that was largely unexpected. As has been widely discussed, in the weeks leading up to the vote, betting odds suggested that the probability of Brexit averaged around only 30% and was never higher than 40%."[35]

Best Practice: Know the impact of your decisions.

After the election, government and banking officials published separate forecasts about the impact of Brexit, which painted a series of dire pictures that seemed to go from bad to worse. The scenarios included a weaker economy, a loss of jobs, the departure of many businesses, a less attractive investment climate, and uncertainties about the relationship that the country would have with the European Union.[35]

SISTER ACT

Crisis Trigger:	Embezzlement
Category:	Religion
Country:	United States
Organization:	Catholic Church

Reality Check:

If you can't trust nuns, who can you trust?

What Happened:

Two nuns at St. James Catholic School in Torrance, California, were accused of embezzling hundreds of thousands of dollars from the school and using the money for personal purposes—including gambling at a casino.[36]

Edward's Take:

If the two women had stolen from a business instead of a church, I doubt that the company would have been as forgiving.

Best Practice: Pay attention to telltale signs of a problem.

The embezzlement of funds was uncovered in part because of a series of red flags that were raised about the school's finances and a tip that was received on an archdiocese ethics hotline.[36]

Best Practice: Get the facts.

School officials conducted an internal investigation, financial review, internal audit of procedures, and review of staff records. The auditor later confirmed suspicions that there was a problem. An outside forensics auditor was retained to do a more comprehensive review and a retired FBI agent was hired to interview school officials and the nuns.[36]

Best Practice: Notify the appropriate authorities.

School officials notified the police that the two nuns had used school funds for personal purposes.[36]

Best Practice: Tell people what happened.

Church officials met with parents and alumni of the school to tell them about the embezzlement.[36]

Best Practice: Assume that you are being recorded.

The two-hour meeting was audio recorded, and a copy later found its way into the hands of a news organization.[36]

Best Practice: Do what you think best.

Church officials said they would not seek criminal charges against the two nuns, who were removed from the ministry and sent to different convents.[36]

Best Practice: Take steps to prevent the crisis from happening again.

School officials promised to implement improvements and reforms to guard against similar financial issues from occurring in the future.[36]

THIS IS NOT WHY WE HIRED THEM

Crisis Trigger:	Employees
Categories:	Accounting, Entertainment
Country:	United States
Company:	PricewaterhouseCoopers
Organization:	Academy of Motion Picture Arts and Sciences

Reality Check:

Companies need employees in order to make products and provide services. But people who fail to do what they were hired to do can create all kinds of crisis situations for organizations.

What Happened:

The wrong movie was announced as the Best Picture at the 2017 Academy Awards show, watched by tens of millions of people.[37]

Edward's Take:

There are not too many crisis situations I can think of that have played out before a live international television audience. And even if you did not see the mistake as it happened, you could watch as it was reported and repeated countless times by news organizations and late-night talk shows.

Best Practice: Explain what happened, and why.

Warren Beatty told the stunned audience, "I wanted to tell you what happened. I opened the envelope, and it said, 'Emma Stone, *La La Land*.' That's why I took such a long look at Faye [Dunaway], and at you, I wasn't trying to be funny."[37]

Best Practice: Move quickly to address the crisis.

It did not take too long to figure out the employees of the accounting firm of PricewaterhouseCoopers had handed the wrong envelope to the presenters, who, not knowing anything differently, went ahead and announced the name that was in the envelope.[37]

Best Practice: Take responsibility for your actions.

The accounting firm did the only thing they could do—they took full responsibility for the snafu and "breaches of established protocols." They issued the following statement: "The presenters had mistakenly been given the wrong category envelope and when discovered, [it] was immediately corrected. We are currently investigating how this could have happened, and deeply regret that this occurred."[37]

TOO BIG A GAP

Crisis Trigger:	Equal Pay
Categories:	Entertainers, Entertainment
Country:	United States
Individuals:	Mark Wahlberg, Michelle Williams

Reality Check:

It's an unfortunate and regrettable fact that women usually make less money for doing the same job as men. Although it's not fair under any circumstances, glaring examples of the discrepancy can generate lawsuits and occasional actions to make things right.

What Happened:

Actor Mark Wahlberg was reported to have received $1.5 million more than his colleague Michelle Williams for their work in reshooting scenes for the motion picture *All the Money in the World*. Williams received less than $1,000—or about one-tenth of 1 percent of what Wahlberg was paid. The scenes, which originally featured actor Kevin Spacey, had to be redone after he was fired from the picture because of allegations of sexual assault. See page 91 for details.[38]

Edward's Take:

The issue of unequal pay is a systemic problem that will take years to fix. Some individuals do what they can to call attention to the issues and address glaring examples of this inequity.

Best Practice: Do the right thing right away.

In an apparently unprecedented act, Wahlberg announced that he would donate the money he received to the TIME'S UP Legal Defense Fund. "Over the last few days my re-shoot fee for *All the Money in the World* has become an important topic of conversation," Wahlberg said in a statement. "I 100 percent support the fight for fair pay and I'm donating the $1.5 million to the TIME'S UP Legal Defense Fund in Michelle Williams' name."[38]

On top of that, the agency that represented both Wahlberg and Williams said they would contribute an additional $500,000 to the TIME'S UP fund.[38]

Best Practice: Put the problem in perspective.

The agency said, "The current conversation [about unequal pay] is a reminder that those of us in a position of influence have a responsibility to challenge inequities, including the gender wage gap. It's crucial that this conversation continues within our community, and we are committed to being part of the solution."[38]

PAY UP, OR ELSE

Crisis Trigger:	Extortion
Category:	Entertainers
Country:	United States
Individual:	David Letterman

Reality Check:

When high-profile individuals are the target of illegal activities, they need to do what's necessary to protect their images, reputations, and careers.

What Happened:

Late night comedian David Letterman was the target of an extortion plot in which someone demanded $2 million in exchange for keeping information about Letterman's extramarital affairs quiet.[39]

Edward's Take:

Extortion can put the victim between a rock and a hard place: Is it worse to pay the extortionist or to have your secret exposed?

Best Practice: Tell your side of the story.

The comedian admitted to the affairs in a very public way by announcing his indiscretions on his TV show. His admission was widely reported by news organizations.[39]

According to a statement released by his production company, Letterman received a package from an individual who claimed to have information about Letterman's alleged sexual relationships with female employees of the *Late Show with David Letterman* and threatened to reveal them if Letterman did not pay the individual a large sum of money.[39]

Best Practice: Get the help you need.

Letterman contacted the Manhattan district attorney's office, which conducted an investigation and arrested the alleged extortionist.[39]

Best Practice: Don't be a hypocrite.

Letterman had previously made jokes on his show about others who had extramarital affairs.[39]

RED FACED

Crisis Trigger:	Facebook Posts
Categories:	Politicians, Social Media
Country:	United States
Individual:	William Calloway

Reality Check:

Facebook can be both a boon and a curse. It's boon for those who want to immediately share their opinions or activities with millions of people around the world. It's a curse when people post things that put them or their organization in a questionable or bad light.

What Happened:

Old homophobic Facebook posts made by a Chicago political candidate became public.[40]

Edward's Take:

Time is critical in any crisis. The longer you wait, the worse it can get.

Best Practice: Don't wait to apologize.

More than a week passed after the posts became public and the candidate, William Calloway, apologized for them. He said he no longer believed in what he had written.[40]

Best Practice: Apologize.

To his credit, Calloway met reporters at a local hotel to apologize and explain his comments. He said, "I think an apology here is really really important, but what's more important that I want to do, convey and come across is my heart and my heart [sic] for people and my heart to serve [sic], and I want to continue to serve this city.

I'm sorry...I apologize, it was wrong, it was offensive. I said a lot of things even in my teenage years from how I grew up...I had to evolve from that. We have to allow our people...room and space to evolve, to grow."[40]

EVERY DAY CAN BE APRIL FOOLS' DAY

Crisis Trigger:	Fake News
Category:	Government
Country:	Thailand
Companies:	*The Thaiger, The Phuket News*

Reality Check:

Fake news—news about people, things, or events that never really happened—can generate legitimate reactions such as shock, dismay, or amusement. Sometimes the fake news can have real and serious consequences.

What Happened:

Several news organizations, including *People*, reported that tourists could be subject to the death penalty if they took selfies in front of low-flying planes at Thailand's Phuket International Airport.[41]

Edward's Take:

A news organization got to the bottom of a fake news story and corrected what others had gotten wrong—or apparently assumed was true.

Best Practice: Set the record straight.

Travel Weekly dispelled the fake news by explaining what really happened: "Early last month, when *The Thaiger* [newspaper] and later *The Phuket News* broke the news that Phuket's well-known airport selfie spot would be moved to another section of Mai Khao beach, there was no reference to the selfies incurring the death penalty. A month later, the story has taken on a life of its own, with media outlets around the world claiming that selfie-takers will be put to death by capital punishment."[41]

"Apichet Buatong, the secretary to Deputy Director of Phuket International Airport (corporate side) Kanyarat Sutipattanakit, has since confirmed that tourists taking selfies will not face the death penalty."[41]

Best Practice: Explain what caused the problem.

The fake news might have been created when news organizations mistakenly linked violations of the country's air navigation act—which are punishable by death—to moving the site at the airport where people could take selfies. "The international tabloids have added 2 plus 2 together and come up with 17!" *The Thaiger* said.[41]

JUMPING THE GUN

Crisis Trigger:	False Alarms
Category:	Government
Country:	United States
Organization:	Hawaii State Government
Individual:	David Ige

Reality Check:

Why would anyone get upset for being warned about an imminent event that could hurt or even kill them? When that warning turns out to be nothing more than a false alarm that got people concerned or upset for no reason at all, that's why. False alarms can create real problems for the people and organizations that issue them.

What Happened:

The State of Hawaii sent a false alert that was picked up by television, radio, and cell phones that there was a pending missile attack.[42]

The reason for the scare? A confused employee[42] who apparently pushed the wrong button.[42]

Edward's Take:

The silver lining to this short-lived crisis was that it showed people were paying attention. As the *Washington Post* reported, "When the false alarm splashed across cellphones...people began frantically trying to determine how long they might have to reach safety. Some sought shelter in their homes, while others described 'mass hysteria' on the roads."[42]

Best Practice: Respond immediately.

It took several minutes for state officials to tweet that there was "NO missile threat to Hawaii." Governor David Ige later admitted that he had forgotten his Twitter password, which is why it took so long for him to assure the public that it was a false alarm.[42]

Best Practice: Take steps to ensure the problem is not repeated.

The governor tweeted that he was going to meet with his top aides to find out what caused the false alarm and what could be done to prevent a similar incident in the future.[42]

State officials said they would require the approval of a second person before an alarm could be issued.[42]

Best Practice: Have a contingency plan.

It took almost a half-hour after the false alarm was sent for state officials to decide how to tell the public that everything was okay.[42] After they had figured it out, it took another 18 minutes for the correction to be sent via email, and more than a half-hour until a follow-up text message was sent.[42]

DOWN THE DRAIN

Crisis Trigger:	Financial News
Category:	Manufacturing
Country:	United States
Company:	General Electric

Reality Check:

The financial reports that are prepared and distributed by corporations provide important information and insights about how well—or poorly—the companies are doing. When the news is good, news coverage can help attract investors and shareholders. When the news is bad, it can scare them away, drive down stock prices, and reduce the value of the company.

What Happened:

General Electric announced it had reduced the value of the company by $23 billion.[43]

Edward's Take:

Some bets in business pay off, and some don't. General Electric made a calculated decision about acquiring a company that did not work out as planned.

Best Practice: Be aware of the possible consequences of your decisions.

The *Wall Street Journal* reported that "the industrial giant misjudged how profitable its 2015 acquisition of Alstom SA's power business would be and took a $22 billion goodwill impairment charge in the third quarter, forcing the company to post a $22.8 billion loss."[43]

General Electric's decision to write down the value of the company spurred two government investigations into their accounting practices.[43]

Best Practice: Explain what happened.

"Our outlook for power has continued to deteriorate driven by the significant over-capacity in the industry, lower market penetration, uncertain timing of deal closures due to deal financing, and the complexities of working in emerging markets," the company said in its third-quarter earnings filings.[43]

Best Practice: Express confidence in the future.

"This is a strong company," Chief Executive H. Lawrence Culp said on a conference call with analysts. "We can do better, but this is an important company, and I'm pleased to be on the team. Everything is on the table" with respect to the power business, he added.[43]

PAY UP

Crisis Trigger:	Fines
Category:	Oil and Gas
Country:	United States
Company:	ExxonMobil

Reality Check:

Companies are often caught doing things they shouldn't have been doing and can be penalized by courts or government agencies.

What Happened:

A judge fined ExxonMobil $20 million for releasing millions of pounds of hazardous chemicals into the atmosphere. The court also ruled that the company had saved millions of dollars by not following federal Clean Air Act rules and regulations.[44]

Edward's Take:

What people say or do when a company is fined depends, of course, on whether they were on the winning or losing side of the decision.

Best Practice: If you're happy with the result, put the victory in perspective.

Luke Metzger, director of Environment Texas, said he believed the fine was the "largest penalty resulting from a citizen suit in US history....It means that private citizens victimized by the world's biggest polluters can get justice in the American court system, even when government regulators look the other way."[44]

Neil Carman, clean air program director for the Sierra Club's Lone Star Chapter, said the decision sent "a resounding message that it will not pay to pollute Texas....We will not stand idly by when polluters put our health and safety at risk."[44]

Best Practice: If you are on the losing side of the argument, don't take it laying down.

ExxonMobil issued a statement saying, "We disagree with the court's decision and the award of any penalty." The company said it would look at its legal options and would consider appealing the court's decision.[44]

OUSTED

Crisis Trigger:	Fired
Category:	Entertainment
Country:	United States
Company:	Netflix
Individual:	Jonathan Friedland

Reality Check:

High-profile corporate executives can find themselves in a precarious position when they say or do things that raise eyebrows, offend people, and create the kind of publicity that no company wants to receive.

What Happened:

A top Netflix executive was fired because of the racist remarks he made in a meeting.[45]

Edward's Take:

Words matter. If you think that what you say in the privacy of a meeting will stay private, think again. When people are upset by what you say or how you say it, do not be surprised when they report your offensive remarks to others—and when there are consequences for your poor choice of words. And don't be surprised when your words are reported to a much larger audience.

Best Practice: When you are wrong, say so.

Friedland did the right thing by giving the following statement to the *Hollywood Reporter:* "Leaders have to be beyond reproach in the example we set and unfortunately I fell short of that standard when I was insensitive in speaking to my team about words that offend in comedy. I feel awful about the distress this lapse caused to people at a company I love and where I want everyone to feel included and appreciated."[45]

Best Practice: Tell people what you did, and why you did it.

Netflix CEO Reed Hastings announced to his staff in a memo that was reprinted by the *Hollywood Reporter* that he had fired Jonathan Friedland, the company's chief communications officer. "His descriptive use of the N-word on at least two occasions at work showed unacceptably low racial awareness and sensitivity."[45]

Best Practice: Tell people what you will do to fix the problem.

In that same memo, Hastings said, "Going forward, we are going to find ways to educate and help our employees broadly understand the many difficult ways that race, nationality, gender identity and privilege play out in society and our organization. We seek to be great at inclusion, across many dimensions, and these incidents show we are uneven at best. We have already started to engage outside experts to help us learn faster."[45]

For another example of what happened with an executive who used the N-word, go to page 196.

UP IN FLAMES

Crisis Trigger:	Fires
Category:	Religion
Country:	France
Organization:	Catholic Church

Reality Check:

Fire is both a boon and bane to civilization. It can keep us warm but also destroy the things we love and think will last forever. The bigger the loss, the more news it will make. This is especially true when beloved structures such as churches and cathedrals are almost burned to the ground.

What Happened:

Hundreds of firefighters battled a raging blaze that partially destroyed the Notre Dame Cathedral in Paris.[46]

Edward's Take:

Hindsight is 20/20.

Best Practice: Do everything you can to prevent a crisis.

According to news reports after the tragedy, there were steps that could have been taken to help prevent or fight the fire or alert officials to a blaze much faster. This included fire walls, the use of modern detection equipment, posting firefighters permanently on site, and the installation of fire sprinklers. These options were not pursued for various reasons.[46]

"We could have avoided all this with a modern detection system," said Guillaume Poitrinal, president of Fondation du Patrimoine, an organization that promotes French architectural heritage.[46]

Best Practice: Don't assume anything.

According to the *New York Times*, officials "appeared to have miscalculated what was needed to protect such an unusual, complex and irreplaceable building from a fire. Scientists consulted by [the newspaper] said fire dynamics indicated that, while the dense timbers may take time to burn completely, a fire would naturally race across the original timbers at Notre-Dame. It was a mistake to assume otherwise, they said."[46]

Best Practice: Set realistic deadlines.

French President Emmanuel Macron said he wanted the 856-year-old structure to reopen within five years.[46]

However, experts expect that it may take at least two decades before it is reopened.

"It's going to be a case of assessing the damage, strengthening everything that's there, do a full inventory of what we've lost, and then find the building materials," Dr. Emily Guerry, senior lecturer in medieval European history at Britain's University of Kent, told CBS News. "In the modern world, we don't build like we used to."[46]

A RIVER RUNS THROUGH IT

Crisis Trigger:	Floods
Categories:	Agriculture, Government, Weather
Country:	United States
Organization:	US Army Corps of Engineers

Reality Check:

Floods can devastate the lives of millions of people, destroy communities, impact businesses, and test their resolve and resources.

What Happened:

Record-breaking rainfall caused the Mississippi River to overflow its banks, shutting down all shipping on the river, delaying the delivery of important goods and materials for a variety of businesses, and preventing farmers from planting their crops.[47]

Edward's Take:

How governments and companies respond to floods will affect their reputations.

Best Practice: Explain the process for addressing the crisis.

As reported by Fox News, "The US Army Corps of Engineers said it will take at least three weeks without any rain in the forecast before the water goes down low enough within the Rock Island, Ill. district before they can open the locks up again. So they are hoping it reopens towards the end of June—if the rain holds off.

"When the water does go down, there's a lot of work to do to restore the locks to an operational status," Tom Heinold, chief of operations for the US Army Corps of Engineers, said. "There's a lot of [debris] that piles up on the walls, there's logs and trees that come down in pieces on the docks. Right now, that work is at least two or three weeks off."[47]

Best Practice: Explain how a crisis will impact your business.

Because the flood prevented farmers from planting their crops as scheduled, Deere & Co., which makes tractors and harvesting equipment, said it reduced its profit and sales forecasts to account for the decreased demand for its products.[47]

SICK TO THE STOMACH

Crisis Trigger:	Food Safety
Category:	Restaurants
Country:	United States
Company:	Chipotle Mexican Grill

Reality Check:

People assume that the food they buy and eat is safe, whether it's from a grocery store or restaurant. When it's not, the companies that made or produced the food need to take steps to alert the public and fix the problem.

What Happened:

Chipotle Mexican Grill experienced a series of food safety issues in 2015 and 2016,[48] which led them to implement several improvements and reforms.[48]

The company had an apparent relapse in 2018 when more than 600 people got sick after eating at a Chipotle restaurant in Powell, Ohio. It was not immediately clear what caused these people to become ill.[48]

Edward's Take:

Speed is important when responding to any disaster or scandal. When a crisis hits a restaurant company, the health and safety of customers can be at stake along with the image and reputation of the corporation. It's just as important to ensure that once corrected, the problem does not return.

Best Practice: Act quickly.

Chipotle did the right thing by voluntarily closing the restaurant for 24 hours so it could replace all the food and clean and sanitize the facility.[48]

Best Practice: Tell people what you did to address the problem.

CEO Brian Niccol said in a statement that "Chipotle has a zero-tolerance policy for any violations of our stringent food safety standards, and we are committed to doing all we can to ensure it does not happen again. Once we identified this incident, we acted quickly to close the Powell restaurant and implemented our food safety response protocols that include total replacement of all food inventory and complete cleaning and sanitization of the restaurant."[48]

Best Practice: Take steps to make sure the problem is not repeated.

Chipotle Mexican Grill provided food safety training to all of its workers across the country and planned to test employees on a regular basis to help guarantee they knew and understood basic food safety procedures.[48]

DUPED

Crisis Trigger:	Fraud
Category:	Crowd Funding
Country:	United States
Company:	GoFundMe.com

Reality Check:

People buy or do things based on the assumption that the product, event, or activity is real and legitimate. When it turns out to be otherwise, there can be serious consequences.

What Happened:

Three individuals—a homeless veteran in Philadelphia and a couple in New Jersey—were charged with defrauding 14,000 people of more than $400,000 in donations on the GoFundMe website. Instead of using the funds to help the homeless man as they had promised, the couple spent the money on vacations and a new car for themselves.[49]

Edward's Take:

The homeless man and GoFundMe.com were as much victims of the scam as the thousands of people who were tricked into making the donations. Although the company did not lose money, their image and credibility as a crowdfunding site took a significant hit. The man claimed he did not receive any of the money and sued the couple.[49]

Best Practice: Do the right thing.

After the fraud was discovered, GoFundMe.com did the right thing and returned the money to the donors under its guaranteed refund policy. They also worked with law enforcement agencies.[49]

Best Practice: Fix the problem that caused the crisis.

GoFundMe Chairman and CEO Rob Solomon told NBC News that the company created new safeguards to protect against such scams. "We wouldn't let the money leave the building," Solomon said, "until we could figure out how to get the flow of funds to the beneficiary."[49]

Best Practice: Put the crisis in perspective.

Company spokesperson Bobby Withorne did a good job placing the incident in the right context, telling one news organization that such frauds "make up less than one tenth of one percent" of all GoFundMe campaigns.[49]

Best Practice: Be transparent.

The GoFundMe website features a pledge by the company that contributions will be returned to donors if the money goes to the wrong place or person. It says that the guarantee "ensures that donations are protected if campaign funds are not delivered to the intended beneficiary or donors are misled by a campaign organizer or beneficiary."[49]

SHOW ME THE MONEY

Crisis Trigger:	Funding Cutbacks
Category:	Sports
Country:	Australia
Organizations:	Australian Institute of Sport, Australian Olympic Committee

Reality Check:

Money is an important ingredient of success for corporations and organizations. They need to make it and spend it wisely in order to continue to exist. But when the money runs out or funds are cut back, how an organization responds can send important messages to the public about its future.

What Happened:

The government-funded Australian Institute of Sport (AIS) cut back funding for the Australian Olympic Committee (AOC).[50]

Edward's Take:

The AOC did what needed to be done when they went public with their concerns about the impact of the reduced funding on their activities.

Best Practice: Sound the alarm.

An official of the AOC said in a statement that reductions in their budget would create big problems, coming as it did prior to the 2020 Olympic Games in Tokyo.[50]

"Sports that are lifting performance through well thought-out strategic plans, employing coaches and driving improvement in their systems have found themselves abandoned or facing great uncertainty," AOC chief executive Matt Carroll said in a statement. "It would be naive to think that high-performance athletes can enjoy their best preparation when there is financial pressure on coaching, programs, competitions and rising costs," he said.[50]

Best Practice: Explain what you did and why you did it.

The AIS justified the cutbacks by explaining they had a new funding model that would increase funding for some sports, while cutting it back for a small number of others that have a lesser chance of bringing home medals.[50]

"Having advised these sports and organizations about our funding decisions, we are giving them time to digest the information and advise their athletes and stakeholders before public announcements are made," AIS director Peter Conde said. "We are confident that these changes will not impact on Olympic or Paralympic podium success."[50]

HE SAID *WHAT?*

Crisis Trigger:	Gaffes/Misspeaking
Category:	Politicians
Country:	United States
Individual:	Barack Obama

Reality Check:

People can say surprising things that they do not mean to say or even realize they are saying.

What Happened:

In his first campaign for president in 2008, then senator Barack Obama told a crowd that he had visited 57 states and also misstated the number of potential victims of a cyclone in Burma. The next day the *Los Angeles Times* ran this headline with a story about the gaffe: "Barack Obama wants to be president of these 57 United States."[51]

Edward's Take:

People can get important facts, figures, or other information wrong or go on the record saying things that they have no right or business saying. If they are high-profile individuals or work with well-known companies or organizations, the mistakes can result in unflattering headlines. Occasionally the verbal miscues can raise troubling or unintended questions and issues or have serious consequences.

Best Practice: Acknowledge your mistakes.

Obama apparently realized that he had misspoken, telling reporters later, "I hope I said 100,000 people the first time instead of 100 million [cyclone victims]. I understand I said there were 57 states today. It's a sign that my numeracy is getting a little, uh [sic]."[51]

Best Practice: Ensure that you do not repeat the same mistake.

Help guarantee you are never surprised or embarrassed by anything you say by going through as many of these steps as possible:

- Think through what you want to say before you say it and why you want to say it.
- Ask yourself how someone could criticize what you want to say, then temper your remarks accordingly.
- Write it down, then read it aloud several times. If possible, record yourself saying it. Does it sound as good as it looks? If not, why not?
- Read it to one or more people and ask them what they think.
- Get enough rest before making a speech, presentation, or talking with reporters.

But even when a mistake happens, do not dwell on it. It happens to even the best speakers. Learn from it and move on.

DO YOU SMELL SOMETHING?

Crisis Trigger:	Gas Leaks
Category:	Utility Companies
Country:	United States
Company:	Columbia Gas

Reality Check:

Millions of people depend on natural gas to help warm their homes and businesses, heat their water, and power their appliances. Unfortunately, some of the pipes that transport the gas to our homes and businesses may be prone to leaks and explosions. The leaks or the disasters they cause can create havoc for days or weeks.

What Happened:

Natural gas explosions in three Boston suburbs killed one person, injured dozens of others, and set at least 39 homes on fire.[52]

Edward's Take:

In disasters such as this, public officials and organizations often work on parallel tracks to ensure that people are safe while trying to recover from the crisis as soon as possible.

Best Practice: Be realistic.

It's important to set achievable and realistic goals and milestones to address and recover from a crisis. Some experts doubted that was the case when Columbia Gas announced that it would take them 60 days to replace 48 miles of pipelines that were impacted by the incident. "It's [now] the end of September, and we're conscious of the fact that we're getting into the season where people are going to need their gas more than they do now," Columbia Gas spokesperson Scott Ferson said.[52]

Ferson said the work would be completed "as quickly as is humanly possible" and "will be held to the same [quality] standards as if it were drawn out longer."[52]

The *Boston Globe* reported that according to safety expert Bob Ackley of Gas Safety USA, the utility company's timetable was "unrealistic and unfair to businesses and residents who will need to plan for the prospect of cold weather setting in before their heat returns. 'People need to start making preparations for winter now,' [Ackley] said."[52]

"I questioned whether Columbia Gas had the resources to get the job done," he later told me. "Organizations that do not set and meet realistic deadlines to address and recover from a crisis can inconvenience people—or worse."[52]

Best Practice: Be prepared.

Having enough of the right resources is important when preparing for a possible crisis. "I don't think that the utility company was ready for this disaster," Ackley said. "How they responded—and the fact that the governor asked a different company to help with the immediate recovery efforts—did nothing to restore the public's confidence in Columbia Gas."[52]

Best Practice: Put things in perspective.

Columbia Gas noted in a news release that it was "in the midst of a multiyear program to modernize its gas distribution system and replace cast iron and bare steel pipeline systems across the state. Our commitment to accelerate that work in the Merrimack Valley [where the explosions occurred] while larger in scale than a typical modernization project, is necessary in light of recent events. We remain committed to the modernization of all of our pipeline systems."[52]

INTOLERABLE

Crisis Trigger:	Hate Speech
Categories:	Government, Social Media
Continent:	Europe
Organization:	European Union

Reality Check:

Americans enjoy almost unlimited freedom of speech. And while hate-related speech is protected under the US Constitution, that is not always the case in other countries.

What Happened:

The European Union launched a Code of Conduct to help pressure social media platforms to combat the growing issue of hate speech.[53]

Edward's Take:

Some crisis situations can last much longer than others.

Best Practice: Provide updates about your progress in addressing the crisis.

Three years later, the European Union announced that technology companies such as Facebook, Twitter, and Microsoft were identifying and removing a majority of the offensive comments within 24 hours of them being posted online.[53]

Best Practice: Go the extra distance.

Some European countries enacted even more stringent laws against hate speech. France, for example, passed legislation that requires social media sites to delete hateful content within 24 hours and gives people the option of flagging offensive language. Companies can now be fined $1.4 million if they do not follow the law.[53]

Germany passed their own hate speech legislation under which they fined Facebook $2.3 million for failing to comply with provisions of the law.[53]

Best Practice: Manage expectations.

"The fight against illegal online hate speech is far from over," said Věra Jourová, European commissioner for justice. "We have no signs that such content has decreased on social media platforms. But we do have signs that the Code of Conduct is a tool which can contribute to [a] robust response to the challenge."[53]

MY DEMANDS

Crisis Trigger:	Hostage Situations
Category:	Package Delivery
Country:	United States
Company:	UPS

Reality Check:

Like many crimes, a hostage situation often makes news. How a company responds when one of its employees is held against their will can put the corporation into the public spotlight as much as the hostage situation itself.

What Happened:

A man took two people hostage at a UPS facility in Logan Township, New Jersey. The man was shot and killed by police; the two female hostages did not suffer serious injuries.[54]

Edward's Take:

Companies whose employees or customers have been taken hostage should do exactly as told by the police.

Best Practice: Defer to the proper authorities.

If you find yourself anywhere near a hostage incident, law enforcement officials may tell you to shelter in place until further notice. In this particular case, the police sealed off streets and put nearby schools and businesses into lockdown, and news crews were kept at a safe distance from the UPS building.[54]

Best Practice: Express your appreciation to law enforcement.

After the episode was over, the company issued the following statement: "UPS greatly appreciates the work of the law enforcement personnel who responded to this morning's active shooter situation at the company's supply chain processing facilities in Logan Township, New Jersey."[54]

Best Practice: Let people know when the crisis is over.

In that same statement, the company noted, "The incident is concluded, and all of the employees are accounted for and being attended to by local officials."[54]

Best Practice: Offer help to those affected by the crisis.

UPS said, "Support services for employees who work at the site will be provided as they recover from this unfortunate incident."[54]

NO LAUGHING MATTER

Crisis Trigger:	Humor
Category:	Entertainers
Country:	United States
Individual:	Kathy Griffin

Reality Check:

Comedians live for laughter and are always trying out new jokes on audiences to see what kind of reactions they will generate. But there can be limits to what people think is funny or appropriate humor. Those who cross the line can pay a stiff price for their over-the-top quest for laughs.

What Happened:

Comedian Kathy Griffin staged what she thought was a humorous photo of her holding what appeared to be the severed head of President Donald Trump. The reaction was immediate and fierce—CNN fired her as host of their New Year's Eve broadcast, her bookings dried up, she was attacked by Trump and his family as well as many Trump supporters, and she was investigated by the US Secret Service.[55]

To see how Griffin bounced back from this crisis, go to page 235.

Edward's Take:

Everyone may not share your sense of humor or appreciate who or what you make fun of.

The bigger the target of the humor, the bigger the potential blowback. Sometimes the reactions may be completely out of proportion to the joke.

Best Practice: Apologize.

Griffin apologized profusely in a video message posted to her official Twitter account, saying that as a comic she routinely seeks to "cross the line" but realized that in this case, "I went too far. The image is too disturbing. I understand how it offends people. It wasn't funny. I get it," she said, adding that she was seeking to have the images taken down from social media.[55]

If misery loves company, then Griffin was not alone. Barbra Streisand had to take back her words and apologize profusely for her apparently thoughtless comments about two boys who said they were abused by pop icon Michael Jackson. (Read the full story on page 97.)

BLOWN AWAY

Crisis Trigger:	Hurricanes/Cyclones/Tornadoes
Categories:	Government, Weather
Country:	India
Organization:	Government of Odisha

Reality Check:

People depend on their governments to do the right things the right way. That's especially true when it comes to preparing for and responding to weather and natural disasters.

What Happened:

Cyclone Fani was one of the strongest such storms to strike the Indian state of Odisha in many years.[56]

Edward's Take:

The Indian state of Odisha did an excellent job preparing for the worst that Mother Nature could throw. According to theconversation.com, the government has a "zero casualty" policy for natural disasters and has built an accurate meteorological early warning system.[56]

Best Practice: Take action.

More than one million people were evacuated within two days, and thousands of kitchens and shelters were quickly provided. More than 45,000 volunteers pitched in to help.[56]

Best Practice: Overcome obstacles.

The United Nations Office for Disaster Risk Reduction and others praised the Odisha state government and thousands of volunteers for their work in limiting the death and destruction caused by Fani. As one news organization noted, "Considering the power of the cyclone, it is remarkable that more lives have not been lost."[56]

This was no small feat, considering that it was one of the largest evacuations related to a natural disaster in the country's history.[56]

Best Practice: Get ready.

Odisha's success in responding to the crisis can be traced to the steps they had taken to prepare for it.[56] Among other things, they:

- Prepared a detailed plan for dealing with the cyclone.
- Had a system in place to alert them to the oncoming cyclone.
- Communicated quickly and clearly to key audiences about the crisis.
- Managed and supervised those who were responsible for responding to and handling the situation.[56]

NO PAPERS

Crisis Trigger:	Immigration/Undocumented Immigrants
Categories:	Government, Food Processing
Country:	United States
Company:	Koch Foods
Organization:	Immigration and Customs Enforcement (ICE)

Reality Check:

Undocumented immigration has been a hot button issue for many years and is not likely to go away anytime soon. Businesses that knowingly hire undocumented immigrants can be fined by the federal government and company officials can go to prison.[57] But even if they weren't aware employees were undocumented, companies can find themselves in the middle of this crisis.

What Happened:

Immigration and Customs Enforcement agents arrested more than 240 people at a Koch Foods poultry processing plant[57] in what was called "the largest workplace immigration enforcement action in more than a decade.[57]

Koch is one of the largest poultry processing companies in the United States.[57]

The Koch employees were among 680 people arrested in raids at seven food processing plants in Mississippi. No charges were brought against the four companies or their officials, but government authorities said charges could be filed later.[57]

Edward's Take:

Politicians continue to debate the nation's immigration policies and how to deal with undocumented immigrants. If businesses find themselves involved in the controversy, and to help ensure that they are not perceived as contributing to the problem, they should be prepared to explain or defend their hiring policies, practices, and procedures.

Best Practice: Tell your side of the story.

Koch Foods said that while the government's search warrant affidavit suggests undocumented immigrants have worked at the plant, it didn't demonstrate Koch Foods knew it was hiring them.[57]

Best Practice: Go on the offensive.

Koch Foods said law enforcement officials illegally searched its chicken processing plant, and therefore any evidence it may have collected should not be used against the company.[57]

Best Practices: Issue a warning.

"If this search is allowed to stand, lawful businesses across the nation who legally hire immigrants are exposed to illegal searches founded on suspicion rather than probable cause," Koch attorney Michael Dawkins said.[57]

CAUGHT IN THE CROSS FIRE

Crisis Trigger:	Innocent Bystander
Categories:	Entertainers, Pharmaceuticals
Country:	United States
Company:	Sanofi

Reality Check:

Some people—and companies—have the bad luck to wind up in the middle of a scandal for which they are totally blameless. Although they did nothing wrong, they find themselves in the public spotlight where their character, values, and conduct are being called into question.

What Happened:

Actor Roseanne Barr partially blamed Ambien, which is made by Sanofi, for causing her to post racist tweets that led to the cancellation of her popular TV sitcom.[58]

Edward's Take:

Sanofi did a good job responding quickly and appropriately to Barr's tweet that apparently blamed the company's product for her racist comments.

Best Practice: Don't make excuses.

Barr appeared to blame Ambien for her actions when she tweeted this message: "It was 2 in the morning and I was Ambien tweeting—it was Memorial Day too—I went 2 [sic] far & do not want it defended—it was egregious indefensible. I made a mistake and I wish I hadn't done it...don't defend it please."[58] She was roundly criticized for her tweet to the point that some people posted their own tweets mocking her.[58]

Best Practice: Tell your side of the story.

Sanofi, which makes Ambien, tweeted: "People of all races, religions and nationalities work at [the company] every day to improve the lives of people around the world. While all pharmaceutical treatments have side effects, racism is not a known side effect of any Sanofi medication."[58]

For more about Barr's use of Twitter, go to page 214.

TRYING TO GET TO THE TRUTH

Crisis Trigger:	Investigations
Categories:	Government, Pharmaceuticals
Country:	United States
Company:	Rochester Drug Cooperative, Inc.

Reality Check:

It is never a good sign for an organization when a government agency launches an investigation into its activities or operations. People often jump to the conclusion that the company is guilty of something. And it is never good news when investigators conclude that something is amiss.

What Happened:

Federal and state agencies investigated Rochester Drug Cooperative Inc. (RDC) and its role in the opioid crisis. The investigation led to criminal charges being filed against the company, which agreed to pay a fine of $20 million and adhere to a strict compliance monitoring system.[59]

The company became the first pharmaceutical distributor to face federal criminal charges for its role in the opioid epidemic. "The charges are a result of a two-year investigation that began after it was found that RDC ignored pill limits for pharmacies and catered to doctors who over-prescribe," according to NPR.[59]

Edward's Take:

Companies and organizations in regulated industries and professions should consider taking extra precautions to ensure that they are operating within the law.

Best Practice: Admit your mistakes.

A company spokesperson said, "We made mistakes, and RDC understands that these mistakes, directed by former management, have serious consequences."[59]

Best Practice: Don't repeat your mistakes.

This was the second time in four years that the Drug Enforcement Administration (DEA) found issues with how the company monitored purchases of their products In 2015, RDC paid $360,000 in federal penalties after admitting it failed to report thousands of purchase orders as required to the DEA.[59]

SO, SUE ME!

Crisis Trigger:	Lawsuits
Category:	News Organizations
Country:	United States
Company:	Charter Communications

Reality Check:

Lawsuits are important and accepted ways for people and organizations to seek a redress of their grievances, correct a wrong, or call attention to a problem or issue. For the companies that are sued, lawsuits can create legal and PR headaches.

What Happened:

Five veteran female news anchors in New York City filed an age and gender discrimination lawsuit, alleging that television station NY1 was giving them less airtime and replacing them with younger women.[60]

Edward's Take:

It was ironic that a news organization which often reports on the alleged wrongdoing of others found itself charged with wrongdoing by their own employees.

Best Practice: Tell your side of the story, part 1.

The women, who were between the ages of 40 and 61, said in their lawsuit, "It is not surprising that a company without female leadership acquiesces to a workplace where discrimination thrives and fails to take appropriate measures to ensure that these issues are taken seriously and appropriately addressed when raised."[60]

Best Practice: Tell your side of the story, part 2.

The company denied the charges. A spokesperson for Charter Communications, which owns NY1, told Vox, an online news site, that "some journalists ended up with less time on the air because the station added news shows and shifted coverage after the merger."[60]

'We take these allegations seriously and as we complete our thorough review, we have not found any merit to them. NY1 is a respectful and fair workplace and we're committed to providing a work environment in which all our employees are valued and empowered.'[60]

DOWNSIZED

Crisis Trigger:	Layoffs
Categories:	Automobiles, Manufacturing
Country:	United States
Company:	General Motors

Reality Check:

Companies will do what's necessary to help ensure they are successful. But efforts to generate profits—such as laying off employees—can also generate headlines.

What Happened:

General Motors announced that it would eliminate about 14,000 jobs in North America.[61]

Edward's Take:

An ounce of prevention is worth a pound of cure, which could have been the rationale behind the carmaker's move to reduce its workforce. Although it was bad news for GM employees, the decision may have prevented a different kind of corporate crisis down the road.

Best Practice: Explain the reasons behind your actions.

Mary T. Barra, chairwoman and CEO of General Motors, told analysts, "We are taking these actions now while the company and the economy are strong to stay in front of a fast-changing market."[61]

In a news release, Barra said, "The actions we are taking today continue our transformation to be highly agile, resilient and profitable, while giving us the flexibility to invest in the future. We recognize the need to stay in front of changing market conditions and customer preferences to position our company for long-term success."[61]

Best Practice: Place announcements in context with other actions you are taking.

According to the news release, "Today, GM is continuing to take proactive steps to improve overall business performance, including the reorganization of its global product development staffs, the realignment of its manufacturing capacity and a reduction of salaried workforce. These actions are expected to increase annual adjusted automotive free cash flow by $6 billion by year-end 2020 on a run-rate basis."[61]

WHO'S IN CHARGE?

Crisis Trigger:	Leadership Failures
Categories:	Automobiles, Entrepreneurs, Manufacturing, Start-ups
Country:	United States
Company:	Tesla
Individual:	Elon Musk

Reality Check:

CEOs, presidents, and other top corporate officials need to be very careful about what they say or do in public. Their questionable behavior can impact people inside and outside the organization and draw unwanted scrutiny.

What Happened:

Tesla founder and CEO Elon Musk was named one of the worst leaders of 2018 by *Fast Company* magazine.[62]

Edward's Take:

How corporate and other leaders run their organizations and conduct themselves in private or public can lead to unflattering publicity. Any error in judgment can damage an individual's image, reputation, and credibility.

Best Practice: Set a good example.

Musk was scrutinized or criticized from all quarters—staff, investors, the media, and the public—for his behavior, his management style, conditions at his factory, and the financial health of the company. He apparently did not take it well and responded by calling investors names and snapping back via Twitter.[62]

Best Practice: Tell your side of the story.

Musk defended his leadership style in an interview with CBS News, telling reporter Lesley Stahl, "I am somewhat impulsive. And I didn't really want to try to adhere to some CEO template.... I'm just being me. I mean, I was certainly under insane stress and crazy, crazy hours [over the summer]. But the system would have failed if I was truly erratic."[62]

"I think there was like literally one week [during the Model 3 production push] where I actually worked 120 hours and just didn't leave the factory. I didn't even go outside. I wanted to make it clear to the team. They needed to see that however hard it was for them, I would make it worse for me."[62]

SPILLING THE BEANS

Crisis Trigger:	Leaked Emails and Documents
Categories:	Automobiles, Manufacturing, Start-ups
Country:	United States
Company:	Tesla

Reality Check:

There is good news and bad news about email. The good news is that email is an easy and effective way to instantly share news and information with hundreds or thousands of employees. The bad news is that it is just as easy for employees to leak bad news or embarrassing information about the company with the world. Unfortunately, bad news can generate more publicity about an organization than good news.

What Happened:

Tesla sent an email to employees warning them to stop leaking information about the company. That email was leaked, of course, to the media.[63]

Edward's Take:

Companies should not assume that their employees understand the consequences of sharing confidential and sensitive information with others.

Best Practice: Tell and remind employees about your policies.

To its credit, Tesla's security team was specific in telling employees about the dangers of leaking emails. According to the leaked email: "If you read the news, you know that there is an intense amount of public interest in anything related to Tesla. As a result of our success, we will continue to see an interest from people who will do anything to see us fail. This includes people who are actively seeking proprietary information for their own gain, targeting Tesla employees through personal networks or on social networks like LinkedIn, Facebook, or Twitter."[63]

Best Practice: Make sure people know about their responsibilities and the consequences of their actions.

In that same leaked email, the company said, "These solicitations are not only potentially damaging to our company, they can also be illegal, putting you and your colleagues/friends at risk for termination or even the possibility of criminal charges.

"As an employee and a shareholder, each of us has a responsibility to safeguard all information and technology we use and generate every day."[63]

Best Practice: Take steps to prevent a likely crisis scenario from coming true.

If you don't want to see embarrassing or confidential information leaked to the press, don't send it out in the first place. Otherwise, you will have to live with the consequences.

A BOLT OUT OF THE BLUE

Crisis Trigger:	Lightning Strikes
Category:	Computers
Country:	United States
Company:	Microsoft

Reality Check:

It is useless to argue with Mother Nature. She will do what she wants, when she wants, how she wants, and where she wants. All any company can do is to take as many prudent steps as possible to prepare for the worst Mother Nature can throw at them. They need to respond quickly so they can get back on their feet as soon as possible and limit the damage to their activities, operations, reputations, and bottom lines.

What Happened:

A Microsoft data center was knocked out of service after being hit by lightning.[64]

Edward's Take:

It's not often that you can find something ironic or humorous in a crisis situation. In this case it was rather obvious: a Microsoft *Cloud* facility was hit by *lightning*.

Best Practice: Apologize.

Buck Hodges, director of engineering of Microsoft's Azure DevOps, posted this message on a Microsoft blog: "First, I want to apologize for the very long [data center] outage for our customers hosted in the affected region and the impact it had on customers globally. This incident was unprecedented for us. It was the longest outage for [data center] customers in our seven-year history. I've talked to customers through Twitter, email, and by phone whose teams lost a day or more of productivity. We let our customers down. It was a painful experience, and for that I apologize."[64]

Best Practice: Explain what happened.

In that same blog post, Hodges provided a detailed description of what caused the data center to go offline, including this statement: "The incident started with a high energy storm, including lightning strikes, that hit southern Texas near the South Central US data centers. This resulted in voltage sags and swells across the utility fields that impacted cooling systems." He also told people where they could get additional information about the incident.[64]

Best Practice: Keep people updated about the crisis.

Microsoft posted information online with updates about the situation, such as this: "ENGINEERING STATUS: Engineers have successfully restored power to the data-center. Additionally, engineers have recovered a majority of the impacted network devices. While some services are starting to see signs of recovery, mitigation efforts are still ongoing.

NEXT UPDATE: The next update will be provided by 20:00 UTC or as events warrant."[64]

Best Practice: Tell people what you will do to prevent a similar crisis.

In his blog post, Hodges summarized what Microsoft had learned from the incident and the steps they were going to take to prevent a similar situation.[64]

WOULD I LIE TO YOU? APPARENTLY.

Crisis Trigger:	Lying
Categories:	Automobiles, Manufacturing
Country:	Germany
Company:	Volkswagen

Reality Check:

One of the most important assets any organization can have is the trust of their customers and the public. When a company violates that trust, the resulting damage can have far-ranging consequences to its image, credibility, reputation, legal risk, and bottom line.

What Happened:

Volkswagen installed software on millions of diesel engine vehicles that reported false emission readings. The company had to recall a half million cars in the US and more than 8 million automobiles across Europe.[65]

Edward's Take:

Always assume that someone, somewhere, is looking into some aspect of what your company is doing or how you are doing it. In this case, it was a group of scientists working in a laboratory at West Virginia University who discovered VW was cheating.[65] Although the company apologized for what happened, they should have immediately explained what they were doing, or were going to do, to address the problem and ensure it would not happen again.

Best Practice: Know what's happening in your organization.

The company passed the buck and decided to point fingers, saying that engineers were responsible for causing the problem and that no senior managers were involved.[65] VW officials apparently did not know what was happening in their own company, but they should have. That failure paved the way for a crisis that could have been prevented if corporate officials had known what was happening under their noses.

Best Practice: Don't blame others for your mistakes.

Compounding the failure to know what was happening in his company, Michael Horn, the CEO of VW's American division made matters worse by failing to take responsibility and blaming others. He claimed that the decision to deceive regulators "was not a corporate decision, from my point of view, and to my best knowledge today. This was a couple of software engineers who put this in for whatever reasons."[65]

Best Practice: Apologize.

Volkswagen took out full-page newspaper ads across the US to apologize. Beneath a headline that read "We're working to make things right, the ad went on to say, "Over the past several weeks, we've apologized to you, our loyal customers, about the 2.0L VW emissions issue. As we work tirelessly to develop a remedy, we ask for your continued patience."[65]

Best Practice: Take steps to make things right.

In the same ad, VW said that it would offer $500 Visa gift cards to people who owned the vehicles involved, a second $500 gift card for use toward the purchase of a new VW, and free roadside assistance for three years. It noted, "We sincerely hope you see this as a first step toward restoring your invaluable trust."[65]

WRONG LINKS

Crisis Trigger:	Misinformation
Categories:	Religion, Social Media
Country:	United States
Company:	YouTube
Organization:	Catholic Church

Reality Check:

The foundation of any crisis communication plan is the importance of providing accurate information about the crisis—the who, what, when, where, why, and how of the situation. Technology can help to communicate important details and background information. But human error and reliance on technology can lead to the spread of misinformation about an incident.

What Happened:

As it covered the fire that almost destroyed the Notre Dame Cathedral (see page 149), some news outlets aired YouTube video that mistakenly directed viewers to information about the 9/11 terrorist attacks.[66]

Edward's Take:

People depend on news organizations to get things right, especially when reporting a late-breaking crisis. When news outlets make a mistake, they need to set the record straight immediately and explain what went wrong and why.

Best Practice: Explain what caused the problem and what you are doing to fix it.

YouTube sent the following statement to Fox News about the mix-up: "We are deeply saddened by the ongoing fire at the Notre Dame Cathedral. Last year, we launched information panels with links to third party sources like Encyclopedia Britannica and Wikipedia for subjects [that are] subject to misinformation.

"These panels are triggered algorithmically, and our systems sometimes make the wrong call. We are disabling these panels for live streams related to the fire."[66]

Best Practice: Apologize.

YouTube apologized for the algorithm.[66]

TASTELESS

Crisis Trigger:	Offending the Public
Category:	Fashion
Country:	Italy
Company:	Gucci

Reality Check:

Innovation and creativity can help companies stay competitive. But in the race to stay on top in a demanding marketplace, it's important not to upset the very people who you want to buy your products or services.

What Happened:

Gucci sold a sweater that resembled a blackface when worn.[67]

Edward's Take:

Like Avon (see page 94), Gucci should have done a reality check with focus groups to gauge their reaction to the sweater. If the company did solicit feedback before launching the product and ignored it anyway, they should not have been surprised by the reaction they received.

Best Practice: Take action.

In the aftermath of the backlash to the sweater, Gucci removed the product from its website and brick-and-mortar store shelves.[67]

Best Practice: Apologize.

The luxury fashion brand issued the following statement: "Gucci deeply apologizes for the offense caused by the wool balaclava jumper. We consider diversity to be a fundamental value to be fully upheld, respected, and at the forefront of every decision we make."[67]

Best Practice: Tell people what you are going to do going forward.

The company said it would work on "turning this incident into a powerful learning moment for the Gucci team and beyond."[67]

NOT A GOOD LOOK

Crisis Trigger:	Optics/Photos
Category:	Politicians
Country:	United States
Individual:	Ralph Northam

Reality Check:

A picture is worth a thousand words. But sometimes they are the wrong words and send the wrong message.

What Happened:

A racist photo was published on the medical school yearbook page of Virginia Democratic governor Ralph Northam.[68]

Edward's Take:

Looks can be deceiving.

Best Practice: Don't change your mind about the facts.

The first step in responding to a crisis is to find out and confirm the facts about what happened. Northam was apparently so sure that he was one of two people in a college yearbook picture wearing blackface and a Ku Klux Klan costume that he apologized for being in the photo.[68]

That was, of course, until he said that he was sure that it was *not* him. He told a news conference, "I believe now and then that I am not either of the people in this photo. That was not me in that picture. That was not Ralph Northam."[68]

But by then the damage was done, and there were demands that he resign immediately. He decided to stay in office.[68]

Best Practice: Don't dig yourself deeper into a hole.

Northam told a news conference that he once darkened his face with shoe polish to look like Michael Jackson at a dance contest. The governor appeared ready to imitate the dancer's famous moonwalk until he was stopped by his wife, who was standing next to him.[68]

RETURN TO SENDER

Crisis Trigger:	Philanthropy
Category:	Museums
Country:	United States
Organizations:	Metropolitan Museum of Art, Sackler Foundation, Sackler Trust

Reality Check:

Nonprofit organizations run the risk of damaging their own reputations by taking contributions from groups having PR or other problems of their own.

What Happened:

New York's Metropolitan Museum of Art said it would no longer accept gifts from the family that owns the company that makes a painkiller associated with the opioid epidemic.[69]

Edward's Take:

The museum did the right thing in announcing it would stop taking money from the Sackler family. But if you are going to do the right thing, I recommend that you do it sooner rather than later.

Best Practice: Do the right thing right away.

The Metropolitan Museum of Art did not appear to be in any hurry to address the situation. The *New York Times* reported that the museum's decision "was months in the making, and followed steps by other museums, including the Tate Modern in London and the Solomon R. Guggenheim Museum in New York."[69]

Best Practice: Explain your decision.

Metropolitan Museum president Daniel H. Weiss said, "The museum takes a position of gratitude and respect to those who support us, but on occasion, we feel it's necessary to step away from gifts that are not in the public interest, or in our institution's interest," he said. "That is what we're doing here."[69]

Best Practice: Tell your side of the story.

The Sackler family issued their own statement, saying that "while the allegations against our family are false and unfair, we understand that accepting gifts at this time would put the Met in a difficult position.

"We respect the Met and that is the last thing we would want to do," the statement said. "Our goal has always been to support the valuable work of such outstanding organizations, and we remain committed to doing so."[69]

THIS SEEMS FAMILIAR

Crisis Trigger:	Plagiarism
Category:	Online Games
Country:	United States
Company:	IGN
Individual:	Filip Miucin

Reality Check:

Being creative can be difficult for some people. When faced with the need to come up with new and original content, some individuals may decide to copy and paste someone else's work and make it appear as if it were their own.

What Happened:

Online gaming site IGN fired an editor in the wake of allegations he had plagiarized reviews of video games.[70]

Edward's Take:

IGN moved quickly to address the issue and notify people about the situation.

Best Practice: Pay attention to what people are saying.

Dan Stapleton, the IGN reviews editor, said on Twitter that "for days, people had pointed out more similarities between [the editor's] work and various other articles and message board posts."[70]

Best Practice: Investigate.

The gaming site announced that it would review and delete all of the content that had been posted by the editor, then decide what to do after that. They also posted a message that said: "This article has been removed due to concerns over similarities to work by other authors. The author of this article is no longer employed by IGN."[70]

Best Practice: As soon as you know something, do something.

Stapleton posted this message on Twitter: "We've seen enough now, both from the thread and our own searches, that we're taking down pretty much everything [the editor] did."[70]

Best Practice: Don't wait to apologize.

It took almost a year for Filip Miucin, the editor who had plagiarized, to apologize in two videos for what he had done.[70]

BLACKOUT

Crisis Trigger:	Power Outages
Categories:	Government, Utility Companies
Country:	United States
Company:	Con Edison
Individual:	Bill de Blasio

Reality Check:

People assume that when they turn on a switch, the lights will come on and stay on until they are turned off. Power failures can throw this assumption out the window and spell trouble for corporations, organizations, and governments.

What Happened:

In 2019, more than 70,000 people in New York City were thrown into darkness when the power went out.[71]

Edward's Take:

When a crisis happens in the country's largest media market, you can bet that everyone will be watching what you are doing, how you are doing it, and what you will do to make sure it never happens again.

Best Practice: Tell people what happened.

Con Edison provided updates about the blackout that were reported by news organizations.[71]

The utility company issued the following statement soon after the power went out: "Con Edison is responding to extensive power outages affecting approximately 42,700 customers on the west side of Manhattan. The company will provide updates as they become available.

"Company crews are working now to repair the problem. Con Edison advises customers in the affected areas to switch off or unplug electrical appliances to avoid potential damage to the appliances when power is restored."[71]

Best Practice: Keep people informed.

Con Edison issued updates about the status and aftermath of the blackout, assuring people that "the company will provide updates as they become available."[71]

Best Practice: Go to the scene of the crisis.

New York mayor Bill de Blasio was campaigning for president in Iowa when the crisis occurred. He returned to New York the next day and held a news conference about the blackout.[71]

Best Practice: Find out what happened, and why it happened.

Con Edison posted a message on its website that said, "Over the next several days and weeks, our engineers and planners will carefully examine the data and equipment performance relating to this event and will share our findings with regulators and the public."[71]

Best Practice: Apologize.

The utility company released a statement that read in part: "Con Edison sincerely regrets the power disruption to our customers on the west side of Manhattan last night."[71]

Best Practice: Tell people what you will do next.

"When we have an incident like this, we focus first on isolation of the failed equipment or the most likely failed equipment and then restoration of the customers, and then when customers are restored is when we really do the full root cause investigation to identify what may have caused it," Con Edison CEO John McAvoy said.[71]

DELETED

Crisis Trigger:	Pranks
Categories:	Consumer Products, Social Media
Country:	United States
Companies:	Procter & Gamble, YouTube

Reality Check:

Publicity about a product can create awareness and sales for companies. But a PR bonanza can become a PR nightmare when people post videos of themselves misusing the products in dangerous or deadly ways. Two examples include the Tide Pod challenge, in which people swallowed packets of the detergent,[72] and individuals who did the "Bird Box" challenge—wearing a blindfold while they performed activities—that was spurred by a movie of the same name.[72]

What Happened:

YouTube announced that it has banned videos of dangerous pranks.[72]

Edward's Take:

No (sane) company wants to be seen as providing a public forum that promotes or glorifies dangerous stunts or activities.

Best Practice: Express concern.

Procter & Gamble, which makes Tide Pods, said they "are deeply concerned about the intentional and improper use of liquid laundry pacs by young people engaging in intentional self-harm challenges."[72]

Best Practice: Don't wait, part 1.

Rather than immediately shutting down the posting of dangerous videos, YouTube said individuals who had posted these videos would have 60 days to review and delete them. After that, all such videos would be prohibited.[72]

Best Practice: Don't wait, part 2.

Posting videos of dangerous pranks was nothing new. When YouTube announced their updated policy, they made no reference to this long-standing issue.[72]

Best Practice: Tell people what you are doing and why you are doing it.

YouTube posted the following announcement on their site:

"Dangerous challenges and pranks: Reminder—content that encourages violence or dangerous activities that may result in serious physical harm, distress or death violates our harmful and dangerous policy, so we're clarifying what this means for dangerous challenges and pranks.

"YouTube is home to many beloved viral challenges and pranks, but we need to make sure what's funny doesn't cross the line into also being harmful or dangerous. We've updated our external guidelines to make it clear that we prohibit challenges presenting a risk of serious danger or death, and pranks that make victims believe they're in serious physical danger, or cause children to experience severe emotional distress."[72]

TOO PROFITABLE

Crisis Trigger:	Price Fixing
Category:	Pharmaceuticals
Country:	United States
Company:	Teva Pharmaceuticals USA Inc.

Reality Check:

Deciding on the right price to charge for a product or service can help make or break a company. Charge too much, and people may decide to buy it somewhere else. Charge too little and you may not make a profit. A third option—when competitors collude and agree to charge the same price for the same product—can attract the wrong kind of attention.

What Happened:

Teva (the world's largest generic drug manufacturer) and other drugmakers allegedly joined forces to set an artificially high price for their products.[73]

Edward's Take:

Companies who are charged with price fixing, which is illegal in the United States, should be prepared to face the legal and PR consequences and immediately respond to the allegations.

Best Practice: Tell your side of the story.

Although allegations are not proof and companies are entitled to their day in court, it can take months or years until a final verdict is rendered by a judge or jury. A decision in the court of public opinion can come immediately, which is why a company's "plea" to the media and the public should be strong, definitive, and convincing and leave no room for doubt in the minds of the public. This hardly seemed to be the case when Teva vice president Kelly Dougherty denied the charge, saying in a statement that "the allegations in this new complaint and in the litigation more generally, are just that: allegations. Teva continues to review the issue internally and has not engaged in any conduct that would lead to civil or criminal liability."[73]

TAKING UNFAIR ADVANTAGE

Crisis Trigger:	Price Gouging
Category:	Pharmaceuticals
Country:	United States
Company:	Mylan

Reality Check:

Companies that jack up the price of products for no apparent reason other than to make more money run the risk of coming under the scrutiny of the government and incurring the wrath of the public.

What Happened:

Mylan, which makes the EpiPen auto-injector used by almost four million Americans to treat severe allergic reactions, was criticized for raising the price of the product from $100 to $608 over the course of several years.[74]

Edward's Take:

Companies can spend a lot of money to research, create, produce, and market new products. They should be careful, however, when and how they set or raise the price of their products. Otherwise, they may be charged with taking advantage of the people who may desperately need what they are selling. If they are doing something wrong such as price gouging, their standing in the court of public opinion will be improved by correcting the problem and addressing it head on. Circling the wagons does nothing to confront or solve a problem.

Best Practice: Tell your side of the story.

Mylan CEO Heather Bresch told a congressional committee that there was a "misconception" about how much money the company made—only $100 after rebates, fees, materials, and other overhead costs. She claimed that most people who use the drug pay only a fraction of the price.[74]

Bresch said the price increases reflected costs associated with research and development and other expenses, issues related to the distribution of the product, and America's system of healthcare.[74]

Best Practice: Anticipate problems that may cause a crisis.

"Looking back, I wish we had better anticipated the magnitude and acceleration of the rising financial issues for a growing minority of patients who may have ended up paying the full [list] price or more," Bresch told a congressional committee. "We never intended this."[74]

Although the company said, "We never intended this," price gouging is still price gouging, no matter how they may try to get off the hook. You should always consider how your explanation will be received by others. If you don't, you may continue to dig a deeper hole for yourself and your company.

UNDER WARRANTY

Crisis Trigger: Product Defects

Categories: Appliances, Consumer Electronics

Country: South Korea

Company: Samsung

Reality Check:

Nobody is perfect. And neither, apparently, is any product. If it can be made, it can also be made wrong. But consumers continue to expect that the products they buy will be reliable and safe to use. Companies need to be prepared if their products fail to meet those expectations.

What Happened:

Samsung customers reported that their new Galaxy Note 7 smartphones were catching fire and that some phones had exploded. The South Korean company stopped making the phone and issued recalls, refunds, and replacements. Samsung's stock lost billions of dollars in value.[75]

Edward's Take:

Sometimes good may not be good enough. According to news reports, even some of the replacement phones caught fire. Samsung eventually recalled every one of the Note 7 smartphones, including all of the replacement units.[75]

Best Practice: Move quickly.

News reports of Samsung phones that exploded or caught on fire began soon after the phone was rolled out in mid-August. After completing an investigation, the company stopped making the phone in the first week of September and announced the first recall soon thereafter. They announced a second recall in mid-October.[75]

Best Practice: Get the help you need.

Companies even as large as Samsung may not have all the resources they need to look into or address a crisis. Samsung did the right thing and worked with independent groups, including Underwriters Laboratories, to look into the cause of the fires.[75]

Best Practice: Make the best of a bad situation.

The company used the recall of the Note 7 as a communication tool to reach their owners. Samsung America president Tim Baxter said that 23 million text messages were sent to people who owned the phones about the importance of returning the product. According to *Consumer Reports*, "When people plugged in the phones to charge, a message appeared advising them of the recall, and through a series of firmware updates the company and its cellular partners reduced the functionality of the phones, until they were finally rendered inoperable."[75]

Best Practice: Take steps to ensure the problem that caused the crisis is not repeated.

Samsung established an eight-point quality assurance program to help guarantee that the problems that caused the smartphones to explode or catch fire would never happen again.[75]

PICKET LINES

Crisis Trigger:	Protests
Category:	Museums
Country:	Israel
Organization:	Haifa Museum of Art

Reality Check:

Artists express their points of view in their paintings, sculptures, and other formats.

Sometimes people don't understand what an artist is trying to say. On occasion, people might understand all too well—and make their opinions known loud and clear.

What Happened:

Hundreds of people protested against the Haifa Museum of Art in Israel when it exhibited a sculpture depicting Ronald McDonald being crucified.[76]

Edward's Take:

You can't please everyone, especially when it comes to art.

Best Practice: Respond appropriately to new developments and events.

The museum had at first refused to remove the sculpture, but then backed down in the face of protests and violent demonstrations.[76]

Best Practice: Tell people what you will do about the crisis.

The mayor of Haifa announced that the sculpture at the city-owned museum "will be removed and returned as soon as possible."[76]

Best Practice: When appropriate, express remorse or regret.

The mayor said, "We regret the distress experienced by the Christian community in Haifa, and the physical injury and violence that followed."[76]

Best Practice: Express appreciation.

"We thank the heads of the Christian churches and priests in Haifa for the dialogue and desire to bridge, the effort to reach a solution, and to prevent violence," the mayor said.[76]

Best Practice: Put the crisis in perspective.

The museum told the *Times of Israel* that it condemned the violence that broke out in protest of the sculpture. "A discourse about art, however complex it may be, must not spill over into violent territory and must be respected—even in charged situations," the museum said.[76]

FAKING IT

Crisis Trigger:	Publicity Stunts
Category:	Entertainers
Country:	United States
Individual:	Jussie Smollett

Reality Check:

Some people and organizations will do anything to get noticed. What they do and how they do it may generate the kind of publicity that no one wants.

What Happened:

Actor Jussie Smollett was arrested for filing a false police report. Police alleged that he had staged a hate crime against himself.[77] All charges against Smollett were dropped two months later.[77]

Edward's Take:

Not all publicity is good publicity. Smollett was roundly criticized by Chicago's chief of police, civic officials, and others for making it appear that he was a victim of a hate crime on a Chicago street.[77]

Best Practice: Tell your side of the story.

In a statement released after Smollett was charged, the actor's attorneys said he "enjoys the presumption of innocence, particularly when there has been an investigation like this one where information, both true and false, has been repeatedly leaked. Given these circumstances, we intend to conduct a thorough investigation and to mount an aggressive defense."[77]

Best Practice: Don't jump to any conclusions.

After Smollett was arrested, 20th Century Fox and Fox Entertainment said, "We understand the seriousness of this matter and we respect the legal process. We are evaluating the situation and we are considering our options."[77]

Best Practice: Express your concerns.

Apparently concerned about the impact the incident would have on Chicago, the city's police superintendent told reporters, "We will investigate with the same amount of vigor, [but] my concern is now hate crimes will be met with a level of skepticism that previously didn't happen. I only hope the truth about what happened receives the same amount of attention."[77]

IF YOU EVER WANT TO SEE YOUR FILES AGAIN....

Crisis Trigger:	Ransomware
Category:	Government
Country:	United States
Organization:	City of Baltimore, Maryland

Reality Check:

Technology can be used by people to make money off organizations by holding their computer files and other documents for ransom. It can be difficult if not impossible to prevent this information from being held hostage, and it is disruptive, expensive, and time-consuming to recover from ransomware attacks.

What Happened:

Hackers demanded a ransom of about $100,000 in Bitcoin after taking control of thousands of Baltimore city computers.[78]

Edward's Take:

Baltimore city officials took a stand against the hackers and decided not to pay the ransom.[78]

Best Practice: Explain your decision.

Baltimore mayor Jack Young posted this message on Twitter to explain why the city decided not to pay the ransom:

"Why don't we just pay the ransom? I know a lot of residents have been saying we should've just paid the ransom or why don't we pay the ransom?

"Well, first, we've been advised by both the Secret Service and the FBI not to pay the ransom. Second, that's just not the way we operate. We won't reward criminal behavior.

"If we paid the ransom, there is no guarantee they can or will unlock our system.

"There's no way of tracking the payment or even being able to confirm who we are paying the money to. Because of the way they requested payment, there's no way of knowing if they are leaving other malware on our system to hold us for ransom again in the future.

"Ultimately, we would still have to take all the steps we have taken to ensure a safe and secure environment. I'm confident we have taken the best course of action."[78]

Best Practice: Tell people what you are doing about the crisis.

Lester Davis, a spokesperson for the mayor, said, "We have a team of folks who are working with others from the state and federal level. They've quarantined the problem and are working diligently to bring the systems back online."[78]

Best Practice: Notify the appropriate authorities.

City officials told the FBI about the attack, which investigated the matter.[78]

Best Practice: Do what you can as soon as you can.

Baltimore government officials said that they took all of their computer systems offline, "but not before it took down voice mail, email, a parking fines database, and a system used to pay water bills, property taxes and vehicle citations," according to one news report.[78]

Best Practice: Explain the impact of the crisis.

Mayor Young said that "no city services have been affected. People were able to get their cars at the towing yard, people come in and pay in cash or money orders or they can mail their payments in. So all the city is functioning. We're doing it a different way and the citizens of Baltimore are not being affected. [We] just cannot get emails and those kinds of things. We are moving forward and citizens should not notice anything other than they have to come in and do things manually."[78]

SWITCHING TRACKS

Crisis Trigger:	Reorganization
Category:	Railroads
Country:	United States
Company:	Union Pacific Railroad

Reality Check:

Corporations that want to streamline their operations, improve customer service, and generate more profits will often reorganize the way they do business—two things that may help prevent or address larger problems that could lead to a crisis later on.

What Happened:

Union Pacific Railroad announced that it would reduce its number of business units, consolidate subsidiaries, appoint a new leadership team, and make other changes to its operations.[79]

Edward's Take:

Union Pacific did a good job in announcing the reorganization of the company.

Best Practice: Explain your actions.

The company explained why consolidating the subsidiaries made sense. "Merging the subsidiaries yields a company with a more robust portfolio of shipping and logistics services and an employee base with a greater breadth of expertise, both of which help us better serve our customers."[79]

Beth Whited, who was then executive vice president and chief marketing officer, said the leadership changes "more closely align our team structure around the markets we serve, giving us a focused opportunity to provide exceptional transportation products to our customers."[79]

Best Practice: Tell people what will happen next.

"We continue to look for ways to improve the customer experience we provide, and the Customer Care & Support team plays an integral role in that mission," Whited said on the company's website.[79]

QUITTING TIME

Crisis Trigger:	Resignations
Category:	Restaurants
Country:	United States
Company:	Papa John's Pizza
Individual:	John Schnatter

Reality Check:

Before they are forced to deal with a corporate emergency that they see coming—or might have had something to do in creating—some CEOs, presidents, and other top corporate officers may decide to leave the organization before they are fired. Or sometimes they will weather the oncoming storm, only to leave after it has passed—or before they can be fired by their board of directors.

Although their resignation might be welcomed by the board, the departure can still put the company in an awkward position, while creating a leadership void that needs to be filled quickly with the right person.

What Happened:

John Schnatter, chairman of Papa John's, resigned after it became known that he used the N-word during a conference call.[80]

Edward's Take:

It was ironic that he used the N-word during a conference call with the company's marketing agency. The purpose of the call was to coach Schnatter—who previously created a different PR controversy for himself—on how to prevent future self-inflicted public relations problems. Schnatter said he felt pressured to use the word during the call.[80]

Best Practice: Apologize immediately.

Nine hours after *Forbes* reported that he used the N-word, Schnatter issued the following statement: "News reports attributing the use of inappropriate and hurtful language to me during a media training session regarding race are true. Regardless of the context, I apologize. Simply stated, racism has no place in our society."[80]

Best Practice: Tell your side of the story.

Schnatter told a radio station that he felt pressured to use the N-word on the conference call. "The [marketing] agency was promoting that vocabulary....They pushed me. And it upset me," he said.[80]

Best Practice: Tell people what happened.

The company announced that its board of directors had accepted Schnatter's resignation and a new chairman would be appointed "in the coming weeks."[80]

Best Practice: Your actions should reflect your values.

"Papa John's condemns racism and any insensitive language, no matter the situation or setting," a company spokesman told CNBC. "Our company was built on a foundation of mutual respect and acceptance."[80]

Best Practice: Protect your reputation.

In the wake of Schnatter's resignation, the company took steps to eliminate his likeness from their logo and marketing materials. Several organizations, including Major League Baseball and a dozen Major League Baseball teams, terminated their sponsorship agreements with the chain. The University of Louisville even announced that they would take down Schnatter's name from their football stadium.[80]

For another example of what happened when an executive used the N-word, go to page 148.

TRUE OR FALSE?

Crisis Trigger:	Rumors
Category:	Theme Parks
Country:	United States
Company:	The Walt Disney Company

Reality Check:

It can be challenging enough for an organization to communicate with their key audiences without having to deal with rumors for which there is no basis in fact.

What Happened:

Disney World denied rumors that it would replace its classic Tiki Room attraction at their theme park in Orlando, Florida.[81]

Edward's Take:

Unless debunked and disavowed, rumors can take on a life of their own, creating headaches and problems for an organization.

Best Practice: Set the record straight.

Thomas Smith, editorial content director for Disney Parks, posted this humorous and lighthearted denial on the Disney Parks Blog that was picked up and reported by news organizations: "A little birdie told us there are some rumors flying around about our beloved Tiki birds at Walt Disney World Resort. We're sorry that our fans are being fed incorrect information by unscrupulous sources.

"While 'toucan' play at that game, we deal in facts here at the Disney Parks Blog. There are no plans for our feathered friends to fly the coop any time soon. We're constantly evolving our stories, but these birds will continue entertaining our guests at the Magic Kingdom Park just as they have done since 1971."[81]

LISTENING IN

Crisis Trigger: Secret Recordings

Category: Online Shopping

Country: United States

Company: Amazon

Reality Check:

Your private conversations may not be as confidential as you think. You are better off assuming that someone may hear what you are saying or, worse yet, may record and share it with others.

What Happened:

The Bloomberg news service reported that thousands of Amazon employees around the world listen to and transcribe voice recordings of people who use the company's Alexa smart speakers. The online shopping company said they used the recordings to help improve the way Alexa works.[82]

Edward's Take:

Companies seeking to improve their products and services should be careful not to cross the line between research and violating the privacy and confidentiality of their customers.

Best Practice: Tell your side of the story.

Amazon told Bloomberg, "We take the security and privacy of our customers' personal information seriously. We only annotate an extremely small sample of Alexa voice recordings in order [to] improve the customer experience. For example, this information helps us train our speech recognition and natural language understanding systems, so Alexa can better understand your requests, and ensure the service works well for everyone."[82]

Best Practice: Explain what safeguards you have in place.

Amazon told Bloomberg that they have stringent safeguards in place, do not tolerate any abuses, and that there was no way for employees to identify individuals.[82]

OFF LIMITS

Crisis Trigger:	Sexual Abuse/Assault/Harassment
Category:	News Organizations
Country:	United States
Company:	CBS
Individual:	Leslie Moonves

Reality Check:

Sexual behavior that is threatening, unwanted, or harmful creates challenges and problems for corporations whose leaders and employees engage in such illegal conduct. How companies handle this type of behavior can create—or help prevent—a different kind of crisis for organizations.

What Happened:

CBS announced it had dismissed its chairman, Leslie Moonves, after looking into charges of sexual abuse and misbehavior by a growing number of women.[83]

Edward's Take:

After you verify the facts and are satisfied with the outcome of your investigations, move as fast as you can to deal with the problem. The longer you wait, the more likely it is that the public will demand action.

Best Practice: Announce what you are doing to address the situation.

CBS Corporation announced that it fired Moonves because of sexual harassment and assault allegations and refused to pay him a $120 million severance package.[83]

Best Practice: Get the help you need.

Reuters reported that "the decision to deprive Moonves of his severance follows a board of directors review of the findings of an investigation into Moonves' behavior and the CBS culture conducted by two law firms, Debevoise & Plimpton and Covington & Burling, hired by CBS."[83]

Best Practice: Tell people what you did and why you did it.

The CBS board of directors said, "We have determined that there are grounds to terminate for cause, including his willful and material misfeasance, violation of company policies and breach of his employment contract, as well as his willful failure to cooperate fully with the company's investigation."[83]

Best Practice: Tell your side of the story.

Moonves denied any wrongdoing and described his sexual encounters as consensual.

"Mr. Moonves vehemently denies any non-consensual sexual relations and cooperated extensively and fully with investigators," Moonves' attorney Andrew Levander said in a statement, adding that the conclusions of the CBS board were "foreordained and are without merit."[83]

Best Practice: Do the right thing.

In lieu of paying Moonves a $120 million severance package, CBS donated $20 million of it to recipients working to eliminate workplace-based sexual harassment.[83]

TIPPING POINT

Crisis Trigger:	Shortages
Categories:	Real Estate, Trade Associations
Country:	United States
Organization:	California Association of REALTORS®
Individual:	Gavin Newsom

Reality Check:

Some shortages are more serious than others. A lack of housing, for example, can have major consequences for individuals, companies, organizations, and industries. The housing crisis is especially acute in California, which ranks 49th out of the 50 states in existing housing units per resident.[84]

What Happened:

California governor Gavin Newsom called for construction of 3.5 million new housing units over a six-year period.[84]

Edward's Take:

The California Association of REALTORS® (CAR), the state's largest trade association, took appropriate steps to help ensure the construction of more houses throughout the state.[84]

Best practice: When you see something, do something.

In its role as an advocacy organization, CAR launched Californians for Homeownership, a nonprofit organization that helps enforce prohousing laws and increase the state's supply of housing,[84] and established the Center for California Real Estate to influence legislators and the public debate about housing-related issues.[84]

Best Practice: Advocate specific solutions to the crisis.

CAR urged approval of several pieces of legislation that would help spur construction of more housing. The measures would increase housing and apartment development in and around major transit hubs and employers; hold local governments accountable by withholding gas tax revenue if counties did not meet home-building benchmarks; increase housing supply by selling bonds to provide loans to homeowners to construct accessory dwelling units; establish a state housing agency to oversee all housing-related initiatives and activities throughout California; and establish a housing crisis awareness program through the issuance of a specialty license plate to generate revenues for affordable housing programs throughout the state.[84]

Best Practice: Issue a warning if something is not done about the crisis.

CAR president Jared Martin warned, "California is at a tipping point, and the housing crisis threatens to permanently impede the state's economic growth. It's time for California's leaders to take the necessary bold action and support legislative solutions to address the housing shortage and answer the governor's call earlier this year to 'build housing for all.'" Martin also said the failure to pass the legislation the association supported "would put our state's economic future in peril as more and more Californians are priced out of the housing market."[84]

Best Practice: Be willing to work with others to address the crisis.

Martin said the association stands "ready to work with Gov. Gavin Newsom, the Legislature, and key stakeholders during the 2019 legislative session to advance innovative solutions to ensure all Californians can realize the American Dream of homeownership."[84]

THE TRUTH FINALLY COMES OUT

Crisis Trigger:	Skeletons in the Closet
Category:	Education
Country:	United States
Organization:	Georgetown University

Reality Check:

It's hardly unusual for people to have things in their past that they would like to keep hidden from public view. It is rare that a company has information about its past that they prefer stay buried. Sooner or later the truth emerges and must be dealt with whether you are a high-profile individual or a well-known organization.

What Happened:

Georgetown University acknowledged that it had sold hundreds of slaves in order to pay off a debt in 1838.[85]

Edward's Take:

Georgetown University could no longer ignore or hide embarrassing details about their past. How this institution of higher learning responded to their crisis offers important lessons for others when a hidden past comes to light.

Best Practice: Apologize.

The university formally apologized to the descendants of the 272 slaves following the release of a 104-page report from a working group of students and faculty members. "[We] have greatly sinned, in our thoughts and in our words, in what we have done, and what we have failed to do," said Reverend Tim Kesicki, president of the Jesuit Conference of Canada and the United States. "We are profoundly sorry. It is our very enslavement of another, our very ownership of another, which culminated in the tragic sale of 272 women, men, and children that remains with us to this day, trapping us in a historic truth for which we implore mercy and justice, hope and healing," he added.[85]

Best Practice: Put the crisis in perspective.

Georgetown president John J. DeGioia said, "Slavery remains the original evil of our Republic—an evil that our university was complicit in—a sin that tore apart families. Through great violence, [it] denied and rejected the dignity and humanity of our fellow sisters and brothers. We lay this truth bare—in sorrowful apology and communal reckoning."[85]

Best Practice: Do the right thing.

The university administration decided to rename two campus buildings that honored former university presidents involved in the sales of the slaves.[85]

NO EXCUSES

Crisis Trigger:	Surprise (the bad kind)
Category:	Candy
Country:	United States
Company:	Hershey

Reality Check:

There are good surprises and bad surprises. It's the bad ones that can create problems for corporations and organizations.

What Happened:

Bakers complained that the tops of Hershey Kisses were missing.[86]

Edward's Take:

Consumers expect—and often demand—that corporations and organizations immediately tell them about problems or issues that affect them. Any delay in announcing and explaining what happened just makes matters worse for companies—and can stoke anger and resentment among those who buy and depend on their products or services.

Best Practice: Tell the truth.

Hershey initially told people via Facebook that they "are intentionally breaking off the tips of the iconic American Hershey kiss at the factory so the tips don't break off in transit." A baker did not accept that explanation, saying, "This makes no sense."[86]

Best Practice: Tell people that you are looking into the problem.

On Facebook, Hershey responded to individual complaints from bakers in several states, saying that the company was looking into the situation.[86]

Best Practice: Tell people exactly what happened.

Contrary to best practices, Hershey did not immediately explain what happened or why it happened, and their initial public response to the problem did not appear to go down well with some folks. The company used the broken tips to deliver a message about diversity. A social media post showed different varieties of the candy alongside ones with missing tips: "Warm hearts this holiday season and take the time to celebrate our differences," it said.[86]

The company's failure to immediately provide details about the situation irritated some consumers. "American bakers want to have REAL answers: What happened, why it happened, what *exactly* they are going to do about it, and when we may expect a resolution to the problem," a home baker wrote on Facebook.[86]

Best Practice: Provide updates about the problem.

The candy company later issued this update. "After we heard from Hershey's Kisses fans during the Holiday Season, our operations team looked closely at our complete Kisses manufacturing process and made adjustments to the process for shaping the tips," Jeff Beckman, director of corporate communications for Hershey, said in a statement. "Kisses will continue to have their iconic and trademarked conical shape."[86]

Although he did not explain what had caused the problem, Beckman did note that "the equipment needed to be adjusted."[86]

WHAT *OTHER* PEOPLE PAY

Crisis Trigger:	Taxes
Category:	Online Shopping
Country:	United States
Company:	Amazon

Reality Check:

No one likes to pay taxes, including corporations and organizations.

What Happened:

Amazon was among dozens of major companies that did not pay any federal taxes in 2018. That news spurred criticism of the company by politicians and others.[87]

Edward's Take:

When businesses find ways to escape paying any taxes at all, they might please their investors and stockholders but make others mad or upset.

Best Practice: Tell your side of the story.

In a statement, Amazon said it "pays all the taxes we are required to pay in the US and every country where we operate, including paying $2.6 billion in corporate tax and reporting $3.4 billion in tax expense over the last three years."[87]

Amazon told the Reuters news service that "its low tax bill mainly stemmed from stock-based employee compensation, the Republican tax cuts of 2017, carry forward losses from years when the company was not profitable and tax credits for massive investments in R&D."[87]

Best Practice: Put the issue in perspective.

"We pay every penny we owe," Amazon said, adding: "Congress designed tax laws to encourage companies to reinvest in the American economy. We have."[87]

Amazon said it has invested $200 billion since 2011 and created 300,000 US jobs.[87]

FEAR AND LOATHING

Crisis Trigger:	Terrorism
Categories:	Government, Hotels
Country:	Sri Lanka
Organizations:	Sri Lankan security agencies
Companies:	Mandarina Colombo, Onyx Hospitality Group

Reality Check:

Terrorism is designed to create fear and chaos in order to help make a statement, send a message, or achieve political or other objectives. Preparing for and responding to terrorist attacks has become an important priority for governments—and a wake-up call for corporations and organizations.

What Happened:

After hundreds of people were killed in a series of terrorist attacks on churches and hotels in Sri Lanka, there was a steep increase in canceled hotel reservations on the island nation.[88]

Edward's Take:

Although terrorism is not new, each new incident often sparks a wave of international headlines. Companies and organizations need to be prepared if they are affected by a terrorist attack.

Best Practice: Pay attention to the warning signs of a possible crisis.

Several days after the attacks a news organization reported that Sri Lankan officials did not pay attention to early warnings about the terrorist attacks. According to the *New York Times*, Sri Lankan security agencies had monitored a group of radicals that the government later said was responsible for the attacks and which may have had help from overseas.[88]

Best Practice: Issue a warning.

The Mandarina Colombo hotel warned that "guests have to be very vigilant and expect a lot of security."[88]

A US travel advisory for Sri Lanka said, "Terrorist groups continue plotting possible attacks in Sri Lanka. Terrorists may attack with little or no warning, targeting tourist locations, transportation hubs, markets/shopping malls, local government facilities, hotels, clubs, restaurants, places of worship, parks, major sporting and cultural events, educational institutions, airports, and other public areas."[88]

Practice: Tell people what they should do.

The Onyx hotel chain said, "Our recommendation to all guests planning on traveling to the country is to check with their respective governments for travel advisory updates."[88]

The US embassy encouraged American citizens to sign up for safety security alerts through its Smart Travelers Enrollment Program.[88]

MR. CHAIRMAN...

Crisis Trigger:	Testimony before Congress/ Government Agencies
Category:	Banks
Country:	United States
Companies:	Citigroup, JPMorgan Chase, Bank of America, Morgan Stanley, Goldman Sachs, State Street, Bank of New York Mellon

Reality Check:

High-profile organizations that have ties to public policy issues can find themselves being asked to appear—if not subpoenaed—to testify before congressional committees. The CEOs, presidents, and other top officials of these companies can be called on to explain or justify their action—or lack of action—and their policies, procedures, and decisions.

What Happened:

The CEOs of several large US financial institutions testified before a congressional committee about reforms that were implemented in the aftermath of the 2007 financial crisis.[89]

Edward's Take:

Given the contentious and political nature of many congressional hearings and the controversies associated with the banking industry, I would be surprised if these officials did not know and anticipate that they would be on the hot seat.

Best Practice: Tell your side of the story.

The bankers told the committee that their companies were in much better shape since the financial crisis, thanks in part to reforms advocated by then president Barack Obama.

The Hill reported that "Michael Corbat, president and CEO of Citigroup, called the financial crisis 'a searing experience' for the country and his bank, which holds $1.9 trillion in assets."[89]

Corbat testified, "The experience also made it a mission for us never to be in that position again. As we learned, rebuilding trust is much harder than rebuilding our balance sheet."[89]

James P. Gorman, chief executive of Morgan Stanley, agreed. "We are safer, sounder and more resilient than we were before the financial crisis," he said.[89]

Best Practice: Be prepared for tough questions.

Congressional and similar hearings can be political and contentious. In this particular hearing the bank officials were asked a series of tough questions on a variety of issues including diversity, overdraft fees, deregulation, and even whether their banks had benefited from slavery.[89]

WORDS MATTER

Crisis Trigger:	Threats
Category:	Education
Country:	United States
Organizations:	Colorado public schools

Reality Check:

With so much danger in the world, it can be dangerous to ignore threats. Since lives may be at stake, organizations need to have appropriate safeguards in place if they and the people they employ, represent, or are expected to protect are threatened.

What Happened:

On the eve of the twentieth anniversary of the Columbine High School mass shooting, a young woman with an infatuation for the massacre made threats that led to the precautionary closure of hundreds of schools in Colorado.[90]

Edward's Take:

You never know when or from where the next threat will come. School officials in Colorado were attuned to possible dangers and took appropriate steps to respond to them.

Best Practice: Pay attention for danger signs of a possible crisis.

The *Washington Post* reported that as the anniversary approached, officials of the Jefferson County Public School District noticed they were receiving a growing number of threatening emails and phone messages.[90]

Best Practice: Issue appropriate warnings about the crisis.

Law enforcement officials issued public warnings about the woman's mental status and that she was armed and extremely dangerous. Schools increased security and locked their doors.[90]

The woman was later found dead of a self-inflicted gunshot wound.[90]

CLEAR AS MUD

Crisis Trigger:	Transparency (lack of)
Category:	Consumer Electronics
Country:	United States
Company:	Apple

Reality Check:

Corporations can be a lot like people. As shown elsewhere in this chapter, they have been known to lie, cheat, and try to cover up their mistakes. And, like people, sometimes they fail to tell the whole story about a problem involving their products or services. When the truth finally emerges, the company's image, reputation, and credibility can suffer.

What Happened:

In the aftermath of news reports that Apple had intentionally slowed some older iPhones down to save battery life, the company admitted that it had done just that.

Edward's Take:

A lack of transparency does nothing to build trust, credibility, or goodwill with customers or the general public.

Best Practice: Don't wait.

After lawsuits were filed against the company, Apple apologized and offered discounted replacement batteries for those who had certain older iPhones.[91]

Best Practice: Don't hide the truth.

USA Today reported that Apple issued a statement "confirming what many users had suspected—but couldn't verify—that iPhones slowed as they aged. The explanation was new to iPhone owners: Rather than just a reflection of age, the slowing was deliberate, an after-effect of software designed to prevent blackouts."[91]

Best Practice: Tell your side of the story.

Apple posted a lengthy message on its website about the battery issue, which began this way: "Your iPhone is designed to deliver an experience that is simple and easy to use. This is only possible through a combination of advanced technologies and sophisticated engineering. One important technology area is battery and performance. Batteries are a complex technology, and a number of variables contribute to battery performance and related iPhone performance. All rechargeable batteries are consumables and have a limited lifespan—eventually their capacity and performance decline so that they need to be replaced. As batteries age, it can contribute to changes in iPhone performance. We created this information for those who would like to learn more."[91]

Best Practice: Apologize.

Apple posted an apology on their website. "We know that some of you feel Apple has let you down. We apologize."[91]

TAKING A STAND

Crisis Trigger:	Trash/Waste
Category:	Government
Country:	China
Organization:	Government of the People's Republic of China

Reality Check:

Rather than deal with their own trash, some countries send their waste overseas for others to bury or recycle. But there can be limits to how much trash other nations are willing to accept.

What Happened:

China announced it would launch dozens of new recycling centers and expand its ban on importing trash from other countries.[92]

Edward's Take:

China did the right and proactive thing in restricting the overwhelming volume of trash by ending imports of trash from other countries.

Best Practice: Define the problem.

"Large volumes of solid waste are already impacting and restricting the high-quality development of the industrial economy," China's Ministry of Industry and Information Technology said in a policy document.[92]

Best Practice: Be specific about what you will do to solve the problem.

China said that 50 new "comprehensive utilization" facilities would deal with bulk solid waste and another 50 with industrial waste from sectors such as metals production, coal mining, construction, agriculture, and forestry.[92]

Best Practice: Announce a solution.

China said it would tackle its growing problem of trash and buried waste by creating recycling centers and would stop importing trash from other countries.[92]

Best Practice: Prioritize.

China said the centers would deal with items that had the biggest impact on the public such as packaging, batteries, and solar panels.[92]

Best Practice: Set a goal.

China said it wanted to completely eliminate the import of all solid waste by the following year.[92]

TWITS

Crisis Trigger:	Tweets
Categories:	Entertainers, Entertainment
Country:	United States
Company:	ABC
Individual:	Roseanne Barr

Reality Check:

People who post messages on social media platforms—or anywhere else—need to consider the impact of their words before sharing their "words of wisdom" with the world. For high-profile individuals, the reactions to and consequences of ill-conceived rants can ruin reputations and careers.

What Happened:

Comedian Roseanne Barr was fired from her ABC sitcom after she sent a series of racist tweets.[93]

Edward's Take:

Those who live by the tweet run the risk of dying by the tweet—or at least damaging their image, reputation, and credibility. Deleting offensive online messages may not erase the damage they cause.

Best Practice: Apologize.

Barr apologized on Twitter, saying, "I deeply regret my comments from late last night on Twitter. I apologize from the bottom of my heart and hope you can find it in your heart to forgive me."[93]

Best Practice: Don't blame others for your mistakes.

The comedienne later claimed that she had been "Ambien tweeting," which she said was responsible for her racist tweet.[93]

To see how Ambien responded to being blamed by Barr, go to page 166.

Best Practice: Make it clear why you did what you did.

In announcing the show's cancellation, ABC's entertainment president, Channing Dungey, said "Roseanne's Twitter statement is abhorrent, repugnant and inconsistent with our values."[93]

Best Practice: Show your support.

Disney CEO Bob Iger, whose company owns ABC, said, "There was only one thing to do here, and that was the right thing."[93]

ALMOST

Crisis Trigger:	Typos
Categories:	Advertising, Government, Politicians
Country:	South Africa
Organization:	African National Congress

Reality Check:

Some typographical errors are small and may take months before they are noticed. Others can be larger than life and are noticed immediately.

What Happened:

The message on the billboards for the African National Congress (ANC) in the 2019 election was supposed to read "Let's Grow South Africa Together." But two letters were dropped from the last word in the sentence, resulting in this snafu: "Let's Grow South Africa Togher" next to a picture of the ANC's Cyril Ramaphosa, president of South Africa.[94]

Edward's Take:

Anyone can make a mistake.

Best Practice: When you see something, do something.

The ANC said it would immediately remove the billboards.[94]

Best Practice: Put things in perspective.

The ANC minimized the snafu, saying it was the result of human error and was a very minor problem that would have no effect on the political party.[94]

Best Practice: Don't repeat the same mistake.

The ANC released the following statement about the billboard's typos that had, ironically, typos of its own.

"The ANC makes use of service providers to put up it's *(sic)* billboards and have *(sic)* noted with concern that the service provider has put one up containing spelling errors."

The ANC "will not allow a human error that was made by a service provider to derail us" and "will continue to work hard and make strides in gunnering *(sic)* support for the ANC towards the general election as we have been doing."[94]

INSTANT INFAMY

Crisis Trigger: Viral Videos

Category: Airlines

Country: United States

Company: United Airlines

Reality Check:

Viral videos can be gold for businesses by generating millions of dollars of free publicity. But the videos can also make a crisis situation worse by quickly sharing bad news about a company with millions of people around the world.

What Happened:

A video that went viral showed a passenger on a United Airlines flight being forcibly removed from his seat and dragged by airport security—unconscious and bleeding—down the aisle. The airline initially made flimsy excuses for what happened but eventually apologized for the debacle.[95]

Edward's Take:

There are two things that are bound to make a crisis worse: denying the obvious and minimizing what happened. United Airlines chose the latter until the reality of the crisis forced them to deal with it head-on.

Best Practice: Don't do anything that makes a bad situation worse.

In an effort to make room on the last flight of the day for four airline employees, United Airlines chose four passengers to be involuntarily bumped from the trip. When the fourth person refused to get off the plane, airport security yanked him from his seat. As *Forbes* reported, "He was dragged, unconscious and with a bloody mouth, down the aisle and off the plane. Of course, passengers filmed the spectacle on their phones and the images—and the outrage—quickly went viral."[95]

Best Practice: Identify and eliminate company policies that could cause a crisis.

United could have avoided this crisis if it had thought through a "what if" scenario in which a passenger who had paid for their ticket refused to relinquish their seat. In this scenario, a logical question would be "What's the worst thing that could happen?" In retrospect, this crisis was inevitable—and preventable.

Best Practice: Don't downplay the situation or blame the victim.

United CEO Oscar Munoz described the incident as "re-accommodating the customers" and claimed the passenger was "disruptive" and "belligerent."[95]

Best Practice: Get the facts.

The airline said later that it would conduct an internal investigation of the incident.[95]

Best Practice: Don't wait to apologize.

I think Munoz waited too long to apologize for the incident. He eventually did the right thing, however, and later took a more conciliatory approach, saying, "I continue to be disturbed by what happened. I deeply apologize to the customer forcibly removed and to all the customers aboard. No one should ever be mistreated this way."[95]

Best Practice: Apologize as often as necessary.

United Airlines issued another statement in which it apologized again. "This horrible situation has provided a harsh learning experience from which we will take immediate, concrete action," the airline said. "We have committed to our customers and our employees that we are going to fix what's broken so this never happens again."[95]

TICK TOCK

Crisis Trigger:	Waiting Too Long
Category:	Baby Furniture
Country:	United States
Company:	Fisher-Price

Reality Check:

When something goes wrong with the products we buy, the companies that made them ask people to return them to be repaired or receive a refund. But some companies do a better job than others in admitting there is a crisis in the first place.

What Happened:

Dozens of infant fatalities were attributed to Fisher-Price's Rock 'n Play sleepers. The Consumer Product Safety Commission issued a recall for almost five million units of the product.[96]

Edward's Take:

Companies that do not respond quickly and effectively when their products are found to be dangerous or hazardous run the risk of having their image and reputation damaged.

Best Practice: Move quickly to address the crisis.

The first reports about infant deaths tied to the Fisher-Price product were in 2009. But it was not until 10 years later that a recall was issued. By then, more than 30 babies had died.[96]

The delay did not go down well with consumer advocates, who criticized the company for waiting so long to recall the dangerous product. Instead of taking the initiative and recalling the product, they passed the buck to federal bureaucrats and, as reported by one news organization, "let the government issue vague warnings that got little attention."[96]

Best Practice: Tell your side of the story.

Chuck Scoton, general manager of Fisher-Price, posted a video online in which he said, "While we continue to stand by the safety of all of our products, given the reported incidents in which the product was used contrary to safety warnings and instructions, we've decided in partnership with the Consumer Product Safety Commission (CPSC), that this voluntary recall is the best course of action.

"Consumers should stop using the Rock 'n Play Sleeper and can contact Fisher-Price immediately for a refund or voucher...

"With these actions, we want parents around the world to know that safety will always be a cornerstone of our mission, that we are committed to these values, and will continue to prioritize the health, safety and well-being of the infants and pre-schoolers who utilize our products."[96]

RED FLAGS

Crisis Trigger:	Warnings
Category:	Government
Country:	United States
Organization:	US House of Representatives
Individual:	Adam Schiff

Reality Check:

Altered videos—known as deepfake videos—make it appear that people say or do things they did not say or do. Examples include altered footage that made it appear House Speaker Nancy Pelosi was drunkenly slurring her words; a manipulated video showing President Barack Obama kicking down a door; and a realistic—but tampered with—video where Mark Zuckerberg was talking about Facebook's control of data.[97]

What Happened:

Experts and politicians at a congressional hearing issued warnings about the dangers posed by doctored videos.[97]

Edward's Take:

Each new technology comes with its own benefits and potential drawbacks. Experts who raise red flags about these dangers—and companies who do something about it—might help prevent a new kind of crisis from spreading.

Best Practice: If you see something, say something.

At a congressional hearing, Rep. Adam Schiff (D-CA), chair of the House Intelligence Committee, said, "Now is the time for social media companies to put in place policies to protect users from this kind of misinformation." He warned that the companies should not wait to do something until "after viral deepfakes have polluted the 2020 elections. By then it will be too late."[97]

Best Practice: Do what you can about the problem, part 1.

Instagram said, "We will treat this content the same way we treat all misinformation on Instagram. If third-party fact-checkers mark it as false, we will filter it from Instagram's recommendation surfaces like Explore and hashtag pages."[97]

Best Practice: Do what you can about the problem, part 2.

Facebook said it was developing a policy about posting altered videos on the social media platform.[97]

Best Practice: Do what you can about the problem, part 3.

Researchers have developed a way to identify videos that have been doctored or altered in some way.[97]

EXPOSED

Crisis Trigger:	Whistle-blowers
Category:	Airlines
Country:	United States
Companies:	American Airlines, Southwest Airlines

Reality Check:

Allegations of corporate wrongdoing often come from outside an organization in the form of government investigations, lawsuits, or customer complaints. But it is not unusual for those allegations to originate from inside a company by those who blow the whistle on what they perceive to be wrong or illegal practices or policies. Allegations of wrongdoing put the accusers—and the accused—in the public eye.

What Happened:

Airline mechanics at American Airlines and Southwest Airlines said they felt pressured to ignore important safety issues and problems.[98]

Edward's Take:

A crisis can be created as easily by the people inside an organization as by those who work outside it. Whistle-blower laws can provide important protections for employees who want to expose wrongdoing or questionable practices and behavior at their companies.

Best Practice: Tell your side of the story, part 1.

Mechanics told CBS News that the pressure was the result of the fact that airlines do not make money unless the planes are transporting passengers.[98]

Best Practice: Tell your side of the story, part 2.

Southwest Airlines told CBS News that it "is fully committed to ensuring the Safety of our Customers and Employees. We continuously work to create and foster a Culture of Safety that proactively identifies and manages risks to the operation and workplace.

"With a fleet of 750 planes and 4,000 flights a day, we have a rigorous and well-run program. Safety has always been our highest priority—from day one to today and always. We are absolutely confident that our maintenance policies, procedures, and programs ensure the safety and airworthiness of our aircraft."[98]

OUT OF CONTROL

Crisis Trigger:	Wildfires
Category:	Wineries
Country:	United States
Company:	Paradise Ridge Winery

Reality Check:

There are more than 100,000 wildfires in the United States each year that burn through four million to five million acres, threatening people, homes, and businesses.[99]

What Happened:

In 2017, a major wildfire ripped through Sonoma County, California, destroying more than 5,600 structures, killing dozens of people, and costing the local economy more than $1 billion.[99]

The Paradise Ridge Winery is located in Santa Rosa—the largest city in the county. The boutique winery was known as a destination spot for weddings and other special events.

The fire destroyed all of the structures on the 156-acre property, including the event center/tasting room, winery, and three houses.[99]

Edward's Take:

Businesses that are located near forests or areas of heavy vegetation need to be aware of the danger that quick-spreading fires may pose for them, their employees, and their customers. It can take years for people and companies to rebuild and recover.

Best Practice: Try to bounce back as soon as you can.

The day after the fire, the winery talked with their general contractor about rebuilding the destroyed structures.[99]

Best Practice: Make sure you have enough insurance.

Although rebuilding the winery was estimated to cost almost $15 million, the family that owned the winery received only about a third of that amount from their insurance company and had to look for ways to pay for the rest of the expenses.[99]

Best Practice: Have a back-up plan.

The company's wine-making facilities were destroyed in the fire, so they made plans to make wine at a neighboring winery.[99]

Best Practice: Know what has to be done to recover, and in what order.

Because events like weddings helped generate about a third of the winery's business, they worked to reopen the event center/tasting room first.[99]

Best Practice: Make the hard decisions.

Before the fire, Paradise Ridge Winery had about 50 employees. It had to cut back the payroll to 17 after the blaze.[99]

Best Practice: Help prevent the occurrence of a similar crisis.

The winery took steps to make sure their facilities are safer and more fire resistant.[99]

BETTER SAFE THAN SORRY

Crisis Trigger:	Workplace Violence
Categories:	Healthcare, Hospitals, Trade Associations
Country:	United States
Companies:	Cleveland Clinic, MultiCare Tacoma General Hospital
Organizations:	American Society of Association Executives, International Association for Healthcare Security and Safety

Reality Check:

How companies protect their employees from being assaulted on the job is becoming a top priority in many industries and professions. Of the 25,000 incidents of workplace violence that occur every year in the United States, 75 percent of them take place in healthcare settings.[100]

What Happened:

Hundreds of healthcare facilities around the country have enlisted the help of dogs whose presence can be a calm and soothing influence in tense encounters and can help prevent or de-escalate violent situations in the workplace.[100]

Tacoma General Hospital in Tacoma, Washington, "hired" Officer Ben, a three-year-old German Shepherd security dog. He patrols the hospital to help keep visitors, doctors, nurses, and others safe from potentially dangerous situations.[100] The canine spends about 90 percent of his time on patrol. In one three-month period Officer Ben was called on for assistance more than 300 times and helped diffuse 80 potentially abusive and violent situations in the hospital.[100] Although originally hired for security purposes, he does occasional double duty as a therapy dog.[100]

Edward's Take:

It's one thing to acknowledge there is a problem or crisis and something else to take steps to address it. Fourteen percent of US hospitals are now using security dogs to help prevent and address violence in the workplace.[100]

Best Practice: Sound the alarm about the crisis.

Cleveland Clinic CEO Tom Mihaljevic said, "There is a very fundamental problem in US healthcare that very few people speak about, and that's the violence against healthcare workers. Daily—literally, daily—we are exposed to violent outbursts, in particular in emergency rooms."[100]

Best Practice: Know what's causing the crisis.

According to NPR, "Many healthcare workers say the physical and verbal abuse comes primarily from patients, some of whom are disoriented because of illness or from medication. Sometimes nurses and doctors are abused by family members who are on edge because their loved one is so ill."[100]

Best Practice: Be proactive.

The International Association for Healthcare Security and Safety urged healthcare facilities to establish policies, practices, and procedures to help prevent and manage violence in the workplace. The association posted a series of recommendations on their website to help their members implement the reforms.[100]

The American Society of Association Executives offered its members an online training session that included advice on what to do in the case of workplace violence and other threatening situations.[100]

UPSIDE DOWN

Crisis Trigger:	Wrong Priorities
Category:	Government
Country:	Zimbabwe
Organization:	Government of Zimbabwe

Reality Check:

There are limits to what organizations can do with their time, money, and resources, underscoring the need for them to do the right things, in the right ways, and for the right reasons.

What Happened:

The Zimbabwe government spent tens of thousands of dollars on judicial wigs.[101]

Edward's Take:

Organizations can create their own crisis simply by the decisions they choose to make.

Best Practice: Don't make the wrong decisions for the wrong reasons.

The government of Zimbabwe is facing multiple and serious problems: most of their people live in poverty, the economy is in poor shape, and courtrooms are in bad condition.

According to *The Guardian*, "Zimbabweans reacted with anger on social media, questioning the wisdom of the government's expenditure at a time when courtrooms are cramped and ill-equipped, the national economy is crumbling and, according to the World Food Programme, 63% of the population live below the poverty line."[101]

Dumisani Nkomo, chief executive of Bulawayo-based rights organization Habakkuk Trust, told *The Guardian*, "[The wigs] are misplaced priorities. We need to focus on bread and butter issues and avoid expenditure on unnecessary luxuries."[101]

I was not surprised, then, when news outlets ran stories with headlines such as:

"Zimbabwe spent $155,000 on 'hideous' powdered wigs for judges, angering citizens."[101]

Best Practice: Respond to calls from the media in time so that your side of the story will be included in their reports.

Having your side of the story included in news coverage about a crisis is the best—and sometimes only—way to ensure your point of view is heard. Zimbabwe missed an important opportunity to be included in CNN's story about the questionable purchase of the powdered wigs, which reported that "Zimbabwe's Judiciary Service Commission did not immediately respond to CNN's request for comment."[101]

THEY'RE *BAAACK!*

Crisis Trigger:	Zombies
Category:	Social Media
Country:	United States
Company:	Facebook

Reality Check:

Zombies return from the dead to attack and eat people. A zombie-like crisis is when disasters, scandals, or other emergencies keep coming back to eat a company or organization alive.

What Happened:

Over the years Facebook has had to deal with numerous crisis situations that involved issues ranging from data breaches, altered video, and hate speech to fake news, violation of privacy, and Russian meddling in US elections.

Edward's Take:

Most of the crisis examples in this chapter are of corporations and organizations that had one—and only one—crisis to contend with. Imagine, then, what it must be like for those, like Facebook, whose multiple crisis situations have been the subject of books, blogs, websites, and countless news reports.[102]

Given their experience in responding to different types of crises, you'd think the social media giant would have mastered the art of identifying everything that could go wrong and taken steps to address them so they do not become problems later. That is, of course, until their next crisis makes headlines and Facebook responds anew to the latest emergency.

What new lessons will Facebook provide us about crisis management and communication in the days ahead?[102]

Stay tuned!

101 Best Practices

The bad news is that there are dozens of things that can trigger a crisis.

The good news is that there are dozens of best practices that you can use to prevent, prepare for, respond to, manage, and recover from a crisis. I've summarized below the best practices that were followed—or that I think should have been followed—for the crisis triggers in this chapter and elsewhere in the book. The best practices are grouped according to the following categories: prevention, preparation, research, media relations, leadership/management, action, communication, and recovery.

When applied, the 101 best practices and the other advice in this book can help you prevent, respond to, and bounce back from disasters, scandals, and other emergencies.

Prevention

1. Know what's happening in your company or organization.
2. Be aware of events, trends, or developments that may trigger a crisis.
3. Assume nothing.
4. Identify known and possible crisis triggers.
5. Eliminate or reduce known and possible risks.

Preparation

6. Have a crisis management plan.
7. Review and update your plan on a regular basis.
8. Prepare back-up and contingency plans for different crisis scenarios.
9. Conduct regular crisis exercises.
10. Have procedures that enable you to immediately learn about a crisis in your organization.
11. Know when to activate the plan.
12. Appoint a crisis management team.
13. Ensure you can immediately reach key staff and others in event of a crisis.
14. Provide media relations training for your spokesperson.
15. Make sure you have enough of the right kind of insurance.

Research

16. Do your homework.
17. Get all the facts about the crisis.
18. Be sure of your facts.
19. Obtain the latest information about all aspects of the crisis.

Media Relations

20. Engage with and monitor mainstream and social media sites for relevant information.
21. Seek to correct mistakes by news organizations.
22. Respond quickly to media inquiries.

Leadership/Management

23. When you see or hear something, do something.
24. When appropriate, take ownership and responsibility for the crisis.
25. Tell your side of the story.
26. Always tell the truth.
27. Be transparent.
28. Define the problem that caused the crisis.
29. Identify solutions.
30. Do what you think is best to address the emergency.
31. Prioritize steps to address the crisis.
32. Don't jump to conclusions.
33. Don't minimize the crisis.
34. Commit to taking action.
35. Make the hard decisions.
36. When you are wrong, say so—the sooner the better.
37. Put the crisis in context and perspective.

Action

38. Do what you can as soon as you can.
39. Set realistic deadlines.

40. Put the crisis behind you as soon as you can.
41. Do the right things.
42. Do things right.
43. Move quickly.
44. Don't do anything that will make matters worse.
45. Don't assign blame.
46. Define success in dealing with the crisis.
47. Set achievable and realistic goals and deadlines.
48. Overcome challenges and obstacles.
49. Be visible to key audiences.
50. Provide full disclosure about the situation.
51. Justify your actions and decisions.
52. Reinforce your core values.
53. Seek the advice of experts.
54. Make the best of a bad situation.
55. Identify, obtain, and utilize the resources you need.
56. Tell people what they need to do to address the crisis.
57. Announce appropriate solutions to the problem that triggered the crisis.
58. Explain the impact your actions and decisions will have.
59. Exceed expectations.
60. Overcome challenges and obstacles.
61. Expect the unexpected.
62. Take steps to ensure the crisis is not repeated.
63. Set the record straight if necessary.
64. Respond immediately to changing circumstances.
65. Have a contingency plan.
66. Avoid disruptions to your business.
67. Respond quickly and appropriately to criticism.
68. If you think you are innocent, say so.
69. Explain and justify your actions and decisions.
70. Anticipate how others will react to what you do and say.
71. Manage expectations.
72. Don't give up.
73. Set a good example for others.
74. Take steps to make things right.

Communication

75. Apologize.
76. Sympathize.
77. Empathize.
78. Don't say anything until you have and can confirm the facts.
79. Think twice before you say a single word.
80. Promptly announce bad news.
81. Acknowledge that there is a problem or crisis.
82. Explain the impact of the crisis.
83. Don't dig yourself deeper into a hole.
84. Don't blame others for your mistakes.
85. Don't make excuses.
86. Provide updates as necessary.
87. Use all available and appropriate communication tools.
88. Don't speculate.
89. Don't hide bad news or try to cover it up.
90. Keep key audiences posted about your progress.
91. Notify the proper authorities.
92. Explain how you discovered the problem.
93. Express and demonstrate your concerns.
94. Defend your actions when necessary.
95. Make it clear what you are doing and why you are doing it.
96. Explain what safeguards you have in place.
97. Issue appropriate warnings to others if action is not taken.
98. Express appreciation for the help that was provided by others.

Recovery

99. Have a recovery plan with appropriate deadlines and milestones.
100. Apply lessons from your crisis and update your crisis management plan accordingly.
101. Never stop learning from the mistakes and successes of others.

CHAPTER 7
Bouncing Back:
How to Recover from a Crisis

Bouncing back from a disaster, scandal, or other emergency is more than just a possibility—it's done all the time.

Crisis Ahead ends on this positive note: you can bounce back from disasters, scandals, and other emergencies.

If you find yourself in the middle of a crisis, you can be forgiven for doubting that it will ever end or that you will be able to recover from it—especially when your image, reputation, or credibility have taken a major hit or appear to be ruined. The reality is that bouncing back from a disaster, scandal, or other emergency is more than just a possibility—it's done all the time. But first you will have to make sure that the light at the end of the tunnel is in fact daylight—and not the light of another oncoming train. After you are certain the crisis is over, then you can take steps to recover from it. The sooner the better.

Road Map to Recovery

Elsewhere in this book you've learned how to assess your readiness for a crisis (page 7), gauged your response to dozens of different crisis scenarios (page 11), and found out how others responded to their own crisis situations (page 81).

The cause and effect of a crisis depends on the nature of the emergency—as does the amount of time it can take to bounce back from it. Some crises may be nothing more than bumps in the road and will be over and done with in a relatively short period of time. Others may play out seemingly without end in the press, social media, and the legal system.

Although the road to recovery can vary depending on where you've been, here's a basic road map to help you get to where you want to go.

Apologize

- If appropriate, apologize or take responsibility for anything you did that caused or contributed to the crisis.

Prevent

- Create or update policies and procedures to help reduce the likelihood that the crisis will be repeated.

Learn

- Identify, apply, and share the lessons that you learned from the crisis.

Commit

- Promise those who were impacted by the crisis that you will learn from it.

Remember

- Don't forget what made you successful in the first place.

Define

- Define success—how will you know when you have bounced back?

Measure

- Establish milestones to measure your progress on the road to recovery.

Take Stock

- Inventory, evaluate, and use your resources, talents, skills, and abilities to bounce back.

Exploit

- Identify, create, and take advantage of opportunities that enable you to demonstrate, highlight, and promote those talents, skills, and abilities.

Publicize

- Generate positive news coverage and social media awareness about your comeback-related activities and successes.

Repeat

• Repeat all of the above as needed.

Celebrate

• As appropriate, take note when you have fully recovered from the crisis.

Bounce Back Hall of Fame

There are several companies, organizations, and high-profile individuals that I'd nominate to be inducted into the Bounce Back Hall of Fame. Although you may have a tough time believing otherwise, as the following examples show, you *can* come back from a crisis no matter which industry or profession you are in.

Don't assume that after you've recovered you will stay recovered. For some people and organizations, a crisis is like a bad habit or an addiction—it can be all too easy to have a relapse. Once you have managed to dig yourself out of the hole, do what you can to ensure that you do not fall back in—or dig yourself a new, even deeper hole.

Kathy Griffin

As discussed on page 162, comedian Kathy Griffin experienced what could have been a career-ending crisis when she staged a photograph of her holding what appeared to be the severed bloody head of President Donald Trump. Despite her apology, Griffin was investigated by the US Secret Service, attacked by Trump and members of his family, and fired by CNN, and she lost bookings.[1]

It did not take long for the Emmy-winning entertainer to mount an impressive comeback—not in the US, but in Europe. "The picture that ruined me was the picture that allowed me to tour the world for the first time," Griffin said.[2]

A year after the crisis, Griffin had gotten more involved with the business side of her career, generated positive publicity, and built up awareness about herself via email, texting, and social media. As *Forbes* noted in a story about her comeback tour, "It was a savvy move for the comedian, who saw her annual seven-digit income decimated by the photograph. She has already grossed more than $2 million on this tour and could tally up to $4 million, *Forbes* estimates."[3]

Baltimore, Maryland

Several weeks after its computers were held for a ransom that Baltimore refused to pay (see page 193), almost all of the city government's activities were back to normal. It was an expensive experience, costing the city more than $18 million.[4]

The US Conference of Mayors supported Baltimore's decision not to pay the cyber criminals when it passed a resolution opposing the payment of ransoms in similar situations.[5]

Gavin Newsom

In 2007 Gavin Newsom, who at the time was the mayor of San Francisco, admitted to having an affair with the wife of the man who was running his reelection campaign. He told the media, "Everything you've heard and read is true. And I am deeply sorry about that."[6]

After putting the scandal behind him, Newsom went on to be elected lieutenant governor of California and then was elected governor in 2018 with more than 60 percent of the votes.[7]

Although scandals tend to fade with the passage of time, they may not be forgotten entirely. In a televised interview during his run for governor, Newsom was asked about his relationship with the woman with whom he had the affair. He dealt with it head on, saying, "I acknowledged it. I apologized for it. I learned an enormous amount from it. We were very open and honest about it." But it did not end there. He was then asked if there was anything else in his past that could hurt his election chances. His answer: "Absolutely not."[8]

Chipotle

As discussed on page 152, Chipotle faced a crisis that cast doubt about the future of the national restaurant chain. In addition to taking aggressive measures to address the issues raised by food safety-related problems, the corporation made some top-level leadership changes and generated favorable news coverage about what they had done to recover from the crisis while highlighting the company's priorities and core values.

In 2018, Chipotle's new CFO Jack Hartung and CEO Brian Niccol talked about the company's comeback on CNBC's *Mad Money* program, hosted by Jim Cramer.[9]

Hartung acknowledged, "We got knocked on our heels a little bit, so we stopped talking about the things that made Chipotle special. The great thing now…since Brian joined and we brought a new team together, is we're back on our front foot. We're talking about our food."[10]

Niccol agreed, saying, "What we definitely are committed to doing is real ingredients, truly fresh, and that does require different food safety standards to be in place."[11]

In addition to making reforms and improvements, the calendar can be an important ally in helping a company recover its reputation. CNBC's Cramer observed in a 2019 show, "Father Time gets some credit, too. The customers forgot about the health scares. Now they're back and they seem to love Chipotle, as I do, more than ever."[12]

Sears

After emerging from Chapter 11 bankruptcy in October 2018, the retail icon Sears faced and survived another crisis—the imminent threat of liquidation that would have meant the end of the line for the company. A federal judge okayed a proposal to allow the sale of Sears' assets to a hedge fund.[13]

By then the chain was a shadow of its former self—only 425 stores and 45,000 employees—down from 3,500 outlets and almost 300,000 workers in its heyday.[14]

Martha Stewart

In 2003 Martha Stewart was charged by the US Securities and Exchange Commission for allegedly committing illegal insider trading when she sold stock in a biopharmaceutical company after she received an unlawful tip from a stockbroker.[15]

In 2004, a jury convicted her on four counts of obstructing justice and lying to investigators about the sale of the stock.[16]

The verdict did nothing to help Stewart's reputation or finances and put the brakes on what had been a spectacular success story. As the *New York Times* observed,

"She took her company public in 1999, as the internet excitement peaked, and overnight became a billionaire, at least on paper."[17]

Stewart later served five months in jail and five months in home confinement. She was estimated to be worth about $2 billion before her arrest.[17] Although her personal worth is now about a quarter of what it once was, new reports estimate her wealth at more than $600 million. After her release from prison, she wrote more books and has appeared on several network television shows.[18]

As Money Inc noted, "All in all, Stewart is still a major figure in lifestyle matters as well as various businesses that are connected to such things. There are those who would have suffered a serious stumble because of the incident of insider trading, but it seems that Stewart managed to come out in relatively good shape. Moreover, it seems clear that Stewart has no interest in retiring at the moment, so it will be interesting to see how her net worth continues to change in the times to come."[19]

Pepsi

In the wake of widespread criticism of an ad featuring Kendall Jenner that appeared to trivialize the Black Lives Matter protest movement, the soft drink company quickly pulled the TV commercial and issued the following statement: "Pepsi was trying to project a global message of unity, peace, and understanding. Clearly we missed the mark, and we apologize," the statement read. "We did not intend to make light of any serious issue. We are removing the content and halting any further rollout. We also apologize for putting Kendall Jenner in this position."[20]

The ad was responsible for reducing the positive perception of Pepsi to the lowest level in the previous eight years. Less than a year later Pepsi's reputation among one of the company's target audiences—millennials—had apparently been restored, as measured by one market research index.[21]

KFC

The international restaurant chain had to temporarily close most of its restaurants in the UK when it ran out of chicken.[22]

KFC explained that the problem was caused by DHL, their new delivery service. According to the restaurant company, "We've brought a new delivery partner on board, but they've had a couple of teething problems – getting fresh chicken out to 900 restaurants across the country is pretty complex. We won't compromise on quality, so no deliveries has meant some of our restaurants are closed and others are operating a limited menu, or shortened hours."[23]

KFC soon switched back to their old delivery company,[24] reopened all of their restaurants, and ran a humorous ad apologizing for the snafu.[25]

Starbucks

Starbucks responded quickly to the arrest of two black men at a Philadelphia store (see page 124). Among other things, it closed 8,000 stores for a day to provide antibias training to 175,000 employees and apologized to the two men.[26]

Although the company appeared to recover from the incident, the training did not work as well as Starbucks might have hoped. A few months later, six police officers were asked by an employee to leave a Starbucks restaurant in Arizona because they made a customer feel uncomfortable. Starbucks apologized to the police and Rossann Williams, Starbucks' executive vice president and president of US retail, posted this message on Twitter: "What occurred in our store on July 4 is never the experience your officers or any customer should have, and at Starbucks, we are already taking the necessary steps to ensure this doesn't happen again in the future."[27]

Starbucks' comeback and relapse illustrate how easy it can be for a company to dig itself out of one hole, only to fall into another one.

Your Continuing Education

Now that you know how to prepare and bounce back from disasters, scandals, and other emergencies, it's time to talk about your continuing education in crisis management and communication.

You will have some of the greatest teachers in the world—business executives and leaders,. politicians, and other high-profile individuals and organizations who are in the public spotlight because they are the latest victim—or cause—of a crisis. How well or poorly they respond to and manage their crisis situations will likely be reported by mainstream news organizations, social media outlets, trade publications, and at industry events.

If you have an interest in a particular kind of crisis, then all you have to do is set up Google alerts for the latest news about it or subscribe to my newsletter, which has information about the most current examples of crisis-related mistakes and successes. You can sign up to receive the newsletter at PublicRelations.com.

Every time you hear about or read stories of how someone or some company is responding to their crisis, use your newly found knowledge—and the advice in this book—to follow what they do and see how well they do it. And ask yourself this question: "If I were in their shoes, what would I do?"

It's always better to learn from the mistakes of others than to learn those lessons the hard way yourself.

Acknowledgments

I am grateful for the expertise of the many people who helped with various aspects of *Crisis Ahead*. They are:

Pamela Kervin Segal, who has read and edited almost every word I have written since we've been married.

Nancy Kervin, who was incredibly generous with her knowledge and time and used a fine-tooth comb to review and edit the draft manuscript and the advance reading copy.

Stephen Tull, who shared his considerable professional expertise to create the comprehensive index. Anyone who consults that important part of the book will appreciate his thoroughness and attention to detail.

Mary Anne Heffernan, whose insights and suggestions led to a better finished product.

John Willig of Literary Services, Inc., my literary agent, without whose boundless enthusiasm, experience, and expertise this book would not have seen the light of day.

Bob James, Jim Kennedy, Mitch Marovitz, David Nellis, Arnold Sanow, and Nancy Starr, who provided invaluable feedback and suggestions about the manuscript.

Dr. Ann Bonham and Dr. Jesse Joad, who gave important feedback about the book cover.

Dave Stefanides, whose encouragement and enthusiasm for my crisis management workshops led me to write this book.

Joel Singer, CEO, and June Barlow, senior vice president and general counsel of the California Association of REALTORS®, for their help with information about the state's housing shortage.

Robert Eyler, professor of economics and director of the Center for Regional Economic Analysis at Sonoma State University, for his insights about the impact of the devastating wildfire in Sonoma County in 2017.

The opportunity to observe the Pentagon's crisis communication exercise was made possible by US Army Brigadier General Omar Jones, chief of public affairs; US Army

Colonel Eric Bloom, director of army public affairs; US Army Lieutenant Colonel Travis Dettmer; and US Army Lieutenant Colonel Stacy M. Hopwood at the Defense Information School. US Navy Lieutenant Commander Bashon Mann (Ret.) ensured that I took full advantage of the experience.

My thanks to the talented people at the Hachette Book Group family of companies, including Iain Campbell, publishing director of Hodder & Stoughton, who served as the editor for *Crisis Ahead*; copyeditor, Brett Halbleib; proofreader, Jeanne Gibson; attorney, Nicola Thatcher at Keystone Law; Nicholas Brealey Publishing team: editorial assistant, Emily Frisella; production manager, Michelle Morgan; sales manager, Melissa Carl; marketing associate, Sarah Burke; and Alison Hankey, whose recommendations improved and strengthened *Crisis Ahead*.

I also want to express my gratitude to Lewis Csizmazia, the senior designer at Hachette UK who created the attention-getting shark-infested cover of *Crisis Ahead*; Pamela Kervin Segal and Nancy Kervin who suggested doing a video with one of the sharks leaping up to grab the wobbly "D" in the book's title; and Hannah Churn and Todd Churn, the two professional animators who brought the book cover to life online. They created and produced a catchy and engaging action sequence of a great white shark jumping up and carrying off the "D" that teeters precariously over the water. The short video plays in a continuous loop at PublicRelations.com.

Finally, I want to thank Charlie the Wonder Dog, my constant canine companion, who is always nearby to offer her advice and feedback.

In the interest of brevity—and to help limit the length of the book—there is one end-note for each case study in Chapter 6. The citations in that chapter are listed in the order in which they appear in their respective case study and all are based on the guidelines in *The Chicago Manual of Style*, seventeenth edition.

Chapter 2: If You Fail to Plan, You're Planning to Fail

1. Kageyama. "CEO's Tears Win Japan's Empathy." *San Francisco Chronicle.* February 26, 2010. https://www.sfgate.com/business/article/Toyota-CEO-s-tears-win-Japan-s-empathy-3197945.php.
2. "States with Apology Laws," *Sorry Works.* Accessed August 9, 2019. https://sorryworkssite.bondwaresite.com/apology-laws-cms-143.
3. "Corporate Apologies." *JDSupra.* February 13, 2019. https://www.jdsupra.com/legalnews/corporate-apologies-balancing-crisis-85580/.
4. JDSupra.

Chapter 3: Put Your Plan to the Test

1. Davis. "Why NASA Just Destroyed a Simulated New York City with a Huge Fake Asteroid." NBC News. May 7, 2019. https://www.nbcnews.com/mach/science/why-nasa-just-destroyed-simulated-new-york-city-huge-fake-ncna1002476.
2. Thomas. "G7 Countries to Simulate Cyberattacks." Reuters. May 10, 2019. https://www.reuters.com/article/us-g7-france-cyber/g7-countries-to-simulate-cross-border-cyber-attack-next-month-france-idUSKCN1SG1KZ.
3. Kaukuntla. "Mumbai Airport Prepares for Crisis." *The Hindu.* April 26, 2019. https://www.thehindu.com/news/cities/mumbai/mumbai-airport-prepares-for-crisis/article26947165.ece.
4. Myers. "Fort Bragg Power Outage." *Army Times.* April 25, 2019. https://www.armytimes.com/news/your-army/2019/04/25/heres-the-story-behind-that-massive-fort-bragg-power-outage/.
5. Morales. "New York Authorities Test Their Defenses against Cyber Attacks." CNN. July 26, 2019. https://www.cnn.com/2019/07/26/us/nyc-cyber-security-training/index.html.
6. Mann. US Navy Lieutenant Commander (Ret.). Email interview with Edward Segal. June 12 and 27, 2019.
7. Mann.

8. Shear and Schmidt. "Gunman and 12 Victims Killed in Shooting at D.C. Navy Yard." *New York Times*. September 16, 2013. https://archive.nytimes.com/www.nytimes.com/2013/09/17/us/shooting-reported-at-washington-navy-yard.html.

9. Shear and Schmidt.

10. CSX. "Company Overview." Accessed August 4, 2019. https://www.csx.com/index.cfm/about-us/company-overview/.

11. Doolittle. (Former assistant vice president for media and communications for CSX), email interview with Edward Segal. February 10 and March 3, 2019.

Chapter 5: How to Work with the Media during a Crisis

1. Kernis. "Mike Wallace Is Here." CBS Sunday Morning. July 21, 2019. https://www.cbsnews.com/news/mike-wallace-is-here/.

2. Bergin. "BP CEO Apologizes for 'Thoughtless' Oil Spill Comment." Reuters. June 2, 2010. https://www.reuters.com/article/us-oil-spill-bp-apology/bp-ceo-apologizes-for-thoughtless-oil-spill-comment-idUSTRE6515NQ20100602.

3. Bergin.

4. DiFazio. "Philadelphia Made Nearly $1 Billion in Accounting Mistakes Last Year." *Newsweek*. June 13, 2018. https://www.newsweek.com/philadelphia-made-nearly-1-billion-dollars-accounting-mistakes-last-year-974894.

5. McLaughlin. "Man Who Took Hostages Killed by Police." CNN. January 14, 2019. https://www.cnn.com/2019/01/14/us/ups-active-shooter-logan-township-new-jersey/index.html.

6. Stanglin and Madhani. "Fired Factory Worker Goes on Shooting Rampage." *USA Today*. February 16, 2019. https://www.usatoday.com/story/news/nation/2019/02/15/active-shooter-aurora-illinois-says-police-respond-active-shooter/2883754002/.

7. Bowerman. "Kelly Thought Career Was Over After Kids Interrupted Live Interview." *USA Today*. December 20, 2017. https://www.usatoday.com/story/news/nation-now/2017/12/20/bbc-dad-robert-kelly-thought-his-career-over-after-kids-hilariously-interrupted-live-interview/968226001/.

8. Usborne. "The Expert Whose Children Gatecrashed His TV Interview." *The Guardian*. December 20, 2017. https://www.theguardian.com/media/2017/dec/20/robert-kelly-south-korea-bbc-kids-gatecrash-viral-storm.

9. Rogers. "Notre Dame Fire." Fox News. April 15, 2019. https://www.foxnews.com/tech/notre-dame-fire-youtube-slammed-after-live-footage-appears-with-link-to-9-11-info.

Chapter 6: Learn from the Successes and Mistakes of Others

1. Charpentreau. "FAA Defends Its Processes." AeroTime News Hub. May 16. 2019. https://www.aerotime.aero/clement.charpentreau/22646-boeing-737-max-faa

-defends-its-processes-blames-pilots; Charpentreau; Economy. "Boeing CEO Puts Partial Blame on Pilots." *Inc.* April 30, 2019. https://www.inc.com/peter-economy/boeing-ceo-puts-partial-blame-on-pilots-of-crashed-737-max-aircraft-for-not-completely-following-procedures.html; Mokhiber. "Blaming Dead Pilots." Counter Punch. May 24, 2019. https://www.counterpunch.org/2019/05/24/the-boeing-way-blaming-dead-pilots/; Devine, Cooper, and Griffin. "'Inexcusable' to Blame Pilots." CNN. May 23, 2019. https://www.cnn.com/2019/05/23/business/american-airlines-boeing-pilots-union/index.html; Oestreicher. "Boeing Flunks Apology Tour." *O'Dwyer's*, May 21, 2019. https://www.odwyerpr.com/story/public/12540/2019-05-21/boeing-flunks-apology-tour.html.

2. DiFazio. "Nearly $1 Billion in Accounting Mistakes." *Newsweek.* June 13, 2018. https://www.newsweek.com/philadelphia-made-nearly-1-billion-dollars-accounting-mistakes-last-year-974894; DiFazio; DiFazio; Philadelphia City Controller. "Serious Issues with City's Financial Management." June 12, 2018. https://controller.phila.gov/office-of-the-city-controller-finds-serious-issues-with-citys-financial-management/. DiFazio, "Nearly."; Philadelphia City Controller. "Report on Internal Control and Compliance." June 12, 2018. https://controller.phila.gov/philadelphia-audits/report-on-internal-control-and-on-compliance-and-other-matters-city-of-philadelphia-fy-17/; DiFazio, "Nearly."; Newhouse. "Philadelphia's Bookkeeping among Worst in Country." *Metro.* June 12, 2018. https://www.metro.us/news/local-news/philadelphia/phillys-government-bookkeeping-among-worst-country-rhynhart-says.

3. Romano. "Sexual Assault Allegations against Spacey." Vox. December 24, 2018. https://www.vox.com/culture/2017/11/3/16602628/kevin-spacey-sexual-assault-allegations-house-of-cards; Park. "Spacey Apologizes for Alleged Sexual Assault." CNN. October 31 2017. https://www.cnn.com/2017/10/30/entertainment/kevin-spacey-allegations-anthony-rapp/index.html; Park; Weaver and Convery. "Spacey Criticized over Link between Homosexuality and Abuse." *The Guardian.* October 30, 2017. https://www.theguardian.com/culture/2017/oct/30/kevin-spacey-criticised-over-link-between-abuse-and-homosexuality; BBC. "Special Emmy Award Withdrawn." October 31, 2017. https://www.bbc.com/news/entertainment-arts-41816238; Romano. "Spacey Just Got Fired from New Movie." Vox. November 8, 2017. https://www.vox.com/2017/11/8/16626572/kevin-spacey-fired-all-the-money-in-the-world-reshoot-ridley-scott.

4. KSTP-TV. "Gunman Kills 5 People." February 15, 2019. https://kstp.com/news/active-shooter-aurora-illinois/5248240/; Farr. Water Finance & Management. "Shooting at Illinois Henry Pratt Facility." February 18, 2019. https://waterfm.com/shooting-illinois-henry-pratt-facility-leaves-5-dead-5-officers-wounded-mueller-releases-statement/. Pratt. "Aurora/Pratt Survivors' Fund." Accessed July 25, 2019, https://www.henrypratt.com/aurorapratt-survivors-fund/; Farr. "Shooting at Illinois Henry Pratt Facility." Farr. February 18, 2019.

5. Shapiro. "Avon Pulls Marketing Materials." Huff Post. January 20, 2019. https://www

.huffpost.com/entry/jameela-jamil-avon-shaming-women_n_5c44d839e4b0bfa69 3c49bc8; Zoellner. "Avon Issues Apology." *Daily Mail.* January 21, 2019. https://www.dailymail.co.uk/femail/article-6616527/Avon-issues-apology-body-shaming-campaign.html; Shapiro, "Avon."; Shapiro, "Avon."; Shapiro, "Avon."

6. Littleton. "Tsujihara Out as Warner Bros. Chief." *Variety.* March 18, 2019. https://variety.com/2019/biz/news/kevin-tsujihara-warner-bros-sexual-impropriety-1203165653/. Littleton; Littleton; Littleton.

7. Noveck. "Streisand Apologizes for Remarks on Jackson Accusers." AP News. March 23, 2019. https://www.apnews.com/71cbfeaed0014d0b88480933770eb507; Garcia. "Streisand Apologizes for Remarks about Jackson's Accusers." *New York Times.* March 23, 2019. https://www.nytimes.com/2019/03/23/arts/barbra-streisand-michael-jackson.html; Nyren. "Streisand Clarifies Michael Jackson Remarks." Variety. March 23, 2019. https://variety.com/2019/film/news/barbra-streisand-michael-jackson-remarks-backlash-1203170857/.

8. Simko-Bednarski, Frehse, and Romine."Delta Employee Arrests in $250,000 Theft at JFK International." September 26, 2019. https://www.cnn.com/2019/09/26/us/arrest-in-jfk-theft/index.html; Katersky and Crudele. "Delta Baggage Handler Arrested for Alleged Theft of over $250,000 at JFK." ABC News. September 26, 2019. https://abcnews.go.com/US/delta-baggage-handler-arrested-alleged-300000-theft-jfk-story?id=65883239; Katersky and Crudele.

9. Siekierska. "IKEA Apologizes for Selling Map that's Missing New Zealand." Yahoo Finance. February 15, 2019. https://finance.yahoo.com/news/ikea-apologizes-selling-map-thats-missing-new-zealand-181725931.html; Evans. "Ikea Apologizes After Leaving New Zealand off Map." BBC News. February 8, 2019. https://www.bbc.com/news/blogs-trending-47171599; Choudhury. "Ikea Apologizes for Leaving New Zealand off Map." NBC News. February 11, 2019. https://www.nbcnews.com/business/business-news/ikea-apologizes-leaving-new-zealand-world-map-n969941; The Local. "Ikea Apologizes After Leaving New Zealand off Map." February 9, 2019. https://www.thelocal.se/20190209/ooops-ikea-apologises-after-leaving-new-zealand-off-map.

10. Paraskova. "Tesla Owners Protest Price Cuts." Oil Price. March 4, 2019. https://oilprice.com/Latest-Energy-News/World-News/Tesla-Owners-In-Asia-Protest-Against-New-Massive-Price-Cuts.html; Xuanmin."Tesla's Price Cuts Anger Chinese Buyers." *Global Times.* March 3, 2019. http://www.globaltimes.cn/content/1140712.shtml; Lambert. "Tesla Owners Protest Price Cuts." Electrek. March 4, 2019. https://electrek.co/2019/03/04/tesla-owners-protest-price-cuts/; Houser. "Tesla Owners Enraged." Futurism. March 4, 2019. https://futurism.com/the-byte/tesla-protests-company-cut-prices; Houser. "Tesla Reverses Course." Futurism. March 11, 2019. https://futurism.com/tesla-stores-open-raising-car-prices.

11. Isidore. "Sears Declares Bankruptcy." CNN. October 15, 2018. https://www.cnn.com/2018/10/15/business/sears-bankruptcy/index.html; Rothstein.

"Sears Emerges from Bankruptcy." Bisnow. May 28. 2019. https://www.bisnow
.com/national/news/retail/sears-home-and-life-new-store-after-bankruptcy
-99153#ath?utm_source=CopyShare&utm_medium=Browser?utm_source=
CopyShare&utm_medium=Browser.

12. Positively Osceola. "Disney World Bans All Single-Use Plastic Straws." May 4, 2019.
https://www.positivelyosceola.com/walt-disney-world-bans-all-single-use-plastic
-straws-at-its-locations/; Esteves. "How Can Packaging Companies Respond to Global
Bans on Single-Use Plastic?" Maine Pointe. September 5, 2018. https://www.mainepointe
.com/practical-insights/how-can-packaging-companies-respond-to-global-bans-on
-single-use-plastic; Positive Osceola. "Disney World Bans."; Yasharoff. "Disneyland
Paris Gets Rid of Plastic Straws." *USA Today.* April 18, 2019. https://www.usatoday.com/
story/travel/news/2019/04/18/disneyland-paris-officially-banned-plastic-straws-us
-parks-are-next/3506699002/; Penning. "Disney Expands Environmental Commitment."
Disney Parks Blog. July 26, 2018. https://disneyparks.disney.go.com/blog/2018/07/disney
-expands-environmental-commitment-by-reducing-plastic-waste/; Penning.

13. Bellware. "Wells Fargo CEO Blames Fraud on Lowest-Level Employees." Huff Post. September 14, 2016. https://www.huffpost.com/entry/john-stumpf-wells-fargo_n_57d87d54e4
b0fbd4b7bc4c85; Egan. "Workers Tell Wells Fargo Horror Stories." CNN. September 9, 2016.
https://money.cnn.com/2016/09/09/investing/wells-fargo-phony-accounts-culture/;
Egan; Egan.

14. *Los Angeles Times.* "Dozens Charged in College Admissions Scheme." March 12, 2019.
https://www.latimes.com/local/lanow/la-me-college-admissions-scheme-stories
-storygallery.html; Holcombe. "USC Says Students Connected to Cheating Scheme Will
Be Denied Admission." CNN. March 14, 2019.
https://www.cnn.com/2019/03/13/us/college-admission-cheating-scheme-wednesday/
index.html; Holcombe; Speier and Klick. "USC Launches Internal Investigation into
Alleged Bribery Case." *Daily Trojan.* March 14, 2019. http://dailytrojan.com/2019/03/14/
usc-launches-internal-investigation-into-alleged-admissions-bribery-case/; Speier and
Klick.

15. CNBC. "Six Dead After New Pedestrian Bridge Collapses." March 16, 2018. https://www
.cnbc.com/2018/03/15/several-dead-in-florida-bridge-collapse.html;
Miller, *et al.* "Firm that Designed Bridge Promised It Was Safe." *Miami Herald.* May 6, 2019.
https://www.miamiherald.com/news/local/community/miami-dade/article230079344
.html; National Transportation Safety Board. "About." Accessed
August 27, 2019. https://www.ntsb.gov/about/Pages/default.aspx; National Transportation Safety Board. "Pedestrian Bridge Collapse." Accessed August 27, 2019.
https://www.ntsb.gov/investigations/Pages/HWY18MH009.aspx; National Transportation
Safety Board. "Preliminary Report." Accessed August 5, 2019. https://www.ntsb.gov/
investigations/AccidentReports/Pages/HWY18MH009-prelim-.aspx ; National Transportation Safety Board. "Preliminary Report."

16. Good. "More than 1,200 Accounts Banned for Cheating." Polygon. April 20, 2019.

https://www.polygon.com/2019/4/20/18509007/fortnite-world-cup-online-open
-cheating-bans; Tinnier. "Collusion Ban in World Cup." ScreenRant. May 5, 2019.
https://screenrant.com/fortnite-esports-worse-collusion-ban-world-cup/; The Fortnite
Team. "Fortnite Competitive Game Integrity." April 19, 2019. https://www.epicgames
.com/fortnite/competitive/en-US/news/competitive-game-integrity; Davenport. "Cheat-
ers Will Forfeit Winnings." PC Gamers. April 19, 2019.
https://www.pcgamer.com/fortnite-world-cup-cheaters/; The Fortnite Team. "Fortnite
Competitive Game Integrity."; The Fortnite Team; The Fortnite Team.

17. Liebreich, Karen. "Catholic Church Has a Long History of Child Sexual Abuse and Cover-
ups." *Washington Post.* February 18, 2019. https://www.washingtonpost.com/opinions/
the-catholic-church-has-a-long-history-of-child-sexual-abuse-and-coverups/2019/0
2/18/53c1f284-3396-11e9-af5b-b51b7ff322e9_story.html;
Winfield, Nicole. "Pope Tells Abusive Priests to Turn Themselves In." Associated Press.
December 21, 2018. https://www.apnews.com/cafcea3356d64948863e66195c6de4cd;
Rome Reports. "Number of Catholics Worldwide Rises to 1.3 Billion." June 13, 2018.
https://www.romereports.com/en/2018/06/13/vatican-report-number-of-catholics
-worldwide-rises-to-13-billion/; Winfield. "Pope Tells Abusive Priests."; Winfield;Win-
field;Winfield;Winfield;Winfield;Windfield; Winfield.

18. *USA Today.* "Vegetables Recalled for Potential Listeria Risk." *Chicago Sun Times.*
July 2, 2019. https://chicago.suntimes.com/2019/7/2/20679236/trader-joes-green-giant
-signature-farms-vegetables-recall-listeria; Food and Drug Administration. "Growers
Express Issues Voluntary Recall." Accessed August 5, 2019. https://www.fda.gov/safety/
recalls-market-withdrawals-safety-alerts/growers-express-issues-voluntary-recall
-multiple-fresh-vegetable-products-due-potential; Food and Drug Administration;
Food and Drug Administration.

19. Chappell."Uber Pays $148 Million over Yearlong Cover-Up." NPR. September 27, 2018.
https://www.npr.org/2018/09/27/652119109/uber-pays-148-million-over-year-long
-cover-up-of-data-breach; Uber. "2016 Data Incident." November 21, 2017. https://
www.uber.com/newsroom/2016-data-incident/; Uber; Uber.

20. McGeehan. "N.J. Transit: We Let You Down." *New York Times.* August 8, 2018. https://
www.nytimes.com/2018/08/08/nyregion/nj-transit-train-delays.html; McGeehan;
Higgs. "We Won't Get to Nirvana Overnight." NJ.com. December 5, 2018. https://
www.nj.com/traffic/2018/12/we-wont-get-to-nirvana-overnight-nj-transit-says-it
-will-do-a-better-job-alerting-commuters-to-problems.html; Higgs; McGeehan, "N.J.
Transit."

21. BBC. "Aluminum Plants Hit by 'Severe' Ransomware Attack." March 19, 2019. https://
www.bbc.com/news/technology-47624207; BBC; BBC; Meyer. "Norsk Hydro Targeted
by 'Extensive Cyber-Attack.'" *Fortune.* March 19, 2019. http://fortune.com/2019/03/19/
norsk-hydro-cyber-attack/.

22. Andone, Vera, and Reverdosa. "Brazil Dam Collapse." CNN. February 1, 2019. https://
www.cnn.com/2019/01/26/americas/brazil-dam-collapse/index.html; Andone, Vera, and

Reverdosa; Andone, Vera, and Reverdosa; Andone, Vera, and Reverdosa; Andone, Vera, and Reverdosa; Reuters. "Dam Collapse Adds to Long List of Mining Disasters." January 29, 2019. https://www.reuters.com/article/us-vale-sa-disaster-accidents-factbox/factbox-vale-tailings-dam-collapse-adds-to-long-list-of-mining-disasters-idUSKCN1PN1T6.

23. Bernard, *et al.* "Equifax Says Cyberattack May Have Affected 143 Million." *New York Times.* September 7, 2017. https://www.nytimes.com/2017/09/07/business/equifax-cyberattack.html; Yolz and Shepardson. "Criticism of Equifax Data Breach Response Mounts." Reuters. September 8, 2017. https://www.reuters.com/article/us-equifax-cyber/criticism-of-equifax-data-breach-response-mounts-shares-tumble-idUSKCN1BJ1NF; Smith. "We Will Make Changes." *USA Today.* September 12, 2017. https://www.usatoday.com/story/opinion/2017/09/12/equifax-ceo-we-make-changes-editorials-debates/659738001/; Smith.

24. Total Food Service. "Spain Now Leading the US Market of Olive Oil Imports." July 4, 2018. https://totalfood.com/olive-oils-from-spain-leading-us-market-imports/; Burdeau. "Lethal Olive Disease Discovered in Central Spain." Olive Oil Times. April 17, 2018. https://www.oliveoiltimes.com/olive-oil-making-and-milling/xylella-marches-on-lethal-olive-disease-discovered-in-central-spain/62827; Esparza. "Major Spanish Trade Group Looks at Ways to Join Fight against Xylella." Olive Oil Times. January 30, 2018. https://www.oliveoiltimes.com/olive-oil-business/europe/major-spanish-trade-group-looks-ways-join-fight-xylella/62071; Esparza; Gonzalez-Lamas. "Spain's Olive."; Esparza, "Major Spanish."; Esparza, "Major Spanish."

25. Kesslen. "Hard Rock Hotel to Remove Liquor from Minibars." NBC News. June 24, 2019. https://www.nbcnews.com/news/world/hard-rock-hotel-dominican-republic-remove-liquor-minibars-n1020931; Italiano. "Resort Owner Blames Deaths on 'Different Water.'" New York Post. June 30, 2019. https://nypost.com/2019/06/30/hard-rock-resort-owner-blames-dominican-republic-deaths-on-different-water/; Leshan. "Nearly 70 Sickened at Same Dominican Republic Hotel." WUSA9. June 11, 2019. https://www.wusa9.com/article/news/nearly-70-sickened-in-months-at-same-dominican-republic-hotel-where-two-americans-died/65-cc0768fd-2ee1-4e7e-a7ad-c53b7169af87; Leshan;Kesslen, "Hard Rock."; Kesslen, "Hard Rock."; Leshan, "Nearly 70."

26. Bronskill. "CSIS Destroyed Secret File on Trudeau." CBC News. June 15, 2019. https://www.cbc.ca/amp/1.5177205; Bronskill; Bronskill; Bronskill.

27. Stewart. "Two Black Men Arrested in Philadelphia Starbucks." Vox. April 15, 2018. https://www.vox.com/identities/2018/4/14/17238494/what-happened-at-starbucks-black-men-arrested-philadelphia; Johnson. "Reprehensible Outcome." Starbucks. April 14, 2018. https://stories.starbucks.com/press/2018/starbucks-ceo-reprehensible-outcome-in-philadelphia-incident/; Johnson; Madej and Boren. "Starbucks Closes Stores for Anti-Racial Bias Training." *Philadelphia Inquirer.* May 29, 2018. https://www.inquirer.com/philly/news/starbucks-stores-closed-racial-bias-training-20180529.html; Johnson, "Reprehensible."; NBC News. "Starbucks Policy." May 19, 2018. https://

www.nbcnews.com/news/us-news/new-starbucks-policy-no-purchase-needed-sit
-cafes-n875736; Samuelson. "I Personally Apologize." *Time*. April 16, 2018. https://
time.com/5241426/starbucks-ceo-apology-philadelphia/.

28. Centers for Disease Control and Prevention. "Media Statement." April 25, 2019. https://
www.cdc.gov/media/releases/2019/s0424-highest-measles-cases-since-elimination
.html; Centers; Centers; Centers; Centers; Centers.

29. Kang. "Pelosi Criticizes Facebook." *New York Times*. May 29, 2019. https://www
.nytimes.com/2019/05/29/technology/facebook-pelosi-video.html; O'Sullivan. "Doctored
Videos Make Pelosi Sound Drunk." CNN. May 24, 2019. https://www.cnn.com/2019/05/
23/politics/doctored-video-pelosi/index.html; Lagos. "Pelosi: Facebook 'Willing Enablers'
of Russians in 2016." KQED. May 29, 2019. https://www.kqed.org/news/11750792/
nancy-pelosi-doctored-videos-show-facebook-willing-enablers-of-russians-in-2016;
Lagos; Kang. "Pelosi Criticizes Facebook."; Lagos, "Pelosi."

30. Gafni and Sernoffsky. "Video Shows Baer Pulling Wife to Ground." *San Francisco Chron-icle*. March 2, 2019. https://www.sfchronicle.com/giants/article/Video-shows-Giants
-CEO-Larry-Baer-dragging-wife-13656221.php; Crowley and Becker. "Wife of Giants
CEO Issues Statement." *Mercury News*. March 1, 2019. https://www.mercurynews
.com/2019/03/01/wife-of-giants-ceo-larry-baer-issues-statement-in-aftermath-of
-ugly-scene/; Helsel. "Video of Baer Prompts MLB to Gather Facts." NBC News.
March 1, 2019. https://www.nbcnews.com/news/sports/video-s-f-giants-ceo-baer-public
-altercation-wife-prompts-n978421; Helsel; Helsel; Pavlovic. "Baer Taking Personal
Time Away from Team." NBC Sports. March 4, 2019. https://www.nbcsports.com/
bayarea/giants/giants-ceo-larry-baer-taking-personal-time-away-team.

31. Valinsky. "Subway Closed More than 1,000 Stores in US Last Year." CNN. May 2, 2019.
https://www.cnn.com/2019/05/02/business/subway-store-closures/index.html; Isidore.
"Why Subway Could Close Another 500 Restaurants." CNN. April 25, 2018.
https://money.cnn.com/2018/04/25/news/companies/subway-closing/index.html;
Valinsky; Valinsky; Yahoo Finance. February 4, 2019. https://finance.yahoo.com/news/
fast-food-chain-closing-more-215312109.html.

32. Staff Report. "1 in 4 People in Japan over 80 Still Drive." *Japan Times*. June 4, 2019. https://
www.japantimes.co.jp/news/2019/06/04/national/amid-high-profile-car-accidents-in
volving-elderly-survey-finds-1-4-people-japan-80-still-drive/#.XUnAy2cpChA; Staff
Report. "Japan Plans New Driver's License System for Elderly." *Japan Times*. June 11, 2019.
https://www.japantimes.co.jp/news/2019/06/11/national/japan-plans-new-drivers
-license-system-elderly-accidents-surge/#.XR-FZmcpChA; Hyatt. "Japan Working on
New Driver's Licensing System to Help Elderly Drivers." CNET. June 11, 2019. https://
www.cnet.com/roadshow/news/japan-elderly-driver-license-system/; Staff Report, "1
in 4 People."

33. Harig. "Tiger Woods Arrested on DUI Charge." ESPN. May 30, 2017. http://www.espn
.com/golf/story/_/id/19490176/tiger-woods-arrested-dui-florida; Harig, "Tiger."; Ortiz.
"Tiger Woods Arrested." NBC News. August 15, 2017. https://www.nbcnews.com/news/

sports/tiger-woods-dui-arrest-golfer-had-five-drugs-system-toxicology-n792856; Harig, "Tiger."

34. Lam. "How Did Alaska Repair Earthquake-Damaged Roads in Just Days?" *USA Today*. December 6, 2018. https://www.usatoday.com/story/news/2018/12/06/alaska-earth quake-facebook-laud-speedy-road-repairs/2233981002/; Lam; Lam; Lam; Wang. "Earthquake Created Highway Hellscape." *Washington Post*. December 7, 2018. https:// www.washingtonpost.com/transportation/2018/12/07/an-earthquake-created-highwa y-hellscape-alaska-days-later-road-reopened-good-new/?utm_term=.f28aa7981b4d; Wang.

35. BBC News. "Results." Accessed August 5, 2019. https://www.bbc.com/news/politics/ eu_referendum/results; White and Sullivan. "Brexit Deal Resignations." *The Sun*. August 7, 2019. https://www.thesun.co.uk/news/brexit/7745423/theresa-may-brexit -deal-withdrawal-eu/; Low. "Resignations Begin to Surface." Forexlive. August 29, 2019. https://www.forexlive.com/news/!/brexit-resignations-begin-to-surface-over-johnsons -prorogation-of-parliament-20190829; Kirby. "Brexit Agreement Fails for Third Time." Vox. March 29, 2019. https://www.vox.com/world/2019/3/29/18285930/brexit-deal -defeated-parliament-theresa-may-third-time; Bloom, et al. "Brexit Is Already Affect- ing UK Businesses." Harvard Business Review. March 13, 2019. https://hbr.org/2019/03/ brexit-is-already-affecting-uk-businesses-heres-how; Kottasová. "UK Government Says Brexit Deal Will Hurt Economy." CNN. November 28, 2018. November 28, 2018. https:// www.cnn.com/2018/11/28/economy/brexit-economic-impact/index.html.

36. Barnes. "Nuns Improperly Took as Much as $500,000." *Daily Breeze*. December 5, 2018. https://www.dailybreeze.com/2018/12/05/nuns-improperly-took-as-much-as-500000 -from-torrance-catholic-school/; Barnes; Barnes; Barnes; Barnes; Barnes; Barnes; Barnes.

37. Puente, Mandell, Alexander. "Worst Flub in Oscar History." *USA Today*. February 28, 2018. https://www.usatoday.com/story/life/2018/02/28/we-were-there-how-worst-flub -oscar-history-went-down/377305002/; Puente, Mandell, Alexander; Hayden, "Oscars Accountants Apologize for Snafu." *Hollywood Reporter*. February 27, 2017. https:// www.hollywoodreporter.com/news/oscars-we-sincerely-apologize-moonlight-la-la -land-accounting-firm-says-980846; Hayden.

38. Yasharoff. "Williams Felt 'Paralyzed' After Learning of Pay Gap." *USA Today*. April 2, 2019. https://www.usatoday.com/story/life/people/2019/04/02/michelle-williams-felt -paralyzed-over-mark-wahlberg-pay-gap-news/3345072002/; Stefansky. "Wahlberg Donated Hefty Re-shoot Salary to Time's Up." *Vanity Fair*. January 14, 2018. https:// www.vanityfair.com/hollywood/2018/01/mark-wahlberg-donated-his-hefty-all-the -money-in-the-world-reshoot-salary-to-times-up-michelle-williams; Stefansky; Daly. "Wahlberg Gives Reshoot Fee to Time's Up Campaign." NME. January 13, 2018. https:// www.nme.com/news/film/mark-wahlberg-gives-money-world-reshoot-fee-times -campaign-2219117#rexStpsEYw3O00ao.99.

39. Sblendorio, "Letterman Compared Affair Fallout to Car Crash." *Daily News*. April 11, 2017.

https://www.nydailynews.com/entertainment/tv/david-letterman-worried-affairs-destroy-family-article-1.3044381; James and Goldwert. "Letterman Reveals Extortion Plot." ABC News. October 1, 2009. https://abcnews.go.com/Entertainment/david-letterman-admits-sexual-affairs-staffers-details-extortion/story?id=8728424; Katz. "Letterman Shocking Admission." CBS News. October 1, 2009. https://www.cbsnews.com/news/david-letterman-shocking-admission-office-sex-affairs-led-to-2m-extortion-plot/; Katz; James and Goldwert, "Lettermen."

40. Hinton. "Calloway Discusses Homophobic Facebook Posts." *Chicago Sun Times.* March 24, 2019. https://chicago.suntimes.com/2019/3/24/18376266/5th-ward-candidate-calloway-discusses-past-homophobic-facebook-posts; Hinton; Hinton.

41. Pasquini. "Tourists May Face Death Penalty for Taking Photos." *People.* April 5, 2019. https://people.com/travel/tourists-may-face-death-penalty-selfies-phuket-beach/; Fleetwood. "News of 'Death Penalty' for Selfies Labelled 'Fake.'" *Travel Weekly.* April 11, 2019. http://www.travelweekly.com.au/article/news-of-death-penalty-for-thai-airport-selfies-labelled-fake/; Fleetwood; The Thaiger. "Fake News Goes Viral." April 9, 2019. https://thethaiger.com/hot-news/fake-news-goes-viral-about-death-sentence-for-phuket-airport-selfies.

42. Cohen. "Missile Threat for Hawaii a False Alarm." CNN. January 14, 2018. https://www.cnn.com/2018/01/13/politics/hawaii-missile-threat-false-alarm/index.html; Berman and Fung. "Hawaii's Fake Missile Alert." *Washington Post.* January 30, 2018. https://www.washingtonpost.com/news/the-switch/wp/2018/01/30/heres-what-went-wrong-with-that-hawaii-missile-alert-the-fcc-says/?utm_term=.ba76117328af; Cohen, "Missile."; Berman and Fung, "Hawaii's."; Andrews. "Hawaii Governor Didn't Know His Twitter Password." *Washington Post.* January 23, 2018. https://www.washingtonpost.com/news/morning-mix/wp/2018/01/23/hawaii-governor-didnt-correct-false-missile-alert-sooner-because-he-didnt-know-his-twitter-password/?utm_term=.00dd9a8f85ce; Cohen, "Missile."; Berman and Fung, "Hawaii's." Berman and Fung, "Hawaii's."; BBC News. "False Alarm Sparks Panic." January 14, 2018. https://www.bbc.com/news/world-us-canada-42677604.

43. Sutherland. "GE's $23 Billion Write-down." *Bloomberg Business Week.* October 22, 2018. https://www.bloomberg.com/news/articles/2018-10-22/ge-s-23-billion-writedown-stems-from-a-bad-bet-on-fossil-fuels; Shumsky. "GE's $22 Billion Charge." *Wall Street Journal.* October 30, 2018. https://www.wsj.com/articles/ges-22-billion-charge-intensifies-regulatory-scrutiny-1540942603; Shumsky; Shumsky; Biers. Phys.org. "General Electric Reports Huge Loss." October 30, 2018. https://phys.org/news/2018-10-electric-3q-loss-bn-dividend.html.

44. Collier. "ExxonMobil Ordered to Pay $20 million." *Texas Tribune.* April 27, 2017. https://www.texastribune.org/2017/04/27/exxonmobil-ordered-pay-20-million-excess-air-pollution/; Collier; Egan. "Exxon Released 10 Million Pounds of Air Pollution." CNN. April 27, 2017. https://money.cnn.com/2017/04/27/investing/exxon-fined-pollution-texas/index.html?section=money_markets&utm_source=feedburner&utm_medium

=feed&utm_campaign=Feed%3A+rss%2Fmoney_markets+%28CNNMoney
%3A+Markets%29; Egan, "Exxon."

45. Sandberg and Goldberg. "Netflix Fires PR Chief." *Hollywood Reporter.* June 22, 2018.
https://www.hollywoodreporter.com/live-feed/jonathan-friedland-exits-netflix
-1122675; Sandberg and Goldberg, "Netflix."; Sandberg and Goldberg; Sandberg and
Goldberg.

46. Nossiter and Breeden. "Fire Mauls Notre-Dame Cathedral." *New York Times.*
April 15, 2019. https://www.nytimes.com/2019/04/15/world/europe/notre-dame-fire
.html; Bennhold and Glanz. "Notre-Dame's Safety Planners Underestimated Risk."
New York Times. April 19, 2019. https://www.nytimes.com/2019/04/19/world/europe/
notre-dame-fire-safety.html?action=click&module=inline&pgtype=Homepage;
Bennhold and Glanz; Bennhold and Glanz; Matthews. "What Will It Take to Rebuild
Notre-Dame Cathedral?" AFAR. April 18, 2019. https://www.afar.com/magazine/
what-will-it-take-to-rebuild-notre-dame-cathedral; Ott. "Why It Could Take 40
Years to Rebuild Notre Dame." CBS News. April 16, 2019. https://www.cbsnews.com/
news/notre-dame-cathedral-rebuild-in-paris-could-take-40-years/.

47. Hicks. "Flooding Halts Shipping along Mississippi River." Fox News. May 31, 2019.
https://www.foxnews.com/weather/midwest-farmers-in-limbo-as-flooding
-halts-traffic-along-mississippi-river; Hicks; Newman and Bunge. "Floods Swamp US
Farm Belt." *Wall Street Journal.* May 23, 2019. https://www.wsj.com/articles/floods
-swamp-u-s-farm-belt-11558603802.

48. Strom. "Chipotle Food-Safety Issues Drag Down Profits." *New York Times.*
February 3, 2016. https://www.nytimes.com/2016/02/03/business/chipotle-food-s
afety-illness-investigation-earnings.html?rref=collection%2Fbyline%2Fstephanie
-strom&module=inline; Yaffe-Bellany. "Chipotle Recovers Strongly." *New York Times.*
July 23, 2019. https://www.nytimes.com/2019/07/23/business/chipotle-stock-earnings.
html; Bomey and Meyer. "Chipotle to Retrain All Workers on Food Safety." *USA
Today.* August 16, 2018. https://www.usatoday.com/story/money/2018/08/16/chipotle-
mexican-grill-food-safety-retraining/1008398002/; Rosenberg. "More than 600 People Got Sick After Eating at One Chipotle." *Washington Post.* August 7, 2018. https://
www.washingtonpost.com/news/food/wp/2018/08/07/more-than-600-people
-got-sick-after-eating-at-one-chipotle-health-officials-dont-know-why-yet/;
Bomey. "Chipotle Reopens Ohio Restaurant." *USA Today.* August 1, 2018. https://
www.usatoday.com/story/money/2018/07/31/chipotle-closes-ohio-restaurant/
869779002/; Luna. "Chipotle Employees to Be Tested Quarterly on Food Safety."
Nation's Restaurant News. August 21, 2018. https://www.nrn.com/operations/
chipotle-employees-be-tested-quarterly-food-safety.

49. Adams. "Homeless Man and Couple Charged in GoFundMe Scam." *People.*
November 15, 2018. https://people.com/human-interest/homeless-man-gofundme
-couple-scam/; Garcia and Haag. "Homeless Veteran Will Get Money Raised for
Him." *New York Times.* September 6, 2018. https://www.nytimes.com/2018/09/06/

us/gofundme-homeless-man.html; Associated Press. "Donors in Alleged Homeless Scam Refunded." *Chicago Sun Times.* December 25, 2018. https://chicago.suntimes .com/2018/12/25/18345436/donors-in-alleged-homeless-scam-refunded-gofundme -says; Gosk and Ferguson. "GoFundMe Has Answer for Fraud." NBC News. April 8, 2019. https://www.nbcnews.com/news/us-news/after-new-jersey-scam-gofundme-says -it-has-answer-fraud-n992086; Associated Press, "Donors."; Gosk and Ferguson, "GoFundMe."

50.   Reuters. "AOC Slams Funding Cuts." November 26, 2018. https://www.reuters.com/ article/us-olympics-australia-funding/olympics-aoc-slams-funding-cuts-for-minor -sports-ahead-of-tokyo-idUSKCN1NV0AC; Reuters; Reuters; Reuters; Reuters.

51.   Malcolm. "Barack Obama Wants to Be President of These 57 United States." *Top of the Ticket.* [blog]. *Los Angeles Times.* May 9, 2009. https://latimesblogs.latimes.com/ washington/2008/05/barack-obama-wa.html; Malcolm.

52.   CBS News. "Utility Responds After Deadly Gas Explosions." September 14, 2018. https://www.cbsnews.com/news/gas-explosions-massachusetts-evacuations-lawrenc e-and-over-columbia-gas-today-2018-09-14/; Rocheleau and Valencia.
"Columbia Gas Has a Plan for Speedy Pipe Replacement." September 19, 2018. https://www.bostonglobe.com/metro/2018/09/19/gas-company-plan-for-speedy -replacement-work-raises-safety-fears/U84HWSti6FPoBOGJyU7tuM/story.html; Rocheleau and Valencia; Rocheleau and Valencia; Ackley. Gas Safety USA. Email inter- view with Edward Segal. July 25, 2019. Ackley, Interview; NiSource. "Columbia Gas Commits to Complete Replacement of Merrimack Valley Gas Distribution System." Sep- tember 16, 2018. https://www.prnewswire.com/news-releases/columbia-gas-of-mass achusetts-commits-to-complete-replacement-of-merrimack-valley-gas-distribution -system-300713444.html.

53.   DW. "EU Hails Social Media Crackdown on Hate Speech." Accessed August 7, 2019. https://www.dw.com/en/eu-hails-social-media-crackdown-on-hate-speech/a -47354465; DW; Aljazeera English. "France Online Hate Speech Law." July 10, 2019. https://www.aljazeera.com/news/2019/07/france-online-hate-speech-law-puts-pressure -social-media-sites-190710070342024.html; Escritt. "Germany Fines Facebook." Reuters. July 2, 2019. https://www.reuters.com/article/us-facebook-germany-fine/germany-fines -facebook-for-under-reporting-complaints-idUSKCN1TX1IC; DW. "EU Hails Social Media Crackdown."

54.   McLaughlin. "Man Who Took Hostages Killed by Police." CNN. January 14, 2019. https:// www.cnn.com/2019/01/14/us/ups-active-shooter-logan-township-new-jersey/index .html; NBC10 Staff. "Gunman Killed; Hostages Safe." NBC10. January 14, 2019. https:// www.nbcphiladelphia.com/news/local/Logan-Township-Police-Warehouse-504317181 .html; Premack. "Hostage Situation Has Ended." *Business Insider.* January 14, 2019. https://www.businessinsider.com/active-shooter-ups-facility-logan-township-nj -2019-1.; Premack; Premack.

55. Fallon. "Griffin 'Decapitated' Trump. Will Hollywood Welcome Her Back?" The Daily Beast. March 12, 2019. https://www.thedailybeast.com/kathy-griffin-decapitated-donald-trump-will-hollywood-welcome-her-back; Reuters. "CNN Fires Griffin." CNN. May 31, 2017. https://www.newsweek.com/kathy-griffin-donald-trump-severed-head-photo-cnn-fired-barron-trump-melania-618612.

56. New York Times. "Cyclone Fani Hits India." May 2, 2019. https://www.nytimes.com/2019/05/02/world/asia/india-cyclone-fani.html; The Conversation. "India's Cyclone Recovery Offers Lessons." May 13, 2019. http://theconversation.com/indias-cyclone-fani-recovery-offers-the-world-lessons-in-disaster-preparedness-116870; The Conversation; The Conversation; Woodward and Associated Press. "India Preparing for Record-Breaking Cyclone." May 2, 2019. https://www.businessinsider.com/india-prepares-for-extremely-severe-bay-of-bengal-cyclone-2019-5; The Conversation. "India's Cyclone." The Conversation. "India's Cyclone."

57. Gates and Ramseth. "Koch Foods: Mississippi ICE Raid Search Illegal." Clarion Ledger. September 4, 2019. https://www.clarionledger.com/story/news/politics/2019/09/04/mississippi-ice-raid-koch-foods-illegal-search-undocumented-workers/2207811001/; Gates and Ramseth; Editorial Board. "Federal Agents Are Enforcing E-Verify against Employees—But Not Businesses." Washington Post. September 25, 2019. https://www.washingtonpost.com/opinions/federal-agents-are-enforcing-e-verify-against-employees--but-not-businesses/2019/09/25/8b1ba7c6-dbf6-11e9-ac63-3016711543fe_story.html; Gates and Ramseth. "Koch Foods."; Gates and Ramseth; Gates and Ramseth; Gates and Ramseth; Gates and Ramseth.

58. Wolfson. "Ambien Maker Responds to Roseanne Barr." The Guardian. May 30, 2018. https://www.theguardian.com/culture/2018/may/30/roseanne-ambien-racism-tweet-side-effect-response-sanofi; Mazza. "Roseanne Gets Brutal Wakeup Call." Huff Post. May 30, 2018. https://www.huffpost.com/entry/roseanne-ambien-defense_n_5b0e47 1ae4b0802d69cf87b9; Mazza; Woodson, "Ambien."

59. Craig and Taddeo. "Criminal Charges against Rochester Drug Company." Democrat and Chronicle. April 23, 2019. https://www.democratandchronicle.com/story/news/2019/04/23/rochester-drug-cooperative-20-million-opioid-distribution-drug-enforcement-administration/791689002; NPR. "Rochester Drug Cooperative Faces Federal Criminal Charges." April 23, 2019. https://www.npr.org/2019/04/23/716478908/rochester-drug-cooperative-faces-federal-criminal-charges-over-role-in-opioid-ep; Craig and Taddeo, "Criminal."; Craig and Taddeo, "Criminal."

60. Fernández. "News Anchors Say Bosses Are Grooming Younger Women to Take Their Jobs." Vox. June 20, 2019. https://www.vox.com/2019/6/20/18691881/ny1-anchors-sue-age-discrimination; Fernández; Fernández; Fernández.

61. Boudette. "GM to Idle Plants and Cut Thousands of Jobs." New York Times. November 26, 2018. https://www.nytimes.com/2018/11/26/business/general-motors-cutbacks.html; Boudette; General Motors. "General Motors Accelerates Transformation." November 26,

2018. https://media.gm.com/media/us/en/gm/home.detail.html/content/Pages/news/us/en/2018/nov/1126-gm.html; General Motors.

62. Dishman. "Best and Worst Leaders of 2018." *Fast Company.* December 19, 2018. https://www.fastcompany.com/90278934/these-are-the-best-and-worst-leaders-of-2018; Grothaus. "Elon Musk Talks Pot." *Fast Company.* December 10, 2018; https://www.fastcompany.com/90278810/elon-musk-talks-pot-the-sec-and-twitter-flame-wars; Grothaus; Grothaus.

63. Kolodny. "Here's the Email Tesla Sent Employees." CNBC. May 3, 2019. https://www.cnbc.com/2019/05/03/tesla-email-warns-employees-stop-leaking.html; Kolodny; Kolodny.

64. Surur. "Microsoft's Cloud Hit by Lightning." *MS Power User.* September 4, 2018. https://mspoweruser.com/microsofts-cloud-hit-by-lightning/; Service Blog Postmortem. "VS Marketplace outage – 4 September 24, 2018." Service Blog - Azure DevOps. September 24, 2018. https://devblogs.microsoft.com/devopsservice/?p=17535; Service Blog Postmortem; Foley. "Microsoft Datacenter Outages." ZD Net. September 4, 2018. https://www.zdnet.com/article/microsoft-south-central-u-s-datacenter-outage-takes-down-a-number-of-cloud-services/; Service Blog Postmortem.

65. CNN Money Staff. "Volkswagen Scandal." CNN. November 25, 2015. https://money.cnn.com/2015/09/28/news/companies/volkswagen-scandal-two-minutes/index.html; Glinton. "How Little Lab In West Virginia Caught Volkswagen's Big Cheat." NPR. September 24, 2015. https://www.npr.org/2015/09/24/443053672/how-a-little-lab-in-west-virginia-caught-volkswagens-big-cheat; CNN Money Staff, "Volkswagen Scandal."; O'Kane. "CEO Blames Software Engineers." The Verge. October 8, 2015. https://www.theverge.com/2015/10/8/9481651/volkswagen-congressional-hearing-diesel-scandal-fault; D'Orazio. "Volkswagen Apologizes for Emissions Scandal." The Verge. November 15, 2015. https://www.theverge.com/transportation/2015/11/15/9739960/volkswagen-apologizes-with-full-page-ad-in-dozens-of-newspapers; D'Orazio, "Volkswagen."

66. Roberts. "YouTube Flagged Notre Dame Fire Videos as a Conspiracy." *People.* April 15, 2019. https://people.com/travel/notre-dame-cathedral-fire-youtube-allegedly-flags-fake-september-11-videos/; Rogers. "YouTube Slammed." Fox News. April 15, 2019. https://www.foxnews.com/tech/notre-dame-fire-youtube-slammed-after-live-footage-appears-with-link-to-9-11-info; Roberts, "YouTube."

67. Nittle. "Gucci Is Latest Fashion Brand to Spark Blackface Controversy." Vox. February 12, 2019. https://www.vox.com/the-goods/2019/2/7/18215671/gucci-blackface-sweater-apology-prada-virginia; Nittle; Held. "Gucci Apologizes." NPR. February 7, 2019. https://www.npr.org/2019/02/07/692314950/gucci-apologizes-and-removes-sweater-following-blackface-backlash; Held.

68. Wilson and Cain. "Northam Admits He Posed in Yearbook Photo." February 1, 2019. *Richmond Times-Dispatch.* https://www.richmond.com/news/virginia/government-politics/virginia-gov-ralph-northam-admits-he-posed-in-yearbook-photo/article_c29e0f55-6284-5bde-8d93-8804ad507d5d.html; Wilson and Cain;

Moomaw. "Northam Denies He's in Racist Yearbook Photo." *Richmond Times-Dispatch*. February 2, 2019. https://www.richmond.com/news/virginia/government-politics/general
-assembly/resisting-calls-to-resign-northam-denies-he-s-in-racist/article
_f75d342d-e028-586e-8631-70d52424d604.html; Moomaw; Schneider and Vozzella. "How Northam Made Blackface Scandal Even Worse." Washington Post. May 26, 2019. https://www.washingtonpost.com/local/virginia-politics/how-va-gov-ralph-northam
-and-aides-made-his-blackface-scandal-even-worse/2019/05/25/9a096912-7da0-11
e9-8ede-f4abf521ef17_story.html.

69. Arkin. "Metropolitan Museum of Art Will No Longer Accept Gifts from Sackler Family." CNBC. June 11, 2019. https://www.cnbc.com/2019/05/16/metropolitan-museum-of
-art-says-it-will-no-longer-accept-gifts-from-sackler-family.html; Harris. "Met Will Turn Down Sackler Money." *New York Times*. May 15, 2019. https://www.nytimes
.com/2019/05/15/arts/design/met-museum-sackler-opioids.html; Harris, "Met."; Harris, "Met."

70. Schreir. "IGN Pulls Review." Kotaku. August 7, 2018. https://kotaku.com/ign-pulls-review
-after-plagiarism-accusations-1828157939; Schreir. "IGN Pulls Ex-Editor's Posts." Kotaku. August 15, 2018. https://kotaku.com/ign-pulls-ex-editors-posts-after-dozens-more
-plagiarism-1828357792; Schreir; Fogel. "IGN Fires Editor." *Variety*. August 15, 2018. https://variety.com/2018/gaming/news/ign-filip-miucin-plagiarism-1202906110/; Cooper. "Former IGN Editor Admits to Plagiarism." Gamerant. April 22, 2019. https://gamer-
ant.com/ign-plagiarism-dead-cells-filip-miucin-apology-video/.

71. 2 CBS New York. "NYC Blackout." July 14, 2019. https://newyork.cbslocal.com/2019/
07/14/new-york-city-power-outage-cause/; Con Edison. "Con Edison Working to Restore Power." July 13, 2019. https://www.coned.com/en/about-us/media-center/
news/20190713/con-edison-working-to-restore-power-on-west-side-of-manhattan; Con Edison; Con Edison; Con Edison; Con Edison; Con Edison; 2 CBS News New York, "NYC Blackout."

72. Bever. "Teens Are Daring Each Other to Eat Tide Pods." *Washington Post*. January 17, 2018. https://www.washingtonpost.com/news/to-your-health/wp/2018/01/13/teens
-are-daring-each-other-to-eat-tide-pods-we-dont-need-to-tell-you-thats-a-bad-idea/
?utm_term=.45985e41ad03. Ohlheiser. "YouTube's Now Banned Dangerous Pranks." *Washington Post*. January 17, 2019. https://www.washingtonpost.com/technology/2019/01/17/
youtubes-now-banned-dangerous-pranks-were-problem-long-before-bird-box-
challenge/; Ohlheiser; Detrick. "4 Ways P&G Is Trying to Stop People from Eating Tide Pods." *Fortune*. January 22, 2018. https://fortune.com/2018/01/22/pg-stop-eating-tide-
pods/. Desantis. "YouTube Banning Prank and Challenge Videos." *Daily News*.
January 16, 2019. https://www.nydailynews.com/news/national/ny-news-youtube
-banning-dangerous-videos-20190116-story.html; Ohlheiser, "YouTube's"; YouTube Help. "Dangerous Challenges and Pranks Enforcement Update." YouTube. January 28, 2019. https://support.google.com/youtube/thread/1063345?hl=en.

73. McLaughlin and Benmeleh. "Teva Orchestrated Price Fixing Scheme." *Philadelphia Inquirer.* May 13, 2019. https://www.inquirer.com/business/generics-teva-pennsylvani a-new-jersey-drugs-price-fixing-20190513.html; McLaughlin and Benmeleh.

74. Leonard. "Mylan's CEO Hit over Multi-Million Dollar Salary." *US News & World Report.* September 21, 2016. https://www.usnews.com/news/articles/2016-09-21/mylan-head-defends-epipen-price-gouging-in-capitol-hearing; Leonard; Cohen. "Mylan Complains of Overpriced Drugs." *Science.* August 3, 2018. https://www.sciencemag.org/news/ 2018/08/mylan-lambasted-epipen-price-hikes-complains-overpriced-anti-hiv-drugs -us; Lopez and Ramsey. "Congress Railed on Maker of EpiPen." *Business Insider.* September 21, 2016. https://www.businessinsider.com/mylan-ceo-heather-bresch-house -oversight-committee-hearing-epipen-2016-9.

75. Consumer Reports. "Samsung Stops Making Galaxy Note7." October 10, 2016. https:// www.consumerreports.org/smartphones/samsung-stops-making-galaxy-note7 -smartphone/; Hollister. "Why Note 7 Phones are Catching Fire." CNET. October 10, 2016. https://www.cnet.com/news/why-is-samsung-galaxy-note-7-exploding-overheating/; Gikas and Beilinson. "New Details about Note7 Battery Failures." Consumer Reports. January 22, 2017. https://www.consumerreports.org/smartphones/samsung-investigation -new-details-note7-battery-failures/; Gikas and Beilinson; Gikas and Beilinson; Gikas and Beilinson.

76. Sansom. "Christians Protest McJesus Sculpture." *The Art Newspaper.* January 14, 2019. https://www.theartnewspaper.com/news/hundreds-of-christians-protest-against-jani -leinonen-s-mcjesus-sculpture-at-haifa-museum-of-art-in-israel; Dwyer. "'McJesus' Sculpture to Be Pulled from Museum." NPR. January 15, 2019. https://www.npr .org/2019/01/17/686199231/mcjesus-sculpture-to-be-pulled-from-israeli-museum -after-violent-protests; Dwyer; Dwyer; Dwyer; Brice-Saddler. "Sculpture of Ronald McDonald Ignites Clashes in Israel." *Washington Post.* January 15, 2019. https://www. washingtonpost.com/world/2019/01/15/sculpture-ronald-mcdonald-cross-ignites-viol ent-clashes-israel/?utm_term=.66f79d482915.

77. Szalai and Strause. "Smollett 'Staged' Attack, Say Police." *Hollywood Reporter.* February 21, 2019. https://www.hollywoodreporter.com/news/jussie-smollett-under-arrest-custody-chicago-police-say-1188635; Bosman and Deb. "Smollett's Charges Are Dropped." *New York Times.* March 26, 2019.
https://www.nytimes.com/2019/03/26/arts/television/jussie-smollett-charges -dropped.html; Szalai and Strause. "Smollett"; Fieldstadt and Blankstein. "Smollett Arrested for Allegedly Making Up Hate-Crime Attack." NBC News. February 21, 2019. https://www.nbcnews.com/news/us-news/chicago-police-jussie-smollett-considered -suspect-his-report-hate-crime-n973036; Albert. "Smollett Staged Attack as 'Publicity Stunt.'" Daily Beast. February 21, 2019. https://www.thedailybeast.com/jussie-smollett -staged-attack-as-publicity-stunt-over-salary-police; Szalai and Strause, "Smollett."

78. Stewart. "Hackers Holding Baltimore's Computers Hostage." Vox. May 21, 2019. https://www.vox.com/recode/2019/5/21/18634505/baltimore-ransom-robbinhood

-mayor-jack-young-hackers; Stewart; Sussman. "This Is Why We Didn't Pay." Secure World. June 12, 2019. https://www.secureworldexpo.com/industry-news/baltimore -ransomware-attack-2019; Reutter, "Ransomeware." Baltimore Brew. May 7, 2019. https://www.baltimorebrew.com/2019/05/07/ransomware-attack-disables-baltimores -city-government-computers-spares-essential-services/; Warren. "FBI Investigating Baltimore City Ransomware Attack." WJZ13 CBS Baltimore. May 10, 2019. https://balti-more.cbslocal.com/2019/05/10/fbi-investigating-baltimore-city-ransomware-attack/; Warren; Warren.

79. Union Pacific. "Union Pacific Redesigns Marketing & Sales Organization." September 15, 2017. https://www.up.com/media/releases/170915-marketing-redesign.htm; Union Pacific; Union Pacific; Union Pacific.

80. Kirsch. "Papa John's Founder Used N-Word on Conference Call." *Forbes.* July 11, 2018. https://www.forbes.com/sites/noahkirsch/2018/07/11/papa-johns-founder-john -schnatter-allegedly-used-n-word-on-conference-call/#4cbf0b4f4cfc; Kirsch; Harten. "Schnatter Resigns After Apologizing for Racial Slur." *USA Today.* July 12, 2018. https:// www.usatoday.com/story/money/nation-now/2018/07/11/papa-johns-john-schnatter -resigns/777891002/; Helm. "Schnatter Says He Was 'Pushed' to Use N-Word." The Root. July 14, 2018. https://www.theroot.com/papa-john-schnatter-says-he-was-pushed -to-use-the-n-w-1827599519; Meyersohn. "Papa John's Founder Resigns." CNN. July 12, 2018. https://money.cnn.com/2018/07/11/news/companies/papa-johns-pizza-john -schnatter/index.html?iid=EL; Whitten. "Schnatter Apologizes for Using N-Word." CNBC. July 11, 2018. https://www.cnbc.com/2018/07/11/papa-johns-shares-crater-after-report -that-founder-used-a-n-word.html; Stier. "Papa John Says He Was 'Pressured' to Use N-Word." *New York Post.* July 13, 2018. https://nypost.com/2018/07/13/papa-john-says -he-was-pressured-to-use-n-word-during-conference-call/.

81. Puhak. "Disney World Slams Rumor." Fox News. June 29, 2019. https://www.foxnews .com/travel/disney-world-slams-rumor-attraction-replaced.; Puhak, "Disney."

82. Day, Turner, and Drozdiak. "Amazon Workers Are Listening." Bloomberg. April 10, 2019. https://www.bloomberg.com/news/articles/2019-04-10/is-anyone-listening-to-you -on-alexa-a-global-team-reviews-audio; Day, Turner, and Drozdiak; Day, Turner, and Drozdiak.

83. Li. "CBS Fires CEO Leslie Moonves." Reuters. December 17, 2018. https://www.reuters .com/article/us-cbs-moonves/cbs-fires-ceo-leslie-moonves-and-denies-120-million -severance-idUSKBN1OG2F4; Li; Li; Li; Li; Li.

84. Californians for Home Ownership. "Our Work." Accessed August 8, 2019. https:// www.caforhomes.org/work; Salam. "Gavin Newsom's Big Idea." *The Atlantic.* Febru-ary 15, 2019. https://www.theatlantic.com/ideas/archive/2019/02/governor-newsom -addresses-californias-housing-crisis/582892/; California Association of Realtors. "C.A.R. 2019 Legislative Priorities." Accessed August 8, 2019. https://www.car.org/ aboutus/mediacenter/newsreleases/2019releases/legagenda; California Association of Realtors, "C.A.R."; Californians for Home Ownership. "Our Work."; CCRE Center for

California Real Estate. Accessed August 8, 2019. http://centerforcaliforniarealestate
.org/; California Association of Realtors, "C.A.R."; California Association of Realtors,
"C.A.R."

85. Swarns. "272 Slaves Were Sold to Save Georgetown." *New York Times.* April 16, 2016.
https://www.nytimes.com/2016/04/17/us/georgetown-university-search-for-slave
-descendants.html; TRT World. "Universities Come Face-to-Face with Racist Past."
May 13, 2019. https://www.trtworld.com/magazine/british-and-american-universities
-come-face-to-face-with-their-racist-past-26600; Catholic News Service. "University, Jesuits Apologize." April 19, 2017. https://www.catholicnews.com/services/
englishnews/2017/georgetown-university-jesuits-apologize-for-roles-in-sale-of
-slaves.cfm; TRT World, "Universities."

86. Pomranz. "Why Are Hershey's Kisses Suddenly Missing Tips?" *Food & Wine.* December
20, 2018. https://www.foodandwine.com/news/hersheys-kisses-missing-tips-2018;
Pomranz, "Why."; Caron. "Some Hershey's Kisses Are Missing Tips." *New York Times.*
December 22, 2018. https://www.nytimes.com/2018/12/22/business/hershey-kisses
-broken-tips.html?module=inline; Caron, "Some."; Caron, "Some."; Caron, "Some.";
Caron, "Some."

87. Saul and Cohen. "Profitable Giants Pay $0 in Corporate Taxes." *New York Times.* April
29, 2019. https://www.nytimes.com/2019/04/29/us/politics/democrats-taxes-2020
.html; Myers. "60 Companies Paid $0 Taxes." Yahoo Finance. April 12, 2019. https://
finance.yahoo.com/news/companies-paying-zero-taxes-trump-law-155944124.html;
Bose. "Biden Criticizes Amazon for Not Paying Taxes." Reuters. June 13, 2019. https://
ca.reuters.com/article/technologyNews/idCAKCN1TE3BZ-OCATC ; CNN. "Amazon: 'We
Pay Every Penny We Owe.'" WRAL Tech Wire. June 14, 2019. https://www.wraltech-
wire.com/2019/06/14/amazon-to-joe-biden-on-taxes-we-pay-every-penny-we-owe/;
Bose, "Biden."

88. McKirdy, *et al.* "Attack Death Toll Rises to 290." CNN. June 21, 2019. https://www.cnn
.com/asia/live-news/sri-lanka-easter-sunday-explosions-dle-intl/index.html; Gettleman,
Mashal, and Bastians. "Sri Lanka Authorities Were Warned." *New York Times.* April 22,
2019. https://www.nytimes.com/2019/04/29/world/asia/sri-lanka-attack-warning.html;
Oliver. "Sri Lanka Hotels Grapple with Cancellations." *USA Today.* April 26, 2019. https://
www.usatoday.com/story/travel/hotels/2019/04/26/sri-lanka-hotels-cancellations
-tourism-after-bombing-attack/3576016002/; Oliver; Oliver; Oliver.

89. Lane. "Dems Challenge Bank CEOs." *The Hill.* April 10, 2019. https://thehill.com/pol-
icy/finance/438263-dems-challenge-bank-ceos-on-post-crisis-reforms; Lane; Lane;
Merle. "CEOs of Mega Banks Challenged." *Washington Post.* April 15, 2019. https://
www.washingtonpost.com/business/2019/04/10/ceos-mega-banks-will-testify-before
-house-committee-heres-what-expect/?utm_term=.b780de0c7b2b; Merle.

90. Oldham, *et al.* "Woman Sought in Columbine Threats Is Dead." *Washington Post.*
April 17, 2019. https://www.washingtonpost.com/education/2019/04/17/unnerving
-search-continues-armed-year-old-woman-deemed-threat-columbine-high-school/?

utm_term=.e197fef61f9e; Oldham, *et al.*; Oldham, *et al.*; Turkewitz and Healy. "'Infatuated' with Columbine." *New York Times.*

April 17, 2019. https://www.nytimes.com/2019/04/17/us/columbine-shooting-sol-pais
.html; Oldham, "Woman."

91. Graham and Buie. "Apple Sued by More iPhone Owners." USA Today. December 22, 2017.
https://www.usatoday.com/story/tech/talkingtech/2017/12/21/apple-sued-iphone
-owners-over-software-slowed-older-phones/974846001/; Graham and Buie; Graham
and Buie; "iPhone Battery and Performance." Accessed August 8, 2019. Apple. https://
support.apple.com/en-us/HT208387; Nellis. "Apple Apologizes." Reuters. December
28, 2017. https://www.reuters.com/article/us-apple-batteries/apple-apologizes-after
-outcry-over-slowed-iphones-idUSKBN1EM20N.

92. Reuters. "China Starts New Recycling Drive." January 14, 2019. https://www.reuters
.com/article/us-china-waste/china-starts-new-recycling-drive-as-foreign-trash-ban
-widens-idUSKCN1P90A1; Reuters; Reuters; Reuters; Reuters; Reuters.

93. Koblin. "After Racist Tweet, Barr's Show Is Canceled." *New York Times.* May 29, 2018.
https://www.nytimes.com/2018/05/29/business/media/roseanne-barr-offensive
-tweets.html; Nyren. "Barr Returns to Twitter." *Variety.* May 29, 2018.
https://variety.com/2018/biz/news/roseanne-barr-returns-twitter-1202824991/;
Duster, Atkinson, and Johnson. "Barr Blames Racist Tweet on Ambien."
NBC News. May 30, 2018. https://www.nbcnews.com/news/nbcblk/roseanne-barr
-apologizes-tweet-comparing-obama-adviser-ape-n878171; Hipes. "Roseanne Cancellation the Right Thing." Deadline Hollywood News. May 29, 2018. https://deadline
.com/2018/05/roseanne-canceled-bob-iger-reaction-disney-abc-1202399276/; Hipes.

94. O'Donoghue. "South African Election." Breaking News. April 16, 2019. https://www
.breakingnews.ie/discover/bizarre-south-african-election-campaign-sees-cork
-city-suburb-get-international-attention-918172.html; PoliticsWeb. "Billboard Blunder." April 16, 2019. https://www.politicsweb.co.za/news-and-analysis/anc-billboard
-blunder-in-nmb-minor; PoliticsWeb; PoliticsWeb.

95. Goldstein. "Bumping and Beating of Dr. Dao." *Forbes.* December 20, 2017. https://
www.forbes.com/sites/michaelgoldstein/2017/12/20/biggest-travel-story-of-2017-the
-bumping-and-beating-of-doctor-david-dao/#34a63c2ef61f; Goldstein; Goldstein;
Goldstein; Andrews. "Dragging Incident Produces Firings, Suspensions." *Washington Post.* October 17, 2017. https://www.washingtonpost.com/news/morning-mix/
wp/2017/10/17/united-airlines-dragging-incident-that-went-viral-produces-firings
-suspensions-of-officers/?utm_term=.be831b4a7dbd; Zhang. "United Promising to
Make Changes." *Business Insider.* April 13, 2017.
https://www.businessinsider.com/united-airlines-major-changes-response-dao-
2017-4.

96. Consumer Product Safety Commission. "Fisher-Price Recalls Rock 'n Play Sleepers."
Accessed August 8, 2019. https://www.cpsc.gov/Recalls/2019/fisher-price-recalls-rock
-n-play-sleepers-due-to-reports-of-deaths; Consumer Product Safety Commission;

Hsu. "Safety Fears and Dubious Marketing." *New York Times.* April 19, 2019. https://www.nytimes.com/2019/04/19/business/fisher-price-recall.html;
Fisher-Price. Child Safety Is Our Priority. "Rock 'n Play Sleeper Product Recall." Accessed August 8, 2019. https://fisher-pricesafety.com/.

97. Boyd. "CU Denver Helps Pentagon Battle Threat Posed by Deepfakes."4 CBS Denver. July 17, 2019. https://denver.cbslocal.com/2019/07/17/deepfakes-university-colorado -denver-artificial-intelligence/; Kelly. "Congress Grapples with How to Regulate Deep-fakes." The Verge. June 13, 2019. https://www.theverge.com/2019/6/13/18677847/deep -fakes-regulation-facebook-adam-schiff-congress-artificial-intelligence; Kelly; Farrell. "Warning Sign of Things to Come." Silicon Angle. June 12, 2019. https://siliconangle. com/2019/06/12/deep-fake-video-mark-zuckerberg-used-warning-sign-things-come/; Ortutay. "Facebook Evaluating Deepfake Video Policy." Boston Globe. June 27, 2019. https://www.bostonglobe.com/metro/2019/06/27/mark-zuckerberg-says-facebook -evaluating-deepfake-video-policy/uhwq7UUIYSHmexp7GmAd6J/story.html; Harwell. "Researchers Race to Detect 'Deepfake' Videos." Washington Post. June 12, 2019. https://www.washingtonpost.com/technology/2019/06/12/top-ai-researchers-race -detect-deepfake-videos-we-are-outgunned/?utm_term=.463c03cdfc09.

98. CBS This Morning. "Airline Mechanics Feel Pressured." February 4, 2019. https://www. cbsnews.com/news/airline-mechanics-feel-pressured-by-managers-to-overlook -potential-safety-problems-cbs-news-investigation/; CBS This Morning; CBS This Morning.

99. *National Geographic.* "Wildfires, Explained." Accessed August 8, 2019. https://www .nationalgeographic.com/environment/natural-disasters/wildfires/Wikipedia. "Tubbs Fire." Accessed August 8, 2019. https://en.m.wikipedia.org/wiki/Tubbs_Fire; Swindell. "Winery Takes First Steps to Rebuild." *Press Democrat.* October 22, 2018. https:// www.pressdemocrat.com/business/8864187-181/paradise-ridge-winery-takes-first; Advisor. "Groundbreaking Ceremony." October 24, 2018. https://wineindustry advisor.com/2018/10/24/groundbreaking-ceremony-heralds-return-paradise; Swindell, "Winery."; Swindell, "Winery."; Swindell, "Winery."; Swindell, "Winery."; Advisor. "Groundbreaking Ceremony." October 24, 2018.

100. Stephens. AJMC Managed Markets Network. [Blog] *"Violence against Healthcare Workers."* May 12, 2019. https://www.ajmc.com/focus-of-the-week/violence-against -healthcare-workers-a-rising-epidemic; Iida. "Officer Ben." *The News Tribune.* July 26, 2019. https://www.thenewstribune.com/news/local/article233193691.html# storylink=cpy; Iida. "Tacoma Hospital Brings in K-9." *The News Tribune.* August 5, 2019. https://www.asaecenter.org/programs/lms-activities/109869-workplace-security -awareness. Lida; Lida; Edwards, Marce. Executive Director, Corporate Communications. MultiCare Puget Sound. Phone interview with Edward Segal. October 16, 2019; Rege. "Violence Epidemic in Hospitals." *Becker's Hospital Review.* March 13, 2019. https:// www.beckershospitalreview.com/hospital-physician-relationships/cleveland-clinic -ceo-violence-epidemic-happening-in-hospitals-nationwide-4-takeaways.html;

https://www.thenewstribune.com/news/local/article233173551.html;Harris-Taylor. "Escalating Workplace Violence." NPR. April 8, 2019. https://www.npr.org/sections/health-shots/2019/04/08/709470502/facing-escalating-workplace-violence-hospitals-employees-have-had-enough; IAHS.05. "Services – Patient. 03. Violent Patient/Patent Visitor Management." Accessed August 8, 2019.
https://www.jointcommission.org/assets/1/6/05.03_Violent_Patient_Management__.pdf; ASAE. "Workplace Security Awareness." Accessed August 8, 2019.

101. Staff Reporter. "Wigs for Judges." Bulawayo. March 24, 2019.
https://bulawayo24.com/index-id-news-sc-national-byo-159410.html; Chingono. "Zimbabwe Wigs Met with Fury." April 5, 2019. https://www.theguardian.com/global-development/2019/apr/05/zimbabwe-outlay-on-judges-wigs-met-with-fury-colonialism;
Chingono. "Zimbabwe Wigs."; Alsup. "Powdered Wigs for Judges." *Daily News.* April 5, 2019. https://www.nydailynews.com/news/world/ny-zimbabwe-spent-thousands-on-powdered-wigs-for-judges-20190405-v6heuqekxbg3nbnypdfzldnp3u-story.html; Robinson. "Zimbabwe Spent Thousands on Judges' Wigs." CNN. April 5, 2019. https://www.cnn.com/2019/04/05/africa/zimbabwe-judges-wigs-gbr-intl-scli/index.html.

102. Jenkins. "Keeping Track of Facebook's Scandals." *Fortune.* April 6, 2018. https://fortune.com/2018/04/06/facebook-scandals-mark-zuckerberg/; Frenkel, *et al.* "Delay, Deny, Deflect." *New York Times.* Nov. 14, 2018. https://www.nytimes.com/2018/11/14/technology/facebook-data-russia-election-racism.html.

Chapter 7: Bouncing Back: How to Recover from a Crisis

1. Robehmed. "Griffin's Comeback Tour Is on Track to Make Millions." *Forbes.* June 1, 2018. https://www.forbes.com/sites/natalierobehmed/2018/06/01/kathy-griffins-comeback-tour-is-on-track-to-make-millions/#dab884b2cc94.

2. Robehmed.

3. Robehmed.

4. Eiten. "Baltimore Ransomware Attack." WJZ13 CBS Baltimore. June 12, 2019. https://baltimore.cbslocal.com/2019/06/12/baltimore-ransomware-attack-inches-closer-to-normal/.

5. Doctorow. "US Conference of Mayors Adopts a Resolution." Boing Boing. July 12, 2019. https://boingboing.net/2019/07/12/hang-separately.html.

6. McKinley. "San Francisco Mayor Admits He Had Affair with Aide's Wife." *New York Times.* February 2, 2007. https://www.nytimes.com/2007/02/02/us/02newsom.html.

7. *New York Times.* "Election Results." January 20, 2019. https://www.nytimes.com/elections/results/california-governor.

8. Mehta and Willon. "Former Aide to Gavin Newsom Speaks Out about Their Affair." Los

Angeles Times. February 7, 2018. https://www.latimes.com/politics/la-pol-ca-governor s-race-gavin-newsom-affair-20180207-story.html.

9. Gurdus. "Chipotle CEO and CFO: 'We're Back on Our Front Foot.'" CNBC. October 4, 2018. https://www.cnbc.com/2018/10/04/chipotle-ceo-cfo-talk-food-safety-standards -past-messaging-issues.html.

10. Gurdus.

11. Gurdus.

12. Gurdus. "Leadership Changes and Time Helped Drive Chipotle's Comeback." CNBC. February 7, 2019. https://www.cnbc.com/2019/02/07/cramer-leadership-changes-and -time-helped-drive-chipotles-comeback.html.

13. Jones and Bomey. "Sears Saved from Liquidation." *USA Today.* February 7, 2019. http:// www.usatoday.com/story/money/2019/02/07/sears-kmart-eddie-lampert-esl-invest ments-sears-bankruptcy/2804797002/.

14. Jones and Bomey.

15. Securities and Exchange Commission. "SEC Charges Martha Stewart, Broker Peter Bacanovic with Illegal Insider Trading." June 4, 2003. https://www.sec.gov/news/ press/2003-69.htm.

16. CNN. "Stewart Convicted on All Charges." March 10, 2004. https://money.cnn .com/2004/03/05/news/companies/martha_verdict/.

17. Eaton. "Martha Stewart Verdict: The Overview." *New York Times.* March 6, 2004. https://www.nytimes.com/2004/03/06/business/martha-stewart-verdict-overview -stewart-found-guilty-lying-sale-stock.html.

18. Eaton.

19. Berman. "How Martha Stewart Achieved Net Worth of $640 Million." *Money Inc.* Accessed August 4, 2019. https://moneyinc.com/martha-stewart-net-worth/.

20. Maloney. "Pepsi Pulls Ad Featuring Police, Protesters, and Kendall Jenner." *Wall Street Journal.* April 5, 2017. https://www.wsj.com/articles/pepsi-pulls-ad-featuring -police-protesters-and-kendall-jenner-1491414509.

21. Marzilli. "One Year After Jenner Ad Crisis, Pepsi Recovers." YouGov. April 17, 2018. https://today.yougov.com/topics/food/articles-reports/2018/04/17/one-year-after -jenner-ad-crisis-pepsi-recovers.

22. Weaver. "Most KFCs in UK Remain Closed." *The Guardian.* February 19, 2018. https:// www.theguardian.com/business/2018/feb/19/kfc-uk-closed-chicken-shortage- fash-food-contract-delivery-dhl.

23. Weaver.

24. Coghlan. "KFC Goes Back to the Delivery Company It Ditched." Eater London. March 9, 2018. https://london.eater.com/2018/3/9/17099564/kfc-chicken-u-turn-bidvest -logistics-dhl.

25. Petroff. "KFC Apologizes for Chicken Shortage." CNN. February 27, 2018. https://money .cnn.com/2018/02/23/news/kfc-apology-ad-shortage-chicken/index.html.

26. Gabbatt. "Starbucks Closes More than 8,000 US Cafes for Racial Bias Training." *The Guardian.* May 29, 2018. https://www.theguardian.com/business/2018/may/29/starbucks-coffee-shops-racial-bias-training.

27. Knowles. "A Barista Asked Police to Leave Because a Guest Felt Uncomfortable." *Washington Post.* July 8, 2019. https://www.washingtonpost.com/business/2019/07/07/barista-asked-police-leave-because-guest-felt-uncomfortable-starbucks-has-apologized/?utm_term=.d8e81416193c.

Index

M

Macron, Emmanuel, 151
Magic Kingdom Park, 198
Mai Khao beach, 143
Major League Baseball, 130, 197
Mandarina Colombo hotel, 207–208
Mann, Lt. Cdr. Bashon, 44–45
Mariana mine disaster, 117–118
Martin, Jared, 203
May, Prime Minister Theresa, 136
McAvoy, John, 184
McDonald, Ronald, 191
Measles, 126–127
Media interview checklist, 64–69
Media truths, 62
Media, working with the
  exercise, 79–80
  letters to the editor, 77
  media interview checklist, 64–69
  news conference checklist, 73
  newspaper interviews, 74
  online pressrooms, 78
  op-eds and bylined articles, 77
  radio interviews, 75–76
  satellite and Skype media tours, 76–77
  television interviews, 74–75
  when media makes mistakes, 78–79
Mellon, Bank of New York, 209–210
Messaging, 37, 63
Metropolitan Museum of Art, 180–181
Metzger, Luke, 147
Miami, Florida, 98
Microsoft, 160, 173–175
Mihaljevic, Tom, 225
Military leaders, response to simulated
  cyberattack, 43
Millán, Teresa, 121
60 Minutes (TV show), 61
Miucin, Filip, 181–182
Money Inc, 238
Moonves, Leslie, 200–201
Morgan Stanley, 209–210
Mueller Water Products, 93
MultiCare Tacoma General Hospital, 224–226
Mumps, 126
Munoz, Oscar, 218
Murphy, Phil, 115
Musk, Elon, 171–172
Mylan, 187–188

N

NASA scientists, response to crisis simulation, 43
National Public Radio (NPR), 168, 226

National Transportation Safety Board (NTSB),
  107–108
Naval Criminal Investigative Service
  (NCIS), 45
Navy, 45–46
NBC News, 121, 133, 154
Netflix, 92, 148–149
New Jersey, 69, 161–162
New Jersey Transit, 114–115
News conference checklist, 73
Newsom, Gavin, 201–203, 236
Newspaper interviews, 74
News release, 71–73
New York City, 43
New York Times, 45, 150, 181, 208, 237
New Zealand, 99–100
Niccol, Brian, 153, 237
Nkomo, Dumisani, 227
Norsk Hydro, 115–116
Northam, Ralph, 179–180
Northern Ireland, 94–95
Norway, 115–116
Notre Dame Cathedral, Paris, 78, 150, 177
NY1 (TV), 169

O

Obama, Barack, 156–158, 209, 220
Odisha Government, 163–164
Olympic Games, 2020, 156
One-day crisis management simulation, 44
Online pressrooms, 78
Onyx Hospitality Group, 207–208
Op-eds, 77
Opportunities from crisis, 39

P

Papa John's Pizza, 196–197
Paradise Ridge Winery, 33, 223–224
Pelosi, Nancy, 127–128, 220
Pentagon, 45–46
People magazine, 143
Pepsi, 238
Philadelphia, 69, 89–91, 124, 154, 239
Phuket International Airport, Thailand,
  143–144
The Phuket News, 143–144
Poitrinal, Guillaume, 150
Powell, Ohio, 152–153
PricewaterhouseCoopers, 138–139
Procter & Gamble, 185–186
PublicRelations.com, 29, 34, 63, 72, 78, 82, 240,
  242
Punta Cana Casino, 121–122

© Benedict Bacon

Edward Segal has more than 30 years' experience as a crisis management expert. He managed crisis situations as the CEO of two trade associations; advised and helped organizations survive disasters, scandals, and emergencies including the arrest and firing of corporate officers, hate crimes, and sexual harassment; and conducted crisis management and communication training for hundreds of executives and their staffs.

Segal is the former marketing strategies columnist for the *Wall Street Journal*'s StartUpJournal.com and senior media relations consultant for Ogilvy Public Relations. He has provided expert PR advice, counsel, and services to more than 500 corporations and organizations including Marriott, Ford, Airbus, National Association of REALTORS®, and federal and state government agencies.

Crisis Management Services and Workshops

He provides crisis management services and conducts crisis management work-shops, mentoring, and coaching sessions. Contact him at crisisahead@gmail.com or visit his websites at PublicRelations.com and EdwardSegal.com.

Free Tips on Delivering Successful Speeches and Conducting Effective PR Campaigns

Receive information and updates about new crisis situations and Segal's take about how they are being managed. Subscribe to his free crisis management newsletter by going to PublicRelations.com and you will receive his complimentary tip sheets on how to deliver successful speeches and presentations and create effective PR campaigns for your company or organization.